THOU SHALT
NOT BE AWARE

Also by Alice Miller

Prisoners of Childhood
(reissued in paperback as *The Drama of the Gifted Child*)

For Your Own Good: Hidden Cruelty
in Child-Rearing and the Roots of Violence

Pictures of a Childhood:
Sixty-six Watercolors and an Essay

The Untouched Key

Banished Knowledge: Facing Childhood Injury

Breaking Down the Wall of Silence:
The Liberating Experience of Facing the Painful Truth

Paths of Life: Seven Scenarios

THOU SHALT
NOT BE AWARE

Society's Betrayal of the Child

ALICE MILLER

Translated from the German
by Hildegarde and Hunter Hannum

With a Preface by Lloyd deMause
and a new Introduction by the Author

Farrar, Straus and Giroux
New York

Farrar, Straus and Giroux
18 West 18th Street, New York 10011

Copyright © 1981 by Suhrkamp Verlag, Frankfurt am Main
Translation and Afterword to the American edition copyright © 1984 by
Alice Miller
Introduction to the 1998 edition copyright © 1998 by Alice Miller
Preface copyright © 1998 by Lloyd deMause
All rights reserved
Distributed in Canada by Douglas & McIntyre Ltd.
Printed in the United States of America
Originally published in 1981 by Suhrkamp Verlag, Frankfurt am Main,
Germany, as *Du sollst nicht merken*
First American edition published in 1984 by Farrar, Straus and Giroux
First Farrar, Straus and Giroux paperback edition, 1998

Grateful acknowledgment is made to Alfred A. Knopf, Inc., for permission to reprint excerpts from *The Continuum Concept* by Jean Liedloff, copyright © 1975, 1977 by Jean Liedloff, and *Centuries of Childhood* by Philippe Ariès, translated by Robert Baldick, copyright © 1962 by Jonathan Cape Ltd.; to Random House, Inc., for permission to reprint excerpts from *Gods and Heroes: Myths and Epics of Ancient Greece* by Gustav Schwab, translated by Olga Marx and Ernst Morwitz, copyright © 1946 by Pantheon Books, Inc., and renewed 1974 by Random House, Inc.; to Schocken Books, Inc., for permission to reprint excerpts from the following works by Franz Kafka: *Amerika*, copyright © 1927, 1946 by Schocken Books, Inc., *The Complete Stories*, copyright © 1946, 1947, 1948, 1949, 1954, 1958, 1971 by Schocken Books, Inc., *Letters to Felice*, copyright © 1967, 1973 by Schocken Books, Inc., and *Letters to Milena*, copyright © 1953 by Schocken Books, Inc.; to Southern Illinois University Press for permission to reprint excerpts from *Grimms' German Folk Tales*, translated by Francis P. Magoun, Jr., and Alexander H. Krappe, copyright © 1969 by Southern Illinois University Press.

The Library of Congress has cataloged the hardcover edition as follows:
Miller, Alice.
   Thou shalt not be aware : society's betrayal of the child / by
Alice Miller ; translated by Hildegarde and Hunter Hannum.
   Translation of: Du sollst nicht merken.
   Bibliography: p.
      p.   cm.
   ISBN-13: 978-0-374-27646-1
   ISBN-10: 0-374-27646-3
   1. Psychoanalysis.   2. Incest victims.   3. Sexually abused children.
I. Title.

RC506 .M5213 1984
616.85'82—dc19

                                                    84006008

Paperback ISBN-13: 978-0-374-52543-9
Paperback ISBN-10: 0-374-52543-9

Designed by Herbert H. Johnson

www.fsgbooks.com

Contents

THOU SHALT
NOT BE AWARE

Preface

BEFORE there was Alice Miller, there were few voices telling the truth about our betrayal of our children.

As she points out in this book, Freud and most psychoanalysts were little different from others in blaming children for their own abuse. Freud once called a girl patient "hysterical" who was molested by her father (the father was a friend of Freud's) because she complained about her molestation. It was children's sensuousness that was to blame for sexual assaults by adults, he declared, because "the sexual constitution which is peculiar to children is precisely calculated to provoke sexual experiences of a particular kind [seductions]." Karl Abraham, Freud's associate, also believed the molestation of his child patients was "desired by the child unconsciously." Most psychoanalysts since then have continued to label patient reports of childhood sexual abuse merely the victim's "wishes." As one psychiatrist wrote, "I was taught in my . . . early years in psychiatry, as most of us were, to look very skeptically upon the incestuous sexual material described by my patients . . . Any inclination on my part, or that of my colleagues in the training situation, to look upon these productions of the patient as having some reality basis was scoffed at and was seen as evidence of our naiveté."

Nor has opinion really changed much in either academia or psychiatry. Scholarly academic journals have recently praised pedophilia as "nurturant" and advocated abolishing laws against sex with children. The American Psychiatric Association's current diagnostic manual claims pedophilia is only a psychiatric disorder if it bothers the pedophile; otherwise, having sex with children is healthy. In fact, when I gave a speech at a recent A.P.A. convention showing that the majority of children in history were sexually abused, the audience reacted by wondering if incest isn't after all not really pathological, since so many have done it. Alice's insight into the unconscious causes of this almost universal denial of the harm and its costs to society is, unfortunately, still a lonely one today.

Most adults in the past believed that children didn't remember anything of what happened to them up until the age of five, so sexual exploitation, beatings, and other severe abuse had no real effect on them. One particularly widespread belief was that having intercourse with a child would cure one of venereal disease. Up until the early twentieth century, in fact, men who were caught by London police raping little girls were often let go because they thought they were curing themselves of syphilis. Doctors only reinforced the social pact of "thou shalt not be aware." When they treated men for venereal disease, they often found that their children had it too, on their mouths or vaginas or anuses, but they didn't report this to anyone. The attitude was that raping children was an adult prerogative. As one man said coming out of a trial during which a man had been let go after raping a little girl, "What nonsense! Men should not be punished for a thing like that. It doesn't harm the child." Alice Miller demonstrates in this book that one of the far-reaching harms is the lack of awareness and the denial of crimes.

Laws in most countries even today rarely give much protection to children against assault. Incest is usually considered a minor felony, and most sexual abuse still goes unpunished, because it is undiscovered or unprosecuted or routinely plea-bargained. About half of the children raised today in industrial nations have been sexually abused, and the overwhelming majority have been regularly hit, often by dangerous instruments. The statistics proving this high incidence are buried in little-read journals, the better to keep secret the extent of "society's betrayal of the child." But the past two decades of extensive documentation by scores of childhood historians corroborate Alice's conclusions in detail.

Because of her courageous work and studies by others like her, things do change, however slowly. I am told by the bookstore of the Freud Museum in London that the works of Alice Miller are among their best sellers. Many American psychoanalytic institutes now teach therapists to take seriously memories of sexual abuse and not just imagine that they are fantasies. *The Journal of the American Psychoanalytic Association* recently had a whole issue on the reality of sexual abuse of children, showing an awareness unthinkable fifteen years ago. Also, Alice Miller's work on the social effects of child abuse has begun to be documented.

There is even a book, *The Altruistic Personality*, that shows that Nazi sympathizers had very abusive childhoods, whereas rescuers of Jews during the Holocaust had kind, caring parents who didn't discipline them in the brutal manner of most European parents of that time.

Today, the number of caring and well-informed parents is doubtless growing, although not quickly enough. Perhaps if enough people read Alice Miller, we can at long last learn to greet each new child born in the world with a simple "Hello. Welcome to the world! How can I help you grow?" so that we can finally awaken from the nightmare of childhood and put an end at long last to the slaughterbench of history.

Lloyd deMause, author of
The History of Childhood
and editor of *The Journal of Psychohistory*

Introduction

STUDY of the history of cruelty to children reveals that people only mistreat their children if they have been victims of cruelty themselves. We may think that such a situation should be easy to remedy. After all, unlike plants, we have a fully developed conscious mind. We know what we do, why we do it, and what will come of it. Or so we think.

A plant has no influence on its destiny. It grows from a seed, and in its maturity produces new seeds containing the same program as the one from which it grew. Even if the seed is that of an unpleasant and destructive weed, it has no choice but to carry on producing precisely that weed. And if it stems from a beautiful orchid, then it enjoys the undeserved good fortune of basking in its own beauty and giving unalloyed pleasure to others. Weeds provoke our hostility, they encroach on other plants and frequently choke them to death. But they have no choice. They are what they are.

Humans, we are inclined to think, ought to be able to rewrite their programs. And so they can, in theory. But in order to deploy that ability they have to be able to recognize what is destructive about them. And this recognition is something new to our generation. The fact still provokes all kinds of resistance, from lawyers, experts, embattled parents, public foundations, but in the long run there is nothing that can make it disappear from the face of the earth. For it is an insight championed by people who have not grown up in line with the old inherited program. These people have been reared in a family climate consciously chosen for them by parents refusing to conform automatically to the traditional programs.

People still railing against the truth about cruelty to children because they are afraid to face up to their own childhood can hardly be expected to change. But in the course of time they will die out and make room for those whose awareness of what they have been through makes them want to ensure that their children will have a better life. They know that they are not plants, that they have options, that they are not forced to people the world with mentally disturbed criminals. They know that the relevant information is there for the asking. If they want to, they can find out about the positive effects of gentle childbirth and non-violent upbringing. Day by day they are informed by the media about the consequences of childhood cruelty, as manifested by acts of terrorism of all descriptions. Education by fear is still practiced in various religious schools claiming to inculcate a Christian code of morals into their charges. But this pretense has become more and more difficult to uphold. In time, changing education and birth-care methods are bound to swell the numbers of enlightened people able and willing to reveal this hypocrisy for what it is.

Do weeds sense that they are destructive parasites? I do not know. I assume that they have no awareness, that they blindly follow a survival blueprint that is entirely ruthless with respect to the lives of other beings. But what about us humans, so proud of our moral superiority, so ready to read our children improving stories from the Bible? Are we perhaps indifferent to the lives of others too? Do we behave toward our children like mindless plants, obeying preordained programs, doing exactly the same to them as was done to us all those years ago?

To answer this question, all we need to do is to give some thought to the legitimacy of a tradition of education that operates on the principle of "beating some sense" into children. Although this precept has finally been recognized for the absurdity it is, that does not mean that it has been abandoned. Many still hanker after the feeling of power conveyed by taking it out on the children, remaining in a vegetable state of unawareness instead of developing a conscious realization of the consequences of their deeds. They use all the means at their disposal—including law courts and scientific institutions—to prove that human memory is unreliable.

But no such proof is required. It is true that our memories are unreliable, easily manipulated from within (our "wishful thinking") and without. But above all they serve our will for survival. Our will for survival will never push us to invent painful stories, rather the contrary: to make up nice memories in order to *obscure* the painful reality of our childhood. This is something we must never lose sight of. The commandment that says "Thou shalt not be aware of what was done to thee, nor of what thou doest to others" ensures that cruelty suffered in childhood is played down or modified by memory until it becomes unrecognizable.

In this book I have tried to show why that happens. I have also drawn on examples from writers like Kafka, Beckett, and Flaubert to show the precision with which the truth asserts itself in their works without the authors noticing it. Unfortunately, the truth comes out not only in art, in dreams, and in fairy tales, but also in political action, in crime, and—increasingly—in the activities of sects exploiting the ingenuousness and gullibility of maltreated and misguided children for their own financial ends. But this can only happen as long as we let the old traditional programs run on undisturbed. There is nothing inevitable about this. Today we have access to all the information we need in order to put an end to manipulation from outside and to stop denying our own truth at the dictates of our wishful thinking. There is no need to think that we will lose the love of our parents if we assert our allegiance to our own personal truth. The love of a child for its parents is all but indestructible. As children we cannot reconcile this love with the truth, and so we deny that this truth exists. But as adults we can learn to preserve both. In fact we have very little choice, if we want to uphold our verbal tributes to love. It is only in alliance with the truth and the refusal of hypocrisy that authentic love can survive and grow.

Psychoanalysis:
Dogma vs. Experience

❊

Will Françoise ever be told that she nearly died?
Perhaps she will learn that she was rescued by her
wonderful father. . . . She will not be told that he tried
to kill this little girl who was not his own. . . . And so
Françoise will perhaps repeat the story that something
happened to her when she was little, she doesn't know
what, and that since that time she has been going to the
hospital on account of her hip, her leg, or her foot so that
someday she will be able to walk just like everyone else.
. . . In any case, she has been making progress, and she
has been told that she can wear new orthopedic shoes. . . .
—*Leila Sebbar*, Gewalt an kleinen Mädchen (*Violence*
against Little Girls)

⊰ 1 ⊱

Two Psychoanalytic Approaches

I T is of course not classical psychoanalysis alone that suppresses the question of how parents consciously, or more often unconsciously, treat their children in the first years of life; all the disciplines I know of that deal with the human psyche share this characteristic, including those with free access to the relevant facts, i.e., psychiatry, psychology, and various schools of psychotherapy. Probably the main reason I call particular attention to the phenomenon in psychoanalysis has to do with my belief that this discipline could bring about the deepest and most authentic understanding of the subject if its theories did not automatically and unconsciously act as blinders. In order to describe the mechanisms involved, I must go into some detail.

If I as an analyst direct my interest and attention to finding out what drive desires a person who enters my office for the first time is suppressing at the moment, and if I see it as my task to make this clear to him in the course of his analysis, I will listen sympathetically when he tells me about his parents and his childhood, but I will be able to absorb only that portion of his early experiences which is made manifest in his drive conflicts. The reality of the patient's childhood, which has been inaccessible to him all these years, will be inaccessible to me as well. It remains part of the patient's "fantasy world," in which I can participate with my concepts and constructs without the traumas that really took place ever being revealed.

If from the beginning, however, I confront the person who enters my office with questions having to do with what befell him in childhood and if I consciously identify with the child within him, then from the very first hour events of early childhood will open up before us that would never have been able to surface had I based

my approach on an unconscious identification with the parents and
their devious methods of upbringing instead of consciously identifying with the former child. In order to enable these events to come to
light, it is not enough to ask questions about the past; besides, some
questions tend to conceal more than they reveal. But if the analyst
directs his attention to early childhood trauma and is no longer
compelled to defend the position of the parents (his own and those
of his patient), he will have no trouble discovering the repetition of
an earlier situation in the patient's *present* predicament. If, for instance, the patient should describe with complete apathy a current
partner relationship that strikes the analyst as extremely painful, the
analyst will ask himself and the patient what painful experiences the
latter must have had to undergo in early childhood, without being
permitted to recognize them as such, in order to be able to speak
now so impassively about his powerlessness, hopelessness, loneliness,
and constant humiliation in the present-day relationship. It may also
be, however, that the patient displays uncontrollable feelings directed toward other, neutral people and speaks about his parents
either without any show of feeling or in an idealizing manner. If the
analyst focuses upon the early trauma, he will soon ascertain, by
observing how the patient mistreats himself, how the parents once
behaved toward the child. In addition, the manner in which the
patient treats the analyst offers clues to the way his parents treated
him as a child—contemptuously, derisively, disapprovingly, seduc-
tively, or by making him feel guilty, ashamed, or frightened. All the
features of a patient's early training can be detected in the very first
session if the analyst is free to listen for them. If he is a prisoner of
his own upbringing, however, then he will tell his supervisor or
colleagues how "impossible" his patient's behavior is, how much
repressed aggression is latently present, and which drive desires it
emanates from; he will then seek advice from his more experienced
colleagues on how to interpret or "get at" this aggression. But should
he be able to sense the suffering that the patient himself is not yet
able to sense, then he will adhere strictly to his assumption that his
patient's overt attitudes are a form of communication, a code language describing events that for the time being can and must be
reported in exactly this way and no other. He will also be aware that
the repressed or manifest aggression is a response and reaction to

traumas that at present remain obscure but will have to be confronted at the right moment.

I have outlined here two differing, indeed diametrically opposed analytical approaches. Let us assume that a patient or a training analyst in search of psychotherapy speaks with a representative of each of these approaches. Let us further assume that on the basis of the initial session a report has to be submitted, either for the clinic or for the supervisory committee. In itself this is of little importance, for such reports usually remain hidden away in a drawer. What is important is whether the people seen in these sessions are led to regard themselves as a subject or as an object. In the former case, they glimpse, sometimes for the very first time, an opportunity to encounter themselves and their life and thereby come closer to their unconscious traumas, a prospect that can fill them with fear as well as hope. In the latter case, their customary intellectual self-alienation prepares them to see themselves as the object of further pedagogical efforts in the course of which, to use the words of Freud's patient, they can paint themselves as black as necessary but must spare other people.

These differences in a patient's attitude toward himself strike me as having far-reaching significance, not only for the individual, but for society. The way a person perceives himself has an effect on those around him as well, particularly those dependent on him, e.g., his children or his patients. Someone who totally objectifies his inner life will also make other people into objects. It was primarily this consideration that led me to distinguish sharply between these two approaches, although I realize that the motives underlying the "cover-up" approach (defending the parents, denying trauma) have deep, unconscious roots and are unlikely to be altered by books or arguments.

There are other reasons as well that caused me to reflect on the differing approaches of analysts: I frequently encounter the view that analytic work on the self, as I understand the process, can be performed only within the framework of lengthy classical analysis, that it cannot be accomplished by another, perhaps shorter form of psychotherapy. I, too, was convinced of this at one time but no longer am, because I can see how much time the patient may lose if he has to defend himself against his analyst's theories, only to be forced in the end to give in and allow himself to be "socialized" or "educated." The same is true for group therapy. If the therapist assures the members of a group of their right to express their feelings, yet at the same time is afraid of possible outbursts against their parents, he will not be able to understand the participants and may even intensify their feelings of helplessness and their aggressions. He can then either let these feelings remain in a chaotic state or resort to more or less disguised pedagogical measures by calling upon reason, morality, a willingness for reconciliation, etc. The therapist's efforts are often directed toward reconciling patients with their parents because he has been taught—and is also convinced on a conscious level—that only forgiveness and understanding bring inner peace (which in the child's world is actually the case!). Possibly it is the therapist's unconscious fear of his repressed anger against his own parents that leads him to recommend reconciliation to his patients. In this way he is really rescuing (in the therapeutic process) *his* parents from his own anger, which he imagines to have a fatal effect, because he was never allowed to find out that feelings do not kill. If the therapist is able to relinquish entirely his unconscious identification with the parents and their methods of child-rearing and identify instead with the suffering child, serving as his advocate, in a short time his understanding, freed of anxiety, will set in motion processes that at one time were considered miraculous, because their dynamics had not yet been conceptualized.

The difference between the two approaches can be illustrated by a thoroughly banal example of so-called acting out, something every psychoanalyst is familiar with from his practice. Let us assume that a patient in a certain stage of analysis telephones the analyst at home at all hours of the day and night. An analyst with an unconscious pedagogical bent will see in this behavior "insufficient tolerance for frustration" (the patient cannot wait until the next appointment), a distorted sense of reality (the patient doesn't realize that the analyst, in addition to the hours spent with him, also has a life of his own), and other narcissistic "defects." Since the analyst himself is a "well-trained" child, it will be difficult for him spontaneously to impose limits on his patients. He will search for rules and regulations permitting him to eliminate the annoyance caused by the frequent telephone calls; in other words, to "train" the patient.

If, instead, the analyst is able to see in his patient's behavior the active reenactment of a situation passively endured in childhood, he will ask himself how the parents treated this child and whether the patient's behavior may not be telling the story of the totally dependent child, which lies so far back in the past that the patient cannot tell about it in words but only in unconscious behavior. The analyst's interest in the patient's early childhood will have practical consequences: he will not attempt to "take the proper steps" nor will he be in danger of giving his patient the illusion of constant availability, something that the patient never experienced with his parents and that he submissively attempted to offer them in the deluded hope of receiving it in return. As soon as both analyst and patient are able to perceive the latter's earlier situation, the analyst will have no need of pedagogical measures and will nonetheless—or for this very reason—be able to give the proper weight to, and protect, his private life and free time.

It is a reflection of the pedagogical approach that the concept of acting out is virtually synonymous with "bad behavior" among analysts. I prefer not to use this concept and refer instead to reenactments, to which I ascribe a central role and which for me do not signify "misbehavior." For what is involved here is an essential, often dramatic, unconscious message about the early childhood situation.

I know of a patient, for example, who drove her first sympathetic and patient analyst and his family to distraction by calling up at night, only to find out very quickly with her second analyst that these telephone calls were unconscious reenactments of traumatic experiences from early childhood. Her father, a successful artist who often came home when she was already asleep, liked to take her out of her crib and play wonderful and exciting games with her, until he grew tired and put the little girl back to bed. The patient was unconsciously reenacting with her analyst this trauma of suddenly being awakened out of a deep sleep, of being strongly stimulated and then suddenly left all alone; only after they had both realized this was she able to experience for the first time the feelings that situation had aroused in her: indignation at having her sleep disturbed, resentment at the effort she had to make to be a good playmate so that her father wouldn't go away, and finally rage and sorrow at being abandoned. In this reenactment the analyst was assigned the role of the awakened child who wanted to behave correctly in order not to lose the attachment figure she loved and, at the same time, the role of the father, who, when he ends the telephone conversation, hurts the child's feelings by leaving her alone again. The first analyst did not understand the biographical context of this so-called acting out and thus joined in it. The second one listened to the story contained in the reenactment, and this helped him to devote his full attention as a spectator to the drama, without jumping onto the stage and joining in the act. Since he kept his gaze focused on the patient's childhood from this vantage point, he did not see only "resistance" in her transference but also a dramatic re-creation of her father's behavior and her emotional reactions to it.

ᘓ 2 ᘒ

Analysands Describe Their Analysis

I SHALL attempt to illustrate the two different analytic approaches I have delineated with the aid of three autobiographical accounts of the analytic process: Marie Cardinal's *The Words to Say It*; Tilmann Moser's *Lehrjahre auf der Couch* (Apprenticeship on the Couch); Dörte von Drigalski's *Blumen auf Granit* (Flowers on Granite).

As far as I can tell, all the analysts portrayed in these books are sincere, dedicated people who are recognized as highly trained, valued, and respected members of the International Psychoanalytic Association. I know only two of them personally but not well enough to be able to draw any conclusions about their work. Everything I am going to say concerning their methods is based entirely on having read the three books mentioned above. Since the sole concern of all three authors is to present their subjective reality, they are being perfectly honest. In reading their books, I let myself be guided by the authors' feelings, the same way I am by patients' feelings in my analytic work.

The reports of the three analysands gave me the impression that all four analysts (Drigalski had two) devoted themselves to their patients, tried to understand them, and placed their entire professional knowledge at their patients' disposal. Why are the results so different? Can it be explained simply by calling an analysand incurable if the analysis was a four-year-long misunderstanding? Formulations such as "negative therapeutic reaction" or "resentful patients" remind me of the "wicked" (because "willful") child of "poisonous pedagogy,"* according to which children are always guilty if their parents don't understand them. It may be the case that we blame patients in similar fashion and label them as difficult if we cannot understand them. Yet patients are just as little to blame for our lack of understanding as children for the blows administered by their parents. We owe this incomprehension to our professional training, which can be just as misleading as those "tried and true" principles of our upbringing we have taken over from our parents.

In my opinion, the difference between Cardinal's successful analysis on the one hand and Moser's and Drigalski's tragedies on the other is that in the first case the seriously ill patient, whose life was in danger, found out in analysis what her parents had done to her and was able to relive her tragic childhood. Her description is so vivid that the empathic reader goes through the process with her. The boundless rage and deep sorrow she felt at what she had been forced to endure as a child led to relief from the dangerous and chronic uterine hemorrhaging that had previously been unsuccessfully treated by surgery. The result of her sorrow was the full blossoming of her creativity. It is obvious to the professionally trained reader that in Cardinal's case psychoanalysis—not family therapy or transactional analysis, for instance—was used, for the connections can be traced between her tragic emotional discovery about her childhood and what happened in the transference.

The other therapists also used a psychoanalytic approach, but we can sense in them an attempt to interpret whatever the patient says and does from the perspective of the drive theory. If it is an axiom of psychoanalytic training that everything that happened to the patient in childhood was the result of his drive conflicts, then sooner or later the patient must be taught to regard himself as wicked, destructive, megalomanic, or homosexual without understanding the reasons for his particular behavior. For those narcissistic traumas—humiliation, rejection, mistreatment—inflicted on the child and traditionally considered a normal part of child-rearing are not touched upon and thus cannot be experienced by the patient.

---

* "Poisonous pedagogy" refers to that tradition of child-rearing which attempts to suppress all vitality, creativity, and feeling in the child and maintain the autocratic, godlike position of the parents at all costs. See the author's book *For Your Own Good*, especially the section entitled "Poisonous Pedagogy" (pp. 3–91). —Translators' note

Yet it is only by addressing these concrete situations that we can help the patient acknowledge his feelings of rage, hatred, indignation, and eventually, grief.

There are unquestionably many analysands who "successfully" survive the pedagogical approach inherent in their therapy because they are completely unaware of it. As a result of "poisonous pedagogy" they are so accustomed to not being understood and frequently even to being blamed for their fate that they are unable to detect the same situation when it occurs in analysis and will adapt themselves to their new mentor. They will leave analysis having substituted one superego for another. It should not surprise us that Tilmann Moser and Dörte von Drigalski, both creative people, are reduced to despair as a result. In Moser's case, it is true, the despair is still concealed behind idealization of the analyst, but his next book, *Gottesvergiftung* (God Poisoning), shows that he was not able to experience his aggression toward his parents in analysis because obviously the analyst as well as the parents had to be spared. In Drigalski's case, her disappointment with both analyses leads to a rejection of psychoanalysis per se, which is understandable although regrettable, for the case of Cardinal for one demonstrates that psychoanalysis can contribute positively to a person's creative growth.

In Drigalski's report, the tragic traces of "poisonous pedagogy" are particularly striking. They can be seen not only in the approaches of the psychoanalytic training institutes, which often appear to have a veritable horror of originality, but, most tragically, in the years of wasted effort on the part of the patient and both analysts, all of whom were prevented from gaining access to the narcissistic traumas of early childhood because they were inhibited by the unspoken commandment to spare the parents and blame the child. For this reason, what the author reports about her childhood, her parents, and her brothers remains sketchy and devoid of strong feelings, as in the case of Moser, but very unlike that of Cardinal. Now all Drigalski's outrage is directed against psychoanalysis and her second analyst, who did not understand her. Would this woman have been able to struggle against her feelings for four years and bear such torment if she had not been brought up to ignore her inner voice and keep a stiff upper lip? The adults who figured in her early childhood are spared her rage, however. This is the rule, for the more or less conscious goal of adults in rearing infants is to make sure they will never find out later in life that they were trained not to become aware of how they were manipulated. Without "poisonous pedagogy" there would be no "poisonous psychoanalysis," for patients would react negatively from the very beginning if they were misunderstood, ignored, not listened to, or belittled in order to be forced into a Procrustean bed of theories.

There is a good deal else that would not exist without "poisonous pedagogy." It would be inconceivable, for example, for politicians mouthing empty clichés to attain the highest positions of power by democratic means. But since voters, who as children would normally have been capable of seeing through these clichés with the aid of their feelings, were specifically forbidden to do so in their early years, they lose this ability as adults. The capacity to experience the strong feelings of childhood and puberty (which are so often stifled by child-rearing methods, beatings, or even drugs) could provide the individual with an important means of orientation with which he or she could easily determine whether politicians are speaking from genuine experience or are merely parroting time-worn platitudes for the sake of manipulating voters. Our whole system of raising and educating children provides the power-hungry with a ready-made railway network they can use to reach the destination of their choice. They need only push the buttons that parents and educators have already installed.

Crippling ties to certain norms, terminology, and labels can also be clearly observed in the case of many thoroughly honorable people who become passionately engaged in political struggle. For them, political struggle is inseparably associated with party, organization, or ideology. Since the ominous threat child-rearing practices pose to peace and survival has always remained hidden, ideologies have not yet been able to perceive this situation or, if they do perceive it, to develop intellectual weapons against this knowledge. As far as I know, not a single ideology has "appropriated" the truth of the overriding importance of our early conditioning to be obedient and dependent and to suppress our feelings, along with the consequences of this conditioning. That is understandable, for it probably would mean the end of the ideology in question and the beginning of awareness. Accordingly, many ideologues who consider themselves politically active are like people who, if a fire breaks out, would open the windows to try to let out the billowing smoke (perhaps contenting themselves with abstract theories about the fire's origin) and blithely ignore the flames leaping up nearby.

My hypothesis that Adolf Hitler owed his great popularity to the cruel and inhuman principles of infant- and child-rearing prevalent in the Germany of his day* is also proved by the exception. I looked into the background of Sophie and Hans Scholl, two university students in Hitler's Germany who became famous as a result of their activities in the resistance movement, "The White Rose," and were both executed by the Nazis in 1944. I discovered that the tolerant and open atmosphere of their childhood had enabled them to see through Hitler's platitudes at the Nuremberg Rally, when the brother and sister were members of Nazi youth organizations. Nearly all their peers were completely won over by the Führer, whereas Hans and Sophie had other, higher expectations of human nature, not shared by their comrades, against which they could measure Hitler. Because such standards are rare, it is also very difficult for patients in therapy to see through the manipulative methods they are subjected to; the patient doesn't even notice such methods because they are inherent in a system he takes completely for granted.†

What would have happened in the case of a woman such as Marie Cardinal had she gone to an analyst who had explained her hemorrhages as nothing but a rejection of femininity or an expression of penis envy? Here we can only speculate. If the analyst had been a likable person in other respects, Cardinal might have fallen in love with him and temporarily recovered from her symptoms. But if she had not discovered the truth about her mother, she would never have been able to admit to the extent she did the boundless rage and

---

* See the Hitler chapter in *For Your Own Good.*

† In the words of Ilse Aich Scholl: "When my brother came back from Nuremberg he seemed completely changed: tired, depressed, and uncommunicative. Although he didn't say anything, we all sensed that something must have happened having to do with the Hitler Youth. Little by little we learned what it was. The senseless drills, the militaristic parades, the drivel, the vulgar jokes— all this had been shattering for him. Having to line up from morning till evening, speeches and more speeches, and then the artificially whipped-up enthusiasm. There was no time left over for rational discussion.

"What had happened in Nuremberg irritated Sophie, as it did all of us. Nuremberg—this did not yet cause an open break, but it was probably the first step separating us from the world of the Hitler Youth and the German Girls' League" (Hermann Vinke, *Das kurze Leben der Sophie Scholl* [The Short Life of Sophie Scholl], p. 45).

hatred she felt for her. Had she not come to realize that her hostile feelings were *reactive*, she would have considered herself a monster for having them. The outcome probably would have been that in her despair she would have given up analysis after several years or would have ended up in a mental hospital because of her feelings of hatred, misconstrued as "unfounded." It would not have been she who wrote about her case but her analyst, citing it as an example of an incurable illness, a negative therapeutic reaction, or the like. If, on the other hand, she had disliked her analyst from the start, a sado-masochistic transference would soon have emerged, in the course of which his interpretations would increasingly have assumed the character of veiled accusations. However this may be, we are seeing more and more patients like Cardinal whom we cannot do justice to with the usual labels.

The difference between the two opposing attitudes I have tried to illustrate here with my three examples cannot be conveyed by the concept of "reconstructive interpretations." If the analyst is under the sway of the Fourth Commandment* no matter how hard he tries to reconstruct the original situation, he will invariably take the part of his patient's judgmental parents and sooner or later try to "educate" him by urging him to have understanding for them. Without a doubt our parents were victims, too, not of their children, but of their own parents. It is essential for us to perceive the unintentional persecution of children by their parents, sanctioned by society and called child-rearing, if our patients are to be freed from the feeling imposed on them from an early age that they are to blame for their parents' suffering. In order for this to happen, the analyst has to be free from guilt feelings toward his own parents and be sensitive to the narcissistic wounds that can be inflicted in early childhood. If he lacks this sensitivity, he will minimize the extent of the persecution. He will not be able to empathize with a child's humiliation, since his own childhood humiliation is still repressed. If, in keeping with the saying "You'll be the death of me yet," he has learned to accept all the guilt in order to spare his parents, he will try to allay his patient's aggression, which he cannot understand, by repeatedly emphasizing the parents' good sides; this method is referred to as "the establishment of good objects" in the patient.

---

* To honor his father and mother.

If a mother sees her infant as wicked and destructive, then she will have to bring him under control and train him. But if she recognizes his rage and hatred as reactions to painful experiences, whose significance may still escape her, she will not try to train the child but will permit him to experience his feelings. The same is true of the psychoanalytic process. The example of Marie Cardinal demonstrates why it is not necessary "to establish a good object in the patient" and keep telling him that his parents also had their positive sides and were concerned for his welfare. He had never questioned that; on the contrary, the child does not need to repress what is positive for the sake of survival (see my book *The Drama of the Gifted Child*). When the anger of early childhood and the ensuing grief have been experienced, affirmative feelings, which are not based on denial or feelings of duty or guilt, can emerge of their own accord, assuming the right preconditions are present. These affirmative, more mature feelings must be clearly distinguished from the small child's unconditional, dependent, all-forgiving, and therefore tragic love for his or her parents.

We cannot reproach Sigmund Freud for being a child of his times or for not having the opportunity, being the founder of psychoanalysis, to lie on an analyst's couch himself. This was not his fault but his inescapable predicament. To recognize this, however, does not prevent us from seeing the limitations of Freud's self-analysis, limitations revealed in his persistent idealization of the parents and in his tracing the cause of neurotic suffering back to the child's drive conflicts. Freud had no one to help him experience the reactive aggression lurking behind his idealization as a response to narcissistic wounds. Perhaps he later transferred this aggression to followers who did not understand him as well as he thought they should have or who, as he believed, misunderstood him, like Jung and Adler. He was obviously unable to work through his disappointment within the context of early childhood.

But our situation differs from Freud's. Now an analyst has the opportunity of being analyzed, even a second and third time if necessary. Moreover, we are living with a younger generation that is much more open, honest, and critical toward its parents than was ever possible in Freud's day. We can learn a good deal from these young people—from our children, students, and patients—once we have liberated ourselves from our anxious dependence on dogma.

◆§ 3 ✦

Unconscious Pedagogy in
Psychotherapy

C LASSICAL psychoanalysis is not the only place where we find the
triad of shielding the parents, the drive theory, and concealment of trauma. By concealing parents' traumatizing behavior with
the aid of drive interpretations (i.e., essentially by ascribing all guilt
to the child), various psychoanalytic schools appear modern and
progressive at the same time that they continue to fulfill the commandments of "poisonous pedagogy." This can be demonstrated by
countless examples, but I shall refer to only one book, *Selbstanalyse*
(Self-analysis) by Klaus Thomas, for here what patients have to say
is not distorted by interpretations but is communicated directly to
the reader in the form of letters. Thomas, director of a suicide clinic
in Berlin, has successfully treated many adolescents who have attempted to take their own lives. Excessive demands on his time
prompted Thomas to develop a new method of self-analysis based
on having the patient write journal-like letters to the therapist; only
a few of the problems raised in these letters can then be selected for
discussion in the infrequent therapeutic sessions. I can see the possibility of substantial improvement for patients simply in their being
able to articulate their feelings, formulate their resentments, and
experience their rage toward their parents, providing the right conditions for all this are present, e.g., the assurance that someone will
read everything they write, take it seriously, and not judge them for
it. I gained the impression from the cases cited by Thomas that this
kind of writing, followed by discussion, could offer a serious alternative to psychoanalysis, especially for adolescents. Since the sessions
are so infrequent, the patient's realization of the normal (and inevitable) limits of his therapist's understanding can be postponed
for some time, with the result that the patient, thanks to the support

he is being given, may in the meantime be better able to get through to his traumas than in orthodox psychoanalysis, whose preconceived notions can easily impede his discovery of his true feelings. But it can also be the case that the therapist's more or less conscious pedagogical attitude in his relationship with the patient, inherent in this form of treatment as well, comes through strongly and finally blocks the patient's emotional development after all. This may mean that in many cases the resocialization desired by all is attained, i.e., the patient's adaptation to the expectations of both parents and society. His true self then falls victim to these expectations, just as it did in his childhood. This can have negative consequences for artistically gifted people in particular. To demonstrate what I mean, I shall now cite at length from Thomas's book:

> *An example of self-analysis marked by aggressiveness toward the parents and by sexual relations with siblings*
>
> The following case history, in which the names but not the facts have been changed for reasons of professional secrecy, is just as instructive regarding the potential for self-analysis as it is regarding the significance of released aggression.
>
> *Background:* On November 23, 1965, a 28-year-old medical student appears in my office for the first time. He sees himself locked into a situation from which—he believes—only suicide can save him. His parents, who live in a small town . . . sent their oldest son as well as three younger siblings to the university. The father owns the town's only pharmacy and, as a deacon of the church, is highly regarded by the local citizens. It is important that his son complete his studies quickly, since the father also has two older sisters to provide for.
>
> On his visits home—at least once a month—our patient (we'll call him Dieter), in keeping with parental expectations, always spoke of the progress he was making in his medical studies in Frankfurt and at last announced, after his 15th semester, that his final examination had been scheduled, which was untrue. In reality, for the past three years he had attended scarcely any lectures, had not done any clinical rotations or set foot in a hospital; instead, he had spent his time idly daydreaming in bed, occasionally going out to eat with friends, drinking too much, or apathetically watching television. At this point the father made an appointment with the professor from whom Dieter had repeatedly been granted permission to postpone taking his state exams, ostensibly because of work on his dissertation. Now the edifice of lies collapsed. Dieter wanted to escape being disgraced in the eyes of his parents and the whole community by committing suicide.

In his attempt to find information about the most reliable methods of taking his life, he had come upon literature from the Suicide Center in Berlin and came here to seek advice. During the first interview a picture emerged of a rather severe suppressed depression, caused and sustained by an "ecclesiogenic" neurosis. . . .

After the parents' first visit, the report records the following impressions: father—a self-righteous, petit bourgeois, bureaucratic type; mother—a compulsive demon for cleanliness, both of them devout and also suffering from "ecclesiogenic" neurosis. . . .

On October 2 the patient brings in his first recorded and highly symptomatic dream:

"I was lazily lying in bed, half asleep, half awake, when my father came . . . bawled me out, and said I had to make up my mind whether I wanted to stay in bed or have breakfast with the family. Then he turned down the radio and left the room. I turned it back up real loud just to annoy him, stayed in bed, and hoped my father would come back soon and be mad."

As associations to this dream, he reports similar experiences with his family.

The next dream, three days later, touches upon a deeper problem, however. He calls it "Church Dream":

"I was standing in front of a store window that had a sign saying a church service was being conducted inside, but in Japanese or Chinese. Through the window I saw a Japanese clergyman in ecclesiastic robes. From his side there hung a list like the stock-market report in a bank, only written in Japanese characters. I told myself there was no point going inside because I wouldn't understand it anyway."

His associations to this dream reveal—at first without further elaboration—his aggression toward the church in general and in particular to still being expected by his parents to go to church every Sunday: "All they really think about is their business, and no one understands that theological rigamarole anyway" is his harsh judgment. On Nov. 3, after his midday nap, he records as part of his self-analysis the thoughts accompanying his attempt to remember his dream:

"I'm always thinking up situations where I can lash out, even revolt, against somebody because of an enormous inner attitude of defiance; that's why I work so slowly too. And if a professor asks me something, I become practically incapable of thinking, as if I wanted to say, 'If you push and prod me, then I'll be sure not to do what you tell me to.'

"I had this defiant attitude a lot when I was little, first toward my father. Once when I was four I was sitting on the toilet, and it was taking me a long time to do my business; my father suddenly came in, got impatient, and really gave me hell. I can still see him plain as day with the insignia on his uniform and his stern look, just as stern as my mother, who sometimes, half shouting and half crying, beat me with a stick and once even with the fire poker."

In the discussion that follows he sees in these memories, written down as part of his self-analysis, the key to his later attitudes and to his illness.

He drops out of the winter semester; he has done hardly any work. On February 11, 1968, in a violent outburst of emotion, he writes down the beginning of his confession:

"Everything has turned out so badly, nothing goes right, I'm not getting anywhere; all I can think about any more is Inge [his youngest sister], I could play with her by the hour, kiss her c——, f—— [sic] her—awful, awful, awful—I could curse everything, the whole world and her with it, and yet love her forever and be tender toward her. This is something I ought to grow out of. Everything about her is so beautiful and round and soft. And how beautifully she strokes my penis—oh, how awful. I can't help it, the other boys did it too—why shouldn't I do it with my sisters. I always wanted to be in the same room with her as much as possible. After all, I wasn't allowed to have any other girlfriend. For a while Inge slept in the room next to mine. Often in the night I felt such a strong desire that I secretly sneaked over to her. Everything was very still, and all I could hear was my heart pounding, I was so excited. I cautiously reached under the blanket and under her nightgown and put my finger in her vagina. Usually she was sleeping so soundly she didn't notice . . ." (?).

In the 8oth session, when he brings these notes along, he describes memories of extraordinary intensity and oppressiveness. His *incestuous desires and actions* in connection with his two younger sisters reach back from the time when he was 3 until he finally began to have regular sexual intercourse with Inge when he was 16 and she 13. The year after that there was almost a catastrophe: the other sister discovered them in bed together. In mortal fear of punishment, Dieter and Inge were made an offer. If they always included her, the older of the two sisters, in their sex play and subsequent intercourse, she promised to keep quiet. This condition was accepted, leading on the one hand to the obvious pleasure of the three participants, on the other to deep guilt feelings, at least for Dieter; it was no coincidence that in one of his first dreams he saw himself standing at the marriage altar with both sisters.

He now reported other things he had previously concealed. He especially felt panic that his mother might take him by surprise, the way his sister had. In his dreams his mother then replaces his sisters: he finds himself committing incest with his own mother! He is certain of God's punishment. His anxiety also pervades his religious life.

It takes its toll on his sex life as well. When he—by now thirty—has the chance to prove his virility with a girl, he takes it. "I am impotent," he complains in agitation, "I always see my mother standing behind me and sense her presence, and then I can't do anything.

"It's the same when I try to work, then I always think my father is standing behind me, and I simply can't do a thing."

This leads to a growing aggressiveness toward both parents.

"I wish I could write with both hands now," he says, and over the next two weeks brings to each session approximately 20 pages full of the most violent emotional outbursts against his parents. . . .

Between the 85th and 90th sessions, the patient now began to unburden his heart in his writing with an uninhibited display of strong emotions and aggression. After he had written some 60 pages (from which the examples already given are taken) in clear strong language, his obscene vocabulary becomes more and more incoherent. Every day for weeks he wrote at least four pages full of seemingly senseless neologisms in the manner of Dadaism. It was only after this that he experienced inner relief and felt capable of doing academic work for the first time in over ten years. . . .

Yet his obvious improvement is not sufficient to make him think seriously of taking his exams. At first he is advised more and more urgently on ways to make studying easier by means of systematic schedules and study habits and is given numerous other directions on how to study. His success is minimal, and he refuses to cooperate.

He is given one last stern warning: he will not be allowed to postpone his examinations any longer. A position is located for the "eternal student," by now thirty, in a pharmaceutical company that does not require him to finish medical school. He decides to continue putting off both his studies and finding work. After that he is not given any more extensions.

Now, however, his defiance is awakened, which he had already spent ten years directing successfully against his father, who kept urging him to take his exams. "That's just what I'm not going to do," was Dieter's secret attitude. Now parents and doctor were in agreement: he must give up his studies and should forget the idea of a professional career. "That's just what I'm not going to do," he may have thought, perhaps without even realizing it. Nothing more is heard from him for a whole year.

On March 2, 1971, he appears without any appointment. "Yesterday I was awarded my M.D. I've also passed the state exams! I'll tell you the details later, there isn't time today. By the way, I have a girlfriend now too!"

Varying success can be reported in the years that followed: on the one hand Dieter was able to function in his profession, on the other hand his accomplishments were considerably less than those of his colleagues, and his problems in relating to the opposite sex were not satisfactorily resolved. [pp. 77–92]

During his adolescence this man had the strength to use his passivity as a weapon against his parents' lack of understanding. The "inability" of this person of above-average intelligence to perform in medical school was apparently his sole means of salvaging his dignity. The passages from his letters reminiscent of Dada poems reveal an incredible linguistic inventiveness and power that had long been concealed behind his accommodating posture.

> *From his discharges of aggression:* "Old pig-like churl in his pigsty, a heavenhellhound with his Satan's goat, ultrarightleft pigshitfilthy beast, schizophrenic syphilitic, abused assvulture, a.-fucker, gonad pincher . . . churchyard fraud . . . Auschwitz representative, child seducer. . . .* [p. 90]

What the patient had heretofore suppressed was able to come to life with his hope of finding another, understanding father in the person of the therapist; now this new father was put to the test. Like Dieter's real father, however, this one also insisted on achievement, in this case represented by the successful completion of his studies— which did indeed occur. For the young man did not want to lose this father, just as, when a child, he had not wanted to lose his real one. But if I am correct in assuming that the eventual "success" of the therapy signaled the death of a budding writer and that his earliest attachment to his father or mother, which was transferred to

---

* Thomas proceeds to give examples of his patient's epithets for his mother as well as of his other "apparently senseless . . . neologisms." It is impossible to reproduce adequately the puns and linguistic originality involved.—Translators' note

the therapist, remained unresolved, then this will become apparent later in the form of depression. In saying this, I am not questioning the success of Thomas's therapy in social terms. What I am trying to get at here has to do with an entirely different aspect of personality development, for I know how many people who have had marked success in their studies or in other similar areas suffer from severe depression.

Although Thomas is not an orthodox Freudian and, in agreement with Karen Horney, states that he has not found the "death instinct" in a single one of his five thousand suicidal patients, he is nevertheless influenced by Freud's drive theory. For instance, he carefully overlooked the fact that the patient repeats with his sister what his mother did to him earlier. Another of his cases shows to what extent this theory can interfere with the therapist's trust in his patient and hinder or even block the patient's articulation of early trauma.

A case of self-analysis with a great deal of affect and ambivalence

Symptoms and findings: A 25-year-old art student comes to my office after attempting suicide as a reaction to a television program.

First she talks only about her problems with her studies: "I simply can't remember anything," but soon she also tells about her serious neurotic symptoms: "I have a counting compulsion, but usually I only have to count to two, for example, when I'm walking, cleaning, etc., almost in a military fashion, 'one-two, one-two, one-two.'" Her onychophagy or nail biting has become extreme; ever since childhood, she has chewed her nails down to the quick. "Even indoors I usually have to wear gloves, and even then I often chew off their tips," an all too eloquent indication of her strong aggression. This form of self-disfigurement provides a constant source of reinforcement for feelings of inferiority going back to her childhood. Although her looks are far above average, she complains incessantly about being ugly. She writes about her *earliest childhood memories* in her self-analysis: "Every evening and night I prayed, 'Dear God, please make me pretty!'"

Diagnosis: These symptoms, as well as many others, lead to an initial *diagnosis* of an unmistakable *nuclear neurosis with suppressed, moderately severe, secondary depression with frequently anancastic-phobic states (attacks of compulsiveness and anxiety) and with sexual and familial conflicts as well as considerable nicotine abuse (she smokes over 50 cigarettes a day).*

Program of therapy: Cooperating closely with the psychiatrist available to students through the university health plan (he also considers full-scale psychoanalysis indispensable but out of the question for practical reasons), we begin with a *self-analysis* accompanied by *pharmaco-psychiatric treatment*.

Over the next two years she appears on the average of once every two weeks, usually with two to five pages of notes for her *autobiography* and her complaints, her dreams, and her daydreams. The following quotations are taken from this material (only the names have been changed), which reveals a recurrent pattern of ambivalence, i.e., her impulses in opposite directions at the same time. This is especially true for the central area of sexuality but is already apparent in her relationship with her parents.

Parents: Many of the patient's notes bear the stamp of obvious truthfulness, others must be viewed critically, still others are clearly products of a lively imagination and are objectively false (for instance, she writes repeatedly about having been brutally raped, yet the gynecological examination subsequently determined that she was still a *virgo intacta*). To begin with her own words (May 24, 1966): "When I was seven, my parents got a divorce. I lived with my *mother*, who was constantly berating me and calling me her 'coffin nail.' She also was always threatening to commit suicide; that way, she said, an end would be made of her even quicker than if she left it to me. On the other hand, from the time I was eight, my mom always kissed me like a man. I slept in the same bed with her and every night I had to stroke her until she had an orgasm. That went on for years.

"Other favorite expressions she kept repeating were: 'You Satan's morsel, you horny monster, you stupid cow, I'll have to hang myself yet on your account.' " [pp. 40–42]

Although the patient's conscious memories are sufficient to confirm fully her underlying feeling of having been violated (how else can one describe what the mother forced her daughter to do?), the therapist relies on the gynecological examination, which proves to him that the patient is "still a virgin," was therefore lying, and that her fear of being violated again has a paranoid character, i.e., can be seen as the projection of her own desires. This approach was used for decades in treating so-called hysterical female patients, who were portrayed as theatrical, overly dramatic, prone to exaggerate, and whom therapists tried to talk out of their "delusions."

In every psychiatric and psychoanalytic diagnosis, the description of a hysterical patient is inconceivable without the use of the

word "exaggerated." What is meant by this is that these patients'
complaints are out of all proportion to their cause. But how can we
measure the dimensions of the true cause if it is unknown or if it is
ignored by the therapist, as happened, for example, in the case of
the young art student? If we become practiced in overlooking the
sexual abuse that actually took place, we will call our patients' complaints excessive and abandon them to their trauma. Since they cannot confront their trauma without assistance, they must struggle to
keep the cause from becoming conscious. They do this by transferring their feelings to someone in their present life who has nothing
to do with the original trauma, and thus they cover up even more
the situation their parents concealed from them. This also satisfies
their desire—in spite of analysis (or another form of therapy)—to
spare their parents' feelings, albeit at the price of depression or
another set of symptoms. In her reenactments Thomas's patient is
attempting to communicate her trauma to the therapist, and at the
same time to spare her parents, which makes it more difficult for him
to understand her and gives him the impression that she is being
dishonest. Thomas writes:

> Again and again the patient tells about all the times she has allegedly
> been raped. On Aug. 29, 1966, her self-analytic session ends at 8 p.m.
> At 9 she comes back, agitated and in tears, saying that she has just
> been raped by three men in a nearby park. I dissuade her from going
> to the police because I doubt the objective truth of her statement.
>
> On Nov. 4, 1966, she returned from a fall vacation in Romania.
> The first thing she does is to go into the details of how an American
> (???) raped her while she was on the Black Sea coast. She was finally
> able to break free and then reported the man, who has since been
> sent to prison for several years (???) (cf. again the gynecological
> report cited above!). On this particular day she becomes aware during
> the session of several deeper motives behind her frequent ambivalent
> reports of being raped.
>
> But then, on November 25, she tells nervously about the new music
> professor with whom she is studying voice:
>
> "He always explains to me that the nightingale's song is at its most
> beautiful during the mating season. It is essential for humans too to be
> sexually aroused when they sing. He sees to it that this happens during
> every voice lesson, and when it's over he tries to rape me. Usually I
> run away from him, but today he had locked the doors. I couldn't
> defend myself."

A final dream from Feb. 9, 1967, serves as an example for the way she kept returning to variations of the same theme.

"I dream I'm going up the stairs and am calling to my neighbor. At that moment I realize that I have done something wrong. (Association: when I masturbate I often have a guilty conscience.) Then she comes toward me in a flowing nightgown, throws herself passionately into my arms, and tries to pull me into her room. I feel awfully weak and can't defend myself. I'm terribly afraid and cry for help. (Association: I always had the same feeling of helplessness with my mother.) . . .

"Yesterday I dreamed I was leaning way out of an open window; it was raining and was very dark. I wanted to jump out. . . ."

The image of the open window and the urge to jump recur frequently. Once in a dream, looking out the window, she sees far below the corpse of her grandfather, with whom she grew up and who is actually still alive—a clear indication of who the target of her aggression is.

She recalls several reasons for this—which also provide a final example of her ambivalence:

"I was very attached to my grandfather, but some things happened that weren't so nice either. I slept in the same room with my grandma's 55-year-old friend, who often stayed with us. Sometimes at night he would come to this woman's bed and make advances to her and fondle her breasts. Even in the daytime he would often reach under her skirt and would put his arms around her. And he was already 81 at the time." [pp. 45–48]

The question of what the grandfather did to his pretty little granddaughter, who grew up in the same house with him and was "very attached to him," is not even raised in the course of her therapy. Like Freud (after 1897), Thomas makes no attempt to investigate the real background of the patient's ambivalence. Is it any surprise if she uses her symptoms to tell something that at the same time must absolutely remain secret?

Just as educators are convinced that their pedagogical measures are necessary for the child's present and future well-being (and not for fulfilling their own needs), many psychotherapists honestly believe that their manipulative techniques are of life-sustaining importance for the patient and are not aware that they serve as a sometimes grandiose way of defending themselves against their own insecurity. Jay Haley recounts, not without admiration, how his teacher, Milton H. Erickson, used various subtle tricks and traps to make a schizophrenic patient who claimed he had no digestive organs eat and drink. Advocates of such a method will even consider their pedagogical ideas as lifesaving measures if they see the patient's death (in this case from starvation) as the only alternative. It is conceivable, however, that a different therapist might say to this patient: "You firmly believe you have no digestive organs, and you must have a reason for thinking this that neither of us yet knows but can find out. You are trying to tell a story you have no other way of telling that was very tragic and painful for you; otherwise you wouldn't have to submit yourself to an ordeal like starvation in order to keep calling your plight to the attention of others and yourself." I am convinced that if the therapist did not use this strategy as a trick but were really interested in the background of the symptom, the patient would also become interested in his own history and would no longer have to starve himself once he was certain that his unconscious messages were reaching someone.

What must life be like for a person who has been tricked into relinquishing his last chance for self-articulation?

In *Uncommon Therapy: The Psychiatric Techniques of Milton H. Erickson, M.D.*, Haley writes:

> In the middle of this century, in the 1950s, a variety of strategic therapeutic approaches began to proliferate. Various types of family therapy and the conditioning therapies developed with the premise that a therapist should plan what to do. For a time there was controversy over whether it was wrong for a therapist to take action to bring about change, but now it seems clear that effective therapy requires that approach, and the disagreements are over how to go about it. [p. 18]

A pedagogical, manipulative attitude under the sway of the Fourth Commandment could be pointed out behind a great many psychotherapeutic methods, but I do not regard it as my task to track this approach down wherever it occurs, such as in the various forms of hypnosis or in the new directions in the family therapy (cf. Jay Haley or M. Selvini-Palazzoli). Selvini-Palazzoli's paradoxical method, for example, owes much of its success to the fact that patients are well-trained children. It should therefore come as no surprise if many people enthusiastically accept and carry out strict orders given by their therapist. If these people see the disappearance of their symptoms and a better adjustment to their environment as the only goal of therapy, then they have every right to choose a method that allows them to reach this goal as quickly as possible. If, on the other hand, a person has been despondent since childhood because he is unable to be his true self (as I hope to show later in the case of Franz Kafka), he will need someone whose main purpose is to help him find himself and who will not regard him as an object to be socialized. Naturally, we have all been the objects of child-rearing, and although we have a free marketplace with a variety of psychotherapeutic wares to choose from, it cannot be said that a patient is truly free to select the method best suited to him or her. That is why I am trying to awaken a sensitivity to the more subtle forms of unconscious manipulation (for instance, by means of drive theory) in the hope that a critical eye will then automatically detect the more flagrant forms. For this reason, I have taken my examples from a sympathetic therapist like Klaus Thomas, who has no conscious desire to manipulate his patients. It is not my intention to criticize individual therapists or analysts but rather the ideology that shapes the therapist's unconscious attitude, which is unconsciously transmitted by his training and whose roots reach back beyond the time of Sigmund Freud all the way to the Proverbs of Solomon, where we read: "He that spareth his rod hateth his son: but he that loveth him chasteneth him betimes" (13:24). Or: "Chasten thy son while there is hope, and let not thy soul spare for his crying" (19:18); "Foolishness is bound in the heart of a child; but the rod of correction shall drive it far from him" (22:15); "Withhold not correction from the child: for if thou beatest him with the rod, he shall not die" (23:13).

These words were written by a man who is not only regarded as wise but who did in fact express many wise ideas. Yet when we realize, as a result of Freud's discovery of the unconscious, what later happened to these chastised sons, our realization will force us to revise the pedagogical ideology handed down to us, even though it has been venerated for thousands of years.

There are types of psychotherapy that do not deal with childhood at all. But if therapists do take their patients' childhood seriously, sooner or later, perhaps as soon as the next generation, they will have to come to terms with the biblical injunction whose influence has dominated child-rearing practices for so long: "Chastise your child that it may go well with *you* [not him]." In order to prevent this foremost principle of old-style pedagogy from creeping into contemporary psychotherapeutic endeavors (along the lines of "practice therapy on your patients so that your teachers may be pleased with you"), we must first of all become conscious of just what these old principles are. That is the only way we can avoid becoming their victims.

৵ৡ 4 ৡৢ

Why So Radical?

SOME of my readers will perhaps wonder why I present the two psychoanalytic approaches (the one based on drive theory, the other free of pedagogical precepts) as mutually exclusive. Wouldn't it be possible to combine the two; once we have seen through and then abandoned our pedagogic compulsions, couldn't we still retain the drive theory as the basis of our interpretive work? Colleagues whose training and own analysis were dominated by the dogma of the Oedipus complex but who are also immediately struck by the validity of my ideas sometimes attempt to make this sort of synthesis or compromise. I shall describe two cases that illustrate why I believe such a compromise prevents the analyst from performing a supportive role.

A nine-year-old boy develops paranoia immediately following the death of his father, who had given his son a strongly religious upbringing and had treated him very strictly. The boy suffers from pavor nocturnus and awakens in the night thinking his room is filled with large angels who threaten him with long knives. The analyst who told me this story said: "Seen superficially, this would confirm your theory. But we must also take into account that the child has Oedipal wishes and wanted to do away with his father. His father's death fulfilled these wishes and inevitably causes the child deep feelings of guilt. That is why we cannot understand his symptoms unless we interpret the menacing angels as projections of his death wish."

There is much truth to this interpretation. One can hardly deny that the boy had a death wish directed toward his father and feared being punished for it, or.that he even saw himself in the angels with their many knives. But it is inconceivable that a father who played with his child, understood him, and gave him emotional support could, after his death, arouse in his son a hatred of such intensity that it would lead to paranoia. At the same time, even with a tolerant father who showed respect for his son, a boy might wish to separate him from the beloved mother, especially since this type of father would presumably have treated the mother lovingly as well. Nevertheless, after such a father's death, this child would not have visions of punishing angels with knives, because he has not internalized a strict, cruel father.

If a child asks what the difference is between a man and a woman and is told that a man has larger feet and hands than a woman, the answer is not false but it evades the central question (cf. my book *For Your Own Good*, p. 51). The same holds true in this case for the Oedipal interpretation, but something of much greater consequence is also involved, for this interpretation belies the child's own perceptions and robs him of what self-confidence he still has. The boy is trying to tell his story through his pavor nocturnus and delusions of persecution. Since he is not an adult with conscious memories, he cannot say, "I have suffered a great deal from the way my father humiliated me, from his rigidity and his religious bigotry." The boy does not even realize that he has suffered, for every act of cruelty has been explained to him as a part of the religious training God wants him to have in order to become a pious Christian. For this very reason, he needs someone who understands how lonely a child with such a father must feel. If the analyst instead presents the Oedipal interpretation, he passes over in silence the patient's actual torment. He is doing this even if he doesn't explicitly state his opinion but privately regards the patient's Oedipal guilt feelings as the cause of his paranoia.

For centuries, pedagogues have advocated suppressing the child's feelings so that he or she will be able to function better. The destructive effects of this advice on a child's personality go unnoticed as long as most people have been treated in more or less the same fashion. Many readers reacted with horror to the excerpts from child-rearing manuals from past centuries I included in *For Your Own Good*, even though these works have never been kept secret but probably even formed the nucleus of our parents' or grandparents' libraries. Similarly undetected are the detrimental effects on the patient's personality stemming from the approach recommended in much twentieth-century psychoanalytic writing. If the validity of the drive theory and the belief in infantile sexuality must not be questioned, then analysts trained along these lines will not notice the extent to which these dogmas interfere with their supportive role. There are, however, some exceptions, and as an example I shall show the difficulties the drive theory caused one of them, a sensitive, empathic therapist.

A young analyst still in training was treating a severely depressed woman of around fifty; he was delighted when, after a long waiting period, he finally was accepted as a candidate by one of the most renowned supervisory analysts. The long wait and the supervisor's name were enough in themselves to hold the young man's critical faculties in check for quite some time. Then at a certain point it became clear to him why he was always struggling to suppress his feelings in the supervisory sessions.

The woman whose analysis was being supervised had been raped as an adolescent by two soldiers of the occupation forces in Berlin in 1945. She mentioned this fact in the preliminary sessions, but during the course of her analysis she was unable to approach the experience on an emotional level. The supervisor explained the patient's attitude as "an expression of her guilt feelings at the fulfillment of her libidinous desires, which was forbidden by her superego." The training candidate (we shall call him Peter), who had empathized strongly with his patient, was indignant at his teacher's interpretation. Because he was born in 1945 he knew about the war only from books; in spite of this (or perhaps because of it), he was better able than his supervisor to imagine the powerlessness, humiliation, rage, and despair felt by a girl who has been raped. He presented the case in a seminar, hoping to find support, but the seminar leader as well as his other professional colleagues upheld the supervisor's interpretation based on the drive theory. Still Peter did not let himself be dissuaded. At the time, he was reading a novel that took place in the Berlin of 1945, and this helped him to imagine what his patient had undergone. Since he talked to her about her trauma and not about libidinous feelings, and since the patient sensed how seriously her analyst was taking this trauma, she was gradually able to get in touch with her feelings of terrible humiliation and helplessness.

These were followed by feelings of anger and hatred, which finally allowed her to gain access to much earlier traumatizations. Once this had taken place, her depression disappeared.

In fact, Peter's patient was cured, and he himself learned a great deal from the case. His teachers were displeased with him when he referred in seminars to the real events whose existence he suspected and searched for behind his patient's fantasies, and little by little he became aware of the drive theory's inherent hostility toward children. The danger of not being accepted as a member of the Psychoanalytic Association because of his differences with his teachers mattered less to him than what he had learned from this patient and from other patients. He now had the courage to pursue his insights, and no one was able to talk him out of them any longer.

After having survived the repressive atmosphere of the institute, Peter once said: "I can understand that they need compliant candidates if that's what they once were themselves and that it gives them a feeling of greater power if they can undermine the self-confidence of younger, less experienced colleagues with obfuscating, complicated theories, the same way their self-confidence was once undermined. It almost has to be that way. But it overtaxes my tolerance when they even expect us to be grateful for this treatment instead of being grateful to us for putting up with it for so long. Blind obedience is the price we pay now for the right to take our revenge later on a new generation of analysts by treating them the way we were treated."

Anyone who has taken part in training seminars or the conferences of psychoanalytic societies will have no trouble finding many other examples to show how the drive theory diverts an analyst's attention from the patient's trauma and how difficult it is for the analyst, if he is faithful to this theory, to accompany his patient on the very painful but necessary path the latter cannot possibly take alone. But in most cases like Peter's, it is highly unlikely that the training analyst will be able to endure the isolation Peter did; he will be reluctant to incur the official displeasure of the training institute, including the scorn of his teachers and colleagues, and will find it difficult to remain true to his feelings. In order to attain such inner freedom, an analyst has to undergo an exhaustive analysis, one in which he can develop a genuine capacity for judgment free from the strictures of "poisonous pedagogy" instead of sacrificing his independence of thought to his training analyst's theories as he once did to his parents' child-rearing precepts.

Freud himself does not seem to have thought that his theories of infantile sexuality and of the Oedipus complex invalidated his earlier findings, and this point is important enough for him to emphasize it more than once. In an addendum written in 1924 to his "Aetiology of Hysteria" (1896) he says: "All this is true [he is referring to sexual abuse of children]; but it must be remembered that at the time I wrote it I had not yet freed myself from my *overvaluation* of reality and my *low* valuation of phantasy" (Standard Edition, III, 204).

Freud's hope that his drive theory would not prove incompatible with the reality of sexual abuse and that one would not negate the other is shared by many analysts. In my opinion, practical as well as theoretical considerations argue against this sort of linkage between the drive and trauma theories.* I have attempted to show what the practical aspects are in my descriptions of the paranoid boy suffering from pavor nocturnus and of Peter, the young analyst. But on the theoretical level as well I see problems connected with such a compromise. For if a child in the so-called phallic phase really had biologically determined, natural sexual needs directed toward the parent of the opposite sex, there would not be any traumatic consequences if these desires were satisfied; then it would not be necessary to repress the experience of these needs so deeply that years of analysis are later required to uncover it. After all, how can a child have any knowledge of incestuous guilt? He or she comes to suspect it only because of secretive behavior on the part of adults. Only the adult knows there is an incest taboo, and only from the adult's attitude does the child sense that something forbidden is being done to him. His own attitude is at bottom completely free of guilt. Why,

---

* I use the term "trauma theory" (instead of "seduction theory") because it alludes to that part of Freud's theory which I accept. The seduction theory of 1896 as a whole maintains that *all* neuroses are a consequence of sexual abuse before the age of seven; this certainly cannot be true, since there are without any doubt non-sexual traumas as well. I want to make it particularly clear that I do not give credence to the seduction theory of 1896 in its entirety but only to its underlying premise: recognition of the significance of trauma and of its societal suppression as the source of neurosis. Furthermore, the word "seduction" when applied to incest is misleading because it implies that the child is a mature sexual partner, which is not, and can never be, the case.

then, should he experience any "drive conflicts"? The child seeks adults' love because he cannot live without it; he meets all their demands to the extent that he is able—for the sake of survival. He loves his parents, needs their presence, concern, and affection, and will learn to fit his attempt to win these indispensable treasures into the framework provided him by his parents from birth. A child who has been stimulated sexually from the beginning (e.g., by having his genitals massaged, tickled, or sucked, or by having orifices such as mouth and anus used for coitus-like purposes) may under certain circumstances come to regard this type of activity as love because he knows no other form of it. But to brand the child's *reactive* desires as blameworthy, as implied in the drive theory, is undeniably a remnant of the ideology of "poisonous pedagogy," which enables adults to delegate their guilt feelings to the child with the aid of various theories.

The theories of Melanie Klein provide a good illustration of this. The way she describes the infant's world of feeling in her works is an indirect expression of the adult's rejection of his or her own world of feeling, now encountered in the infant. It seems to me that both Klein, with her "cruel infant," and Kernberg, with his theory of the child's "innate pathological narcissism," fail to recognize the very early reactive character of the child's emotional development. They pay insufficient heed to the fact that parents' unfulfilled needs and their attitude toward the child are responsible for the forms taken by his aggressiveness, sexuality, and so-called narcissism in the same way that the analyst's point of view can ultimately determine whether a patient's messages are received with understanding and empathy or are regarded as "psychotic" and "incurable." I have tried to demonstrate elsewhere how perversions or obsessional neuroses with their strange symptoms reflect the incomprehension and dismay of the child's first attachment figure when confronted with the child's natural impulses (see *The Drama of the Gifted Child*). Destructive reenactments in later life can also be understood as a response to the fact that, due to the adult's projections, he or she sees the child's healthy aggressiveness as blameworthy and attempts to stifle it (cf. *For Your Own Good*).

There are forms of sexual abuse of children that entail fear, humiliation, shame, helplessness, powerlessness, and not infrequently physical pain for the child. Not long ago, charges were brought against a man in Switzerland who took each of his six children to the woods when they were four years old (in the Oedipal stage!) and performed anal intercourse with them. Probably the same thing had been done to him at that age. We can only hope that if a son of his should someday require analysis he will not be told by his analyst that the scenes he is describing represent his homosexual "fantasies." It can be just as alienating for the patient if the analyst expresses skepticism less explicitly than this by saying, for example, that it makes no difference whether reality or fantasy is involved here, since the analyst is concerned only with the patient's "psychic reality." This will simply traumatize the patient once again in a very real way (not only in the transference), for he has no one who can fully comprehend his anger and therefore will not be able to comprehend and acknowledge it himself.

Early Childhood Reality and Psychoanalytic Practice

❁

*the god of my childhood wears black robes, has horns
on his head and carries an ax in his hand. how in the
world was I still able to slip past him?
all my life I have been creeping stealthily through
my landscape, under my arm the little bit of life I keep
thinking I have stolen.*
—Mariella Mehr, *Steinzeit* (Stone Age)

In the maternity wards of Western civilization there is little chance of consolation. . . . The newborn infant, with his skin crying out for the ancient touch of smooth, warmth-radiating, living flesh, is wrapped in dry, lifeless cloth. He is put in a box where he is left, no matter how he weeps, in a limbo that is utterly motionless (for the first time in all his body's experience, during the eons of its evolution or during its eternity of bliss in the womb). The only sounds he can hear are the wails of other victims of the same ineffable agony. The sound can mean nothing to him. He cries and cries; his lungs, new to air, are strained with the desperation in his heart. No one comes. Trusting in the rightness of life, as by nature he must, he does the only act he can, which is to cry on. Eventually, a timeless lifetime later, he falls asleep exhausted.

He awakes in a mindless terror of the silence, the motionlessness. He screams. He is afire from head to foot with want, with desire, with intolerable impatience. He gasps for breath and screams until his head is filled and throbbing with the sound. He screams until his chest aches, until his throat is sore. He can bear the pain no more and his sobs weaken and subside. He listens. He opens and closes his fists. He rolls his head from side to side. Nothing helps. It is unbearable. He begins to cry again, but it is too much for his strained throat; he soon stops: He stiffens his desire-racked body and there is a shadow of relief. He waves his hands and kicks his feet. He stops, able to suffer, unable to think, unable to hope. He listens. Then he falls asleep again.

When he awakens he wets his diaper and is distracted from his torment by the event. But the pleasant feeling of wetting and the warm, damp, flowing sensation around his lower body are quickly gone. The warmth is now immobile and turning cold and clammy. He kicks his legs. Stiffens his body. Sobs. Desperate with longing, his lifeless surroundings wet and uncomfortable, he screams through his misery until it is stilled by lonely sleep.

Suddenly he is lifted; his expectations come forward for what is to be his. The wet diaper is taken away. Relief. Living hands touch his skin. His feet are lifted and a new, bone-dry, lifeless cloth is folded around his loins. In an instant it is as though the hands had never been there, nor the wet diaper. There is no conscious memory, no inkling of hope. He is in unbearable emptiness, timeless, motionless, silent, wanting, wanting. His continuum tries its emergency measures, but they are all meant for bridging short lapses in correct treatment or for summoning relief from someone, it is assumed, who will want to provide it. His continuum has no solution for this extremity. The situation is beyond its vast experience. The infant, after breathing air for only a few hours, has already reached a point of disorientation from his nature beyond the saving powers of the mighty continuum. His tenure in the womb was the last he is ever likely to know of the uninterrupted state of well-being in which it is his innate expectation that he will spend his lifetime. His nature is predicated upon the assumption that his mother is behaving suitably and that their motivations and consequent actions will naturally serve one another.

Someone comes and lifts him deliciously through the air. He is in life. He is carried a bit too gingerly for his taste, but there is motion. Then he is in his place. All the agony he has undergone is nonexistent. He rests in the enfolding arms, and though his skin is sending no message of relief from the cloth, no news of live flesh on his flesh, his hands and mouth are reporting normal. The positive pleasure of life, which is continuum normal, is almost complete. The taste and texture of the breast are there, the warm milk is flowing into his eager mouth, there is a heartbeat, which should have been his link, his reassurance of continuity from the womb, there is movement perceptible to his dim vision. The sound of the voice is right, too. There is only the cloth and the smell (his mother uses cologne) that leave something missing. He sucks and when he feels full and rosy, dozes off.

When he awakens he is in hell. No memory, no hope, no thought can bring the comfort of his visit to his mother into this bleak purgatory. Hours pass and days and nights. He screams, tires, sleeps. He wakes and wets his diaper. By now there is no pleasure in this act. No sooner is the pleasure of relief prompted by his innards than it is replaced, as the hot, acid urine touches his by-now chafed body, by a searing crescendo of pain. He screams. His exhausted lungs must scream to override the fiery stinging. He screams until the pain and screaming use him up before he falls asleep.

At his not unusual hospital the busy nurses change all diapers on schedule, whether they are dry, wet, or long wet, and send the infants home chafed raw, to be healed by someone who has time for such things.

By the time he is taken to his mother's home (surely it cannot be called his) he is well versed in the character of life. On a preconscious plane that will qualify all his further impressions, as it is qualified by them, he knows life to be unspeakably lonely, unresponsive to his signals, and full of pain.

But he has not given up. His vital forces will try forever to reinstate their balances, as long as there is life.

Home is essentially indistinguishable from the maternity ward except for the chafing. The infant's waking hours are passed in yearning, wanting, and interminable waiting for rightness to replace the silent void. For a few minutes a day, his longing is suspended and his terrible skin-crawling need to be touched, to be held and moved about, is relieved. His mother is one who, after much thought, has decided to allow him access to her breast. She loves him with a tenderness she has never known before. At first, it is hard for her to put him down after his feeding, especially because he cries so desperately when she does. But she is convinced that she must, for her mother has told her (and *she* must know) that if she gives in to him now he will be spoiled and cause trouble later. She wants to do everything right; she feels for a moment that the little life she holds in her arms is more important than anything else on earth.

She sighs, and puts him gently in his crib, which is decorated with yellow ducklings and matches his whole room. She has worked hard to furnish it with fluffy curtains, a rug in the shape of a giant panda, white dresser, Bathinette and changing table equipped with powder, oil, soap, shampoo, and hairbrush, all made and packed in colors especially for babies. There are pictures on the wall of baby animals dressed as people. The chest of drawers is full of little undershirts, slumbersuits, bootees, caps, mittens, and diapers. There is a toy woolly lamb stood at a beguiling angle on top, and a vase of flowers—which have been cut off from their roots, for his mother also "loves" flowers.

She straightens baby's undershirt and covers him with an embroidered sheet and a blanket bearing his initials. She notes them with satisfaction. Nothing has been spared in perfecting the baby's room, though she and her young husband cannot yet afford all the furniture they have planned for the rest of the house. She bends to kiss the infant's silky cheek and moves toward the door as the first agonized shriek shakes his body.

Softly, she closes the door. She has declared war upon him. Her will must prevail over his. Through the door she hears what sounds like someone being tortured. Her continuum recognizes it as such. Nature does not make clear signals that someone is being tortured unless it is the case. *It is precisely as serious as it sounds.*

She hesitates, her heart pulled toward him, but resists and goes on her way. He has just been changed and fed. She is sure he does not *really* need anything, therefore, and she lets him weep until he is exhausted.

He awakens and cries again. His mother looks in at the door to ascertain that he is in place; softly, so as not to awaken in him any false hope of attention, she shuts the door again. She hurries to the kitchen, where she is working, and leaves that door open so that she can hear the baby, in case "anything happens to him."

The infant's screams fade to quavering wails. As no response is forthcoming, the motive power of the signal loses itself in the confusion of barren emptiness where the relief ought, long since, to have arrived. He looks about. There is a wall beyond the bars of his crib. The light is dim. He cannot turn himself over. He sees only the bars, immobile, and the wall. He hears meaningless sounds in a distant world. There is no sound near him. He looks at the wall until his eyes close. When they open again, the bars and the wall are exactly as before, but the light is dimmer.

—Jean Liedloff, *The Continuum Concept*

I AM sometimes asked where I stand in relation to the psycho-analytic movement, and I also ask myself the same question. When I wrote *The Drama of the Gifted Child*, I still believed my experiences as an analyst were compatible with Freud's drive theory, and I regarded my contribution to the treatment of narcissistic disturbances as groundwork necessary in many cases for dealing with "conflict neuroses." But the more thoroughly I consider the theoretical consequences of my own experiences, the more closely and unbiasedly I examine traditional theoretical concepts for their experiential content, and the more clearly their function in the overall context of societal repression emerges—all the more questionable do I find the validity of Freud's drive theory and all the more urgent my need to distance myself from it.

I owe to Freud's methods insights into the human psyche far surpassing anything my study of philosophy ever had to offer me. But it was my application of these very methods that brought me face to face with certain truths that refuted some of his theories. I cannot abandon the truths I have discovered without abandoning myself, and am therefore compelled to remain true to them, even to those aspects of them that lead me in a different direction from my teachers. In what follows it will become clear that I still share common ground with psychoanalytic theory insofar as I subscribe to these tenets:

1. Everyone is shaped (this does not mean determined) by his or her childhood.

2. Neuroses are rooted in childhood.

3. The methods of free association and of the analytic setting (couch, rule of abstinence) make it possible for the drama of child-

hood to be reenacted in the transference and for a maturation process that has been blocked by neurosis to begin.

4. Changes in personality occurring during analysis do not stem from "corrective emotional experiences" but from insights the patient arrives at by repetition, remembering, and working through relevant material.

These four points may explain in large part why I do not accept C. G. Jung, Alfred Adler, or representatives of countless other schools as my teachers. The analytic psychology of Jung and his followers does not seem to me to give due weight to what I consider the decisive significance of early childhood. Even Adler, who certainly recognized the problem of power vs. powerlessness, did not pay sufficient heed to the many crucial factors of a child's early life, considering that Adler's followers are content with their schematic theories (such as organic inferiority) and overemphasize the teleological point of view. In Frankel's logotherapy, for example, which is oriented toward "the search for meaning," a person's primary concern is to find the meaning awaiting him and live accordingly. It is no doubt true that a person will be subject to depression if he feels his life is meaningless, but the question of *why* he finds his life meaningless will not be answered by logotherapy if it does not take the dimension of childhood into account.

In spite of the common ground I share with Freudian psychoanalysis, I see decisive differences between it and my position:

1. I do not believe that a neurosis originates because a drive conflict has been repressed, as Freud thought, but rather because early traumatic experiences could not be articulated and *therefore* had to be repressed.

2. I do not regard the parents of a patient only as objects of his or her aggressive and libidinous desires but also as real persons, who—often without knowing or intending it—have caused the patient real, not only imagined, suffering.

3. The fact that a patient finally faces his or her parents' personalities and actions and is at last permitted to formulate an emotional response to them leads to an increased capacity for integration on the patient's part.

4. This formulation, emerging in the transference and countertransference and with the aid of fantasies, feelings, and reenactments, is possible only if the analyst listens to the patient without

setting up any pedagogical goals, i.e., if he (a) does not defend the parents against the patient's reproaches because he no longer has to spare his own parents and suppress his own pain; (b) has integrated his awareness of the child's lack of rights in our cultural tradition; (c) does not hide the reactive nature of destructive impulses behind inappropriate theories about the death instinct; (d) retains his role as advocate and does not let himself be turned into a judge, either by the patient or as a result of the criteria acquired in his own training.

5. I cannot consider the problem of "infantile sexuality" in isolation but see it in connection with my knowledge of all the ways children can be used by their parents. I have difficulty separating what Freud interprets as libidinous desires from the child's narcissistic needs for echoing, respect, attention, mirroring, acceptance, and understanding.

6. The child's position between father and mother undoubtedly leads to various feelings, strong emotions, anxieties, conflicts, and problems that can be designated as Oedipal but that I interpret differently from Freud (see Chapter 12). By no means do I consider the "Oedipal conflict" and the need to work it through as the source of neurotic development.

7. The healing process begins when the once absent, repressed reactions to traumatization (such as anxiety, rage, anger, despair, dismay, pain, grief) can be articulated in analysis; then the symptoms, whose function it had been to express the unconscious trauma in a disguised, alienated language incomprehensible both to the patient and to those around him, disappear. This statement goes against the practice of many psychoanalysts who attempt to help their patients gain insight, often of a merely intellectual nature, into their drive conflicts, but it does not go against Freud's methods during the period prior to his discovery of the supposed omnipresence of the Oedipus complex. Therefore, when I distance myself from Freud in these pages, I am thinking of his writing after 1897. In "The Aetiology of Hysteria" (1896), on the other hand, I see a confirmation of my own experience.

⤙ 5 ⤚

Psychoanalysis without
Pedagogy

THERE are many illustrations in *The Drama of the Gifted Child* of what I see as an alternative to orthodox analysis and its manner of interpreting drive conflicts, but since I am repeatedly asked to give a more detailed explanation of my theoretical concepts, I shall do this now as briefly as possible.

1. The analyst endeavors, totally and under all circumstances, to take the patient's part, not to pass judgment, to respect everything the patient says and does, to take him seriously, and to give as much understanding as is humanly possible.

2. This attitude is not to be confused with "love." First it must be said that love for someone is a gift and not something we can produce simply by making a decision or by an act of will. Then, too, love may not even be compatible with the therapeutic relationship, for it would violate the essential rule of abstinence and thus destroy the effectiveness of the treatment. I can love someone when I feel free to show my emotions and at the same time can accept my relative dependence on the person I love. The abstinence rule, which states that the analytic setting must not provide an outlet for the analyst's feelings—excludes both of these possibilities—in analysis only the patient has the right to express *all* his or her feelings.*

3. The analyst does not assume the role of the authoritarian par-

---

* I emphasize this point, which strikes me as obvious, because I have often encountered the view that the analyst, after all, cannot "give love" eight hours a day and must therefore "have a technique handy." Although I myself intentionally do not use the word "technique," an approach that sees love or "mother love" as something one can measure out is just as alien to me. This approach, which displays the presumptuousness and dishonesty of "poisonous pedagogy," has invaded the vocabulary of several forms of therapy but not, so far as I know, that of classical psychoanalysis, where the word "technique" is preferred.

ents in reality, even though he is turned into them in the transference; e.g., he does not wound the patient with his silence, with
authoritarian, one-sided decisions, with unsympathetic, disparaging
interpretations that demonstrate his superiority. He asks questions,
thereby showing that he doesn't know everything. If the patient
points out errors he has made, he admits them; he does not have to
claim the infallibility of an authority figure.

4. The patient discovers (a) that the analyst is interested in the
history of his childhood and is searching for messages and reenactments of repressed traumas in everything occurring in the present
and in the transference, and (b) that he is attempting to learn with
the patient the language of the latter's repetition compulsion.

All this leads to the following steps in the patient's analysis:

1. He finds out, often for the first time in his life, what it means
to have someone on his side, an advocate. This does not represent a
"corrective emotional experience" (for nothing can correct the
past), but it does enable him to break through to his own reality
and to grieve. A person who has never known this support is unlikely to be able to appraise his earlier situation, because he
doesn't realize life can be any other way.

2. The contours of present and past become increasingly sharp.
Through the analyst's understanding, the patient learns for the first
time how lonely he is and how misunderstood he has always been;
through the analyst's honesty, the patient discovers the dishonesty
in his own life; through the respect the analyst shows him, he becomes aware of his lack of respect for himself. Only now, thanks to
experiencing something so different from what he is accustomed to,
does he become aware of the compulsive nature of his customary
life. Without support, the patient would have great difficulty in getting through to his repressed traumas, and he would never be able
to bear them by himself. Patients can even become further traumatized in analysis without being aware of it.

3. An empathic inner object is established that enables the patient to experience sorrow but also curiosity concerning his own
childhood.

4. The patient becomes more and more interested in his past,
and at this point, if not sooner, his depression and suicidal thoughts
disappear.

5. He can deal with partners and parents, both as real persons

and as introjects, using the analyst as the stand-in for all of these people.

6. As a result of the support he receives, the patient now becomes able to express his aggression. Initially, he will express it in the same form in which he experienced it as a child. He may threaten the analyst just as he himself was threatened in early life without being able to remember it (cf. *The Drama of the Gifted Child*). Because he cannot remember, he reenacts the trauma, assigning the role of the child he once was to the therapist. This puts every analyst to the test, particularly in regard to his tolerance for his own feelings of powerlessness. These feelings are less likely to emerge if the patient's "acting out" is understood as a reenactment of real situations from the past (cf. Chapter 7). But if it is interpreted as an expression of "penis envy," of "pathological narcissism," or the like, the analyst can easily develop feelings of powerlessness, which must then be warded off with the full force of his powerful theoretical language.

The patient's numerous reenactments often form the core of the analysis, but I have described the initial phases in considerable detail because I am trying here, among other things, to define my position within psychoanalysis by distinguishing between my approach and the one based on the drive theory. I distance myself, in other words, from an unconscious identification with the parent or pedagogue and consciously identify with the mute child in the patient. I don't do this for "sentimental" reasons but for the sake of clarity, so that together we can locate his repressed traumas, which he has been reenacting all his life and which are inhibiting his vitality; in the process of becoming conscious of these traumas he will make use of repetition compulsion, dreams, and fantasies, as well as transference and countertransference.

The healing power of this process presupposes the kind of emotional development I described in my remarks about the true and false self in *The Drama of the Gifted Child*. If I regard it as my therapeutic goal to have patients experience and articulate their early traumas, I must help them travel the *"via regia,"* i.e., regain their lost ability to feel, for only on the path of feelings can they find their true self. I do not know if it is always possible to take this path. In many cases where the mother makes it a point, as part of her child's upbringing, to instill a fear of feeling from the very beginning, her efforts turn out to be so successful that the effects last for decades. People who have been raised this way from an early age will have to avoid their feelings for the rest of their lives and will sometimes find it necessary to make those around them (including their own children) experience these feelings. Their fear of having to experience their feelings, which they perceived as threatening at such an early age, is not likely to lead them to a psychoanalyst's couch, unless they have decided for some reason to pursue this profession themselves. This occurs more frequently than one would suspect, for this profession in particular offers the opportunity of delegating one's own feelings to others—namely, to patients.

When someone who has not been permitted to be aware of his feelings undergoes a training analysis, he will welcome any theory that keeps him from having to enter dangerous emotional zones. As a result, the analyst will be made to feel the candidate's helplessness, fear, powerlessness, perhaps his anger as well; at the same time the candidate may talk about the cruelest events of his childhood as indifferently as though he were discussing a topic treated in his dissertation. After the completion of the candidate's training, these unwelcome feelings can be relegated to his own analysands, and with the help of the intellectual vocabulary he has mastered they can be directed into safe but ineffectual channels. This is a situation I have frequently encountered, and the numerous directives of supervisory committees can do little to alter its tragic nature. This is one of the reasons why I decided to give up my practice in order to write about the harm caused by traditional child-rearing methods, which may cause irreversible damage in severe cases because it was inflicted at such an early age.

❦ 6 ❧

Why Does the Patient Need an Advocate in the Analyst?

THE more distance I gain from the constraints of psychoanalytic theory, the more I am struck by the frequency with which analysts dispense moral judgments and by how easily and imperceptibly it can come about that they make themselves the judges of their patients. In a group discussion of *The Drama of the Gifted Child,* many of my colleagues were concerned with the question of whom I actually consider the guilty party to be and whom I hold responsible for children's suffering. They could not grasp that I blame neither children nor parents. You cannot, some said, absolve parents of all responsibility; after all, someone must be responsible for all the misery. Others pointed out how difficult some children make it for their parents to love them, be kind to them, and understand them. For this reason parents can't be blamed for everything, they said; you have to be fair and assign guilt to both sides.

Any line of argument that goes around in circles like this shows traces of "poisonous pedagogy." We should not be surprised that pedagogues at the turn of the century thought this way, for they had as yet no inkling of the existence of unconscious compulsions. But when psychoanalysts today attempt to discover who bears the guilt, they are voluntarily relinquishing what is essentially their most precious possession: their knowledge of the unconscious and of the tragedy inherent in human existence. Sigmund Freud sensed this tragedy, and perhaps he was so relieved to "discover" the Oedipus complex because he hoped it would express the universally tragic nature of human life without assigning blame to individual parents. Unfortunately, this theory is better suited to obscure than to illuminate the origins of a neurosis. Since we have all internalized the thought patterns of "poisonous pedagogy," psychoanalysis, in spite of all the progress that has been made, is still haunted by the image of the wicked child, who has to learn to control and even sublimate his wild and destructive energies ("libido" and "death instinct").

The realization that the child's anger is a response to narcissistic disappointments and wounds (caused by parents who reject, humiliate, abuse, or fail to understand their child—again for unconscious reasons) is a relatively recent one. A change seems to occur somewhere between Melanie Klein and Donald Winnicott. For Klein, the "cruelty" of the young child still derives from human drive structure; for Winnicott and Kohut this is not the case, at least not in their practice (cf. Winnicott's article, "Hate in the Counter-Transference"). The latter have much more understanding for the importance of what confronts children in their environment. If I pursue this line of thought and ask how children experience the emotional atmosphere around them, it awakens fear in many that I might want to blame the parents and disregard their difficulties. Since I do not do this, my position sometimes perplexes people. If they do not work through their reaction, their adherence to traditional views on child-rearing may be reinforced.

This is why I keep trying to explain my position with the aid of various images and concepts. I *always* regard myself as the advocate of the child in my patients; whatever they may tell me, I take their side completely and identify fully with the child in them, who usually is not yet able to experience his feelings and delegates them to me. It is rare for patients to reproach their parents, since their illness is a result of not being allowed to do this as a child. If they do reproach them in the early stages of analysis, they soon give this up, torment themselves with guilt feelings, and attempt to defend their parents. If aggression can be experienced at all, it takes adult forms (scorn, irony, intellectual criticism), which originate at a much later date, for the rage felt by a very young child (an ambivalent, impotent rage) can never be experienced initially. It is no different for adolescents who display defiant or even destructive behavior. In the beginning stages of analysis, the feelings stemming from early childhood are always unconscious.

If we keep this in mind we will understand how crucial it is for the analyst not to be judgmental, not to appeal to the patient's reason, not to strive for objectivity, but simply to let himself be guided by the child, who is not yet able to speak. Neither should it be the analyst's goal to bring about the patient's reconciliation with his parents. If the analyst has seen for himself that *his* rage did not kill his parents, he will no longer feel compelled to protect the patient's parents from rage by working toward reconciliation. In most cases the analyst is the first person in the patient's life whom the latter can confide in, and it is important that this person not abuse the trust placed in him, not admonish or blame, not be shocked, but be willing to explore unfamiliar territory of the patient's life along with him. For the patient, too, will become acquainted with his own life for the first time.

It is my belief that by taking into account the parents' child-rearing ideology, the power structure within the family, and the resultant nature of the child's reality, we will reach a deeper understanding of the patient's aggression than by assuming the existence of the Freudian death instinct, also postulated by Melanie Klein and her followers. In her descriptions of the early stages of the child's emotional life, Klein presents us with the portrait of a wicked infant in which she fails to show the connections between the infant's violent feelings (such as hate, envy, and greed) and the unconscious of the parents, as well as the humiliation, mistreatment, and narcissistic wounds the latter inflict on the child.

This view affects the analyst's attitude toward the patient, as can be observed, for example, in the cases presented by Hanna Segal. Whenever her patients have an exaggerated fear of the envy of those around them, she always sees this as a projection of their own feelings of envy onto others. Strangely enough, Segal never considers the possibility that her patients might once have been the objects of a violent parent's envy and are still afraid of that parent.

And yet one might wonder if it can be that only the child (i.e., the patient) is projecting. Why should only the child feel envy and not the adult? What has the adult done with his or her envy? And if it is uncovered in analysis (as it is in numerous cases cited by Segal), why is it assumed that this envy is never directed toward one's own children? And when it is, why is this very real factor (the parents' envy of the child, of his or her greater freedom, spontaneity, minimal responsibilities, abundant leisure, carefreeness) passed over in psychoanalysis and not included in its reconstructions? The infant's anger is appropriate to his situation and free from transference (i.e., directed at the person who is hurting him and not, like adults' hatred, at substitute objects), because—except for the prenatal period—the infant has no history or at the most a very short and less complicated one. In contrast to this, the roots of an adult's hatred reach far back into childhood; it is therefore almost always displaced and usually directed at innocent people in its search for outlets and victims. And these are most easily found in one's own children, who are legally their parents' property.

It is regrettable that considerations of this nature are regarded as "not psychoanalytic" by classical psychoanalysis. Now that we have learned from the most recent literature on the history of childhood what children have always had to endure, we are more likely to be taken aback if someone interprets a child's hatred as an expression of the death instinct—so correct and appropriate will this hatred seem in view of the cruelty and brutality involved.

Once we as analysts have understood the *reactive* nature of this hatred, a great weight will be lifted from us and we shall have made the following decisive gains:

1. We will be better able to understand the patient and to tolerate his aggressiveness.

2. We will no longer need the pedagogical approach.

3. We will be confident that destructive narcissistic rage will of its own accord change into healthy constructive self-defense when the patient no longer experiences his rage as meaningless but sees it as an appropriate reaction to cruelty. In order for this change to take place, the patient needs an analyst who stands behind him wholeheartedly.

For a long time I believed that my own professional experience confirmed the psychoanalytic theory which states that the cruelty of the patient's superego usually surpasses the cruelty of parental behavior because the former is fed by endopsychic aggression (the id). Since I have become more aware of the nature of the young child's feelings, however, I have serious doubts in this regard. Cruelty cannot be measured objectively: what is wounding to one person may not be to another. The way parents' behavior affects a child cannot be detected from the outside, and in later life the former child often does not remember how he reacted to their behavior at the time. But the strictness of the superego will betray how much the child feared his parents *in the past* even if now as an adult he should doubt this and even if his parents do not *at present* seem to the observer to arouse any fear at all.

The self-destructiveness of an addict or a suicidal person is not telling something about his or her present situation, either, but similarly about events long past. Only when we realize how powerless a child is in the face of parental expectations (that he control his drives, suppress his feelings, respect their defenses, and tolerate their outbursts) will we grasp the cruelty of parents' threats to withdraw their love if the child fails to meet these impossible demands. And this cruelty is perpetuated in the child. It can also be detected in the numerous precautions society takes to keep parental exercise of power and violence a secret. According to traditional patterns of child-rearing, the child must regard his or her parents as infallible, must take them as models. As a result, children really are convinced that they, not adults, are the only ones who need to tell lies; that they, not their parents, are the only ones who have to struggle against feelings of hatred.

Because a child experiences feelings much more intensely than an adult, it can sometimes happen (but need not) that a child's sadistic fantasies are much crueler than seems at first glance to be justified by the motivating factors. It may be, for example, that a mother "simply" keeps ignoring her child and as a result he stores up a boundless narcissistic rage, which will later become all the more violent the less the child was able to express it earlier. Sadism may even be a response to a form of treatment that cannot be described as sadistic. But the subjective significance of being ignored, the narcissistic wounding and humiliation of the child can be measured fully only if narcissistic needs for respect, acceptance, and being taken seriously are given due consideration along with his physical needs.

It is not up to the analyst to judge whether the patient is being fair toward his parents or not. The patient will be fair of his own accord as soon as he is able, as soon as he has experienced fully his childhood resentment and overcome it. A push in the right direction, no matter how well intentioned, cannot speed the process but will only delay it. It is not the therapist's task to judge the patient, even though the latter may provoke him to during the transference. I have never known a patient to portray his parents more negatively than he actually experienced them in childhood but always more positively—because idealization of his parents was essential for survival. He can permit himself to be critical and rebellious only if he finds in the analyst someone who gives him unqualified support. Otherwise he will never dare to experience his feelings fully and will be unable to discover his truth (the true nature of his childhood).

Often, a parent's positive sides are also brought to light late in analysis after all his or her negative aspects have been acknowledged. This change simply indicates that the frozen image of a "witch" or "tyrant," for example, was able to be transformed into a many-sided human being, because now the patient has gained access to his feelings and can also integrate the two sides in himself.

The temporary revival of the young child's initial, unconditional, all-forgiving "love" for his parents, which precedes any form of rebelliousness, is also a part of the analytic process. It is this experience that makes the extent of the child's painful disappointment in his parents perceptible and thus makes his ambivalence comprehensible as well. For psychic wounds, humiliation, beatings, and other forms of mistreatment came from those very persons to whom the young child was most attached. Whether the patient's early glorification of his parents turns into a mature love or a calm, hate-free detachment after the storms of analysis depends on countless factors, among them the parents' capacity for growth, should they still be living.

Outside guidance and instruction are not necessary for a child to grow and flourish, yet they are implied in Freud's famous words "Where id was, there shall ego be." The structural model (ego, id, superego) is reminiscent of the traditional family pattern according to which adults are supposed to civilize the wild, wicked child and bring him under control, or at least "tame" his wicked drives.

❧ 7 ❧

The Castrating Woman or the
Humiliated Little Girl?

THE question of what approach an analyst takes to his patient's early childhood is not only a theoretical one but also determines the attitude he will take during treatment as well as his ability to serve as the patient's advocate. The way he reacts to the patient's resistance and to what happens in the transference and countertransference will depend on whether he interprets the patient's aggression, fears, and advances as encoded messages about a real, heretofore concealed situation in the past or as expressions of libidinous and aggressive drives. In the latter case the patient's behavior will strike him as destructive, narcissistic, and neurotic, and his fears as exaggerated, even paranoid, because they are incommensurate to the present situation, especially to the efforts of the well-meaning therapist.

A woman whose analysis I was supervising had previously tried for years to accept her first analyst's diagnosis of penis envy and a castrating attitude in the hope that this would help her to become nicer and more feminine, i.e., less suspicious and critical of men. All her efforts were to no avail. Although she suffered from the way she almost compulsively ruined every relationship with a man by immediately looking for his weaknesses, she was unable to change the pattern. She eventually carried this over to her analyst, whose self-confidence was so undermined by this very intelligent patient that he did not want to continue the therapy.

In her second analysis, which I was able to follow in large part, the transference initially developed along the same lines. The second analyst, however, was not content to see his patient's attacks as expressions of a death instinct or of penis envy but searched for their causes. He understood that his hurt feelings and threatened

64

self-confidence were signs of the countertransference and were telling him something about the patient's father; therefore, he was able
to arrive at reconstructions that were then confirmed by new memories on the patient's part and by a spontaneous change in her attitude toward men.

It turned out that her father had been an insecure and weak
man who was no match for his daughter intellectually, was submissive toward his parents, and was despised by his wife after he
returned from the war. During puberty the patient shared her
mother's scorn and often criticized her father, whom she considered
a coward. She was conscious of all this; why, then, was she fixated
on this attitude and why did she transfer it to other men so that
she was unlikely to marry and have children, although this was what
she really wanted? Her hatred of her father was not unconscious at
all, one might think.

Thanks to her second analyst's interest in what actually tran-
spired in her early childhood, it was revealed that there had at one
time been someone who did not frighten this weak, hypochondriacal,
and ailing man and who had not felt scorn for him, someone on
whom he could take revenge for all the humiliation he had undergone during his childhood, then again as a prisoner of war, and
finally in his marriage: this person was his oldest daughter, the
patient, when she was still very little. Although he couldn't talk to
anyone about his experiences and was very withdrawn, he could
play with his little girl from time to time but then would suddenly
start to scream at her, hit her, put her to shame, and humiliate her.
He could be loving and hold her close when he needed someone,
but then push her aside like a doll or a pet without any explanation
and turn to other things or people. The reconstruction of this period
was made possible by the patient's reenactments in the transference
and was confirmed by her dreams; in addition, she began trying to
find things out from relatives that she had not wanted to know about
before. For the first time she could now listen to details about her
father's membership in the SA without having to run away. She
was searching for her father as he really was and realized that the
SA armband was no longer alien to her because she had found him
within herself (his deep-seated insecurity and his related attempts
to compensate for it) with the aid of the transference.

A period of deep mourning accompanied what she had learned.

The patient kept experiencing herself as a loving child, dependent on a father who was unpredictable—sometimes affectionate and sometimes cruel. Now she was able to detect his immaturity, his vulnerability, and his extreme narcissistic deprivation, to see him as someone who had no understanding for what someone else was feeling and was himself unable to feel, a father who used her like a toy and as an outlet and who had no respect for her soul and no inkling of her true nature. It was *this* father the patient despised in all the men she feared and loved and *his* weakness she had to expose again and again as long as the father of her early childhood was not accessible to consciousness. She was constantly reenacting the drama of her childhood in her repetition compulsion, sometimes with the roles reversed, so that *she* was the one who was superior to men, who wounded and abandoned them. In her encounters with men she also hoped finally to punish her father for his cruelty. After she had experienced her childhood desire for revenge in analysis and had begun to understand that revenge taken on substitute persons in the present can never satisfy the desire for it felt as a child, she was able to experience new kinds of relationships with men that she had never believed possible before.

All this happened without anyone having told her what to do, without any effort on her part, without struggling to be "reasonable." The immeasurable rage she had felt initially toward the first therapist, who she felt had grossly misunderstood her, was slowly transformed into grief over his inability to understand, a limitation she gradually discovered, in other areas, in her new therapist as well but was able to accept. At the same time it became possible for this basically empathic and sensitive woman to accept her father's past. She realized, now on an emotional level and without despising him, that as a child her father had been the plaything of his divorced parents (who were always shunting him back and forth) before he became the plaything of the state and the party in the Third Reich. But true understanding and forgiveness on the part of this woman were possible only because the humiliated little girl's rage and fantasies of revenge were taken seriously by the analyst and not interpreted as an expression of penis envy.

It is not an act of cruelty for an analyst to misunderstand a patient but rather an unfortunate circumstance closely related to his own training analysis; it can therefore be helpful for both parties if the analyst can admit his limitations. The patient is put in a difficult position, on the other hand, if the analyst explains that he understands his patient but that the patient "is refusing" to accept the analyst's interpretation because he, the patient, wants to be more clever, grand, and powerful and make everyone else look small and stupid. Such explanations encourage sadomasochistic transferences or are already a sign of them. They will be repaid with even more vigorous attacks, which can also take the form of hours of silence and make the analyst "lose his patience" completely, which certainly does nothing to increase his empathy.

What is taking place here? A little child who is being abused is not permitted to become aware of it or to talk about it, and this very taboo against experiencing and expressing himself robs him of his self-confidence. As an adult, when he goes to an analyst and is told that he "only thinks" he is misunderstood but actually is not, how will he react? If no foundation for his own feelings has been laid, then the only alternative is total adaptation, and the patient will accept labels for his behavior from his analyst as he once did from his parents. If, however, this foundation exists—i.e., a vital, true self—then the analyst's assertions, which sharply contradict the patient's feelings of not having been understood, will cause the patient serious difficulties and insecurity and will make him angry, perhaps even—and this is preferable—outraged. In the protective setting of analysis, he will for the first time dare to rebel against the I-know-better and I-am-always-right attitude of his parents, which he now sees reflected in the analyst, and to defend his autonomy. His fate now depends on whether the analyst is willing to discard as outdated and useless his previously marketable "wares," letting himself be guided by his patient's feelings, or whether he continues to insist on forcing these wares on the patient. It is not the worst that can happen if a power struggle develops between the two, for this is an indication that the patient is still showing signs of life and is searching for autonomy.

Like the methods used by parents, the methods of therapists (of various schools) can be very subtle. Many of them are not content with talking a patient out of his feeling of not being understood and with using their interpretations to show him that this feeling is only a sign of "willfulness," "stubbornness," etc. There is still another, completely "legitimate" and effective way of destroying his self-confidence and making him submissive, based on the theory that so-called paranoid fears—i.e., the patient's distrust of others—are only a defense mechanism, are only a projection of his own desire to abuse, deceive, seduce, or murder others. This explanation may have some truth to it because the mechanism of projection is in fact a common one. If we are disappointed by someone, for instance, and are not permitted to acknowledge our rage, we are not conscious of being furious ourselves but of the other person as being angry with us. Since such an interpretation, however, encompasses only the final chapter of a long story, it is in most cases not only ineffectual but also wounding, for it does not touch upon the core of the tragedy. It is tragic enough that the beginnings of every human life, insofar as they are influenced by previous generations, are of necessity inaccessible to us and beyond our understanding. But if the truth about the patient's early childhood, which can be pieced together from the repetition compulsion and the interplay between transference and countertransference, is interpreted as the projection of his fantasies, then a new tragedy is created.

What I have shown here in the case of a "castrating woman" and her "penis envy" could be further illustrated with countless and often very cruel stories. It is understandable that women who were humiliated by their fathers and treated like dolls when they were little have the tendency as adults to try to show their superiority over men whenever possible and at the same time to let themselves become hopelessly dependent on them. Likewise, men who were not respected by their mothers will take revenge on women (and little girls). But the biographical origins of this behavior are what make it truly understandable, and one would think it is the task of psychoanalysis to reveal these origins, not to moralize in a pedagogical vein.

When Henry Miller was fifty years old and his mother lay on her deathbed, he sat by her side, hoping with all his heart that she would tell him she had read something he had written. But she died without saying it, for she apparently had never read a single one of his books. Is it any wonder that, as Anaïs Nin has written, in his novels he portrayed women he loved as whores in order to vilify them?

A similar pattern can be found in Baudelaire, who was perhaps

more conscious of his love/hate for his mother than Miller. As a
child, he felt she was being unfaithful to his dead father and to him
by remarrying, and he therefore regarded her as "whore-like" but
at the same time as seductive and desirable. His poem "Lethe" reveals the depth of his ambivalence, with which many people will
be able to identify.

LETHE

Come to my heart, my heartless love, for there
—Tiger adored, monster so indolent—
I long to plunge, trembling and exigent,
My fingers in the richness of your hair;

Within your skirts, so redolent of you,
To bury deep my weary aching head,
And breathe, as though a flower almost dead,
The odor of my withered love, anew.

Ah! more than life itself, I want repose!
I long for sleep as sweet as death, unreigned
To spend my kisses fierce and unrestrained,
Upon your body which like copper glows.

To still my sobs, what rivals the abyss
And all-consuming solace of your bed?
Your mouth unto oblivion is wed
And Lethe flowes from every poppied kiss.

My fate, henceforth my ecstasy, content
I shall, as one ordained for it, obey
—The docile martyr and the guiltless prey
Whose fervor brings the fiercest chastisement—

And I shall suck, to soothe my rancour's smart,
Deep draughts of hemlock and nepenthe blest,
From lovely nipples of this pointed breast,
This fragile prison, empty of a heart.

Two letters Baudelaire wrote to his mother illustrate the tragic
nature of his relationship with her and the emotional honesty characteristic of *Les Fleurs du Mal.*

Who knows if I shall ever again be able to open to you all my soul, *that you never knew or apprecicted!* I write unhesitatingly, so true I know it to be.

There was in my youth a period of passionate love for you, listen and read without fear. I have never said as much to you before. I remember being with you in a carriag⟩, you had come out of a nursing-home to which you had been sent, and you showed me, to prove that you had thought of your son, some pen and ink drawings you had made for me. Do you see how terrible my memory is? Later, the square Saint-André-des-Arts and Neuilly. Long walks, perpetual tenderness! I remember the embankment, so sad at evening. Ah! that was the best time of mother-love for me. I ask your pardon for calling *best time* what was doubtless worst for you. But all the time I was living in you and you were uniquely mine. You were at once my idol and my friend. Perhaps you will be astonished to see me speak with such passion of a time so distant; it astonishes me, too. It is perhaps because I have, once again, conceived a desire to die, that these ancient things present themselves so vividly to my mind [*Letters*, p. 148]

And seventeen years earlier, when his mother wanted to appoint a guardian for him (and subsequently did so), Baudelaire wrote:

I want you to read this very attentively, because it is very serious, and because it is a supreme appeal to your good sense and to that deep tenderness which you say you have for me. I send you this letter, firstly, under the seal of secrecy, and beg you not to show it to anyone.

Secondly, I earnestly beg you not to see in it any intention of trying to be pathetic or of touching you otherwise than by argument. The strange way our discussions have of always turning into bitterness, though it corresponds with nothing real in me, my state of perpetual agitation, your determination not to listen to me, have obliged me to use the form of a letter by which to convince you how much you may be wrong, despite all your tenderness.

I write this with a tranquil mind, and when I think of the state of sickness I have been in during the last days, due to rage and astonishment, I ask myself how, and by what means, I can accept it once it has happened? You do not cease repeating, so as to make me swallow the pill, that there is nothing unnatural in all this, or in any wise humiliating. It may be so, and I believe it; but, truly, what does it matter what it is for most people if it is *quite another thing* for me. You say you look on my rage and my despair as passing things; you think you are only turning me into a mere child for my good. But be sure then of another thing, which you always seem to ignore: it is that, truly, to my sorrow, I am not made as other men. What you regard as a necessity and the misfortune of circumstances, I cannot, I cannot, support. The explanation of that is clear. You can, when we are alone, treat me in whatever fashion pleases you—but I repulse with fury whatever aims at my liberty. Is there not incredible cruelty in submitting me to the arbitration of certain men whom it bores, and who do not even know me? Between ourselves, who can boast of knowing me, knowing where I want to go, what I wish to do, and of what dose of patience I am capable? I believe sincerely that you are making a grave error. I say all this to you coldly, because I regard myself as condemned by you, and because I am sure you will not listen to me: but be certain of this from the first, it is you who voluntarily and knowingly cause me infinite pain and to an extent you cannot imagine. [pp. 12–13]

This plea for understanding was in vain, but the letter does give us a glimpse of the reality behind *Les Fleurs du Mal.* Once we have gained knowledge of the past, the present—no matter how confusing it may have seemed—will often become easy to understand. The drive theory ignores this fact.

Freud's famous description of the case of Dr. Schreber provides a striking illustration here. Freud interprets the man's delusions and persecution complex as the manifestation of his warded-off homosexual love for his father without bothering to find out what this father had done to his child earlier. Morton Schatzman's study of the father's background and personality reveals the son's paranoia to be only a thinly disguised recounting of the tragedy of his childhood. Thus, in his essay about Schreber Freud was actually describing merely the last act of a drama about whose plot up to that point he seemed to know nothing.

❧ 8 ❧

Gisela and Anita

WHAT I describe as the analyst's advocacy function has far-reaching consequences if this designation is taken in a more than superficial sense. In the field of law, too, we expect a client's advocate to do more than translate what his client tells him into acceptable legal language and present it to the court. We also expect him to see connections his client has not yet seen and as a result to discover new, hitherto unnoticed details that enable him to perceive his client's interests better than the client himself. The analyst's function as advocate demands a similar approach, with the decisive difference that his knowledge requires an emotional foundation, one provided by what he has experienced in his own training analysis. Equipped with this sensitivity, the analyst will not only know in theory that childhood plays a decisive role in his patient's life but will also be able to sense what it means for a little child to be totally at the mercy of the needs and demands of adults. Since helplessness and powerlessness are familiar feelings for him, his imagination has free rein; he will even be able to grasp the early childhood situation of a patient who must ward off this period of his life with the aid of fantasies of omnipotence or with grandiose behavior that may be combined with self-scorn.

If the analyst imaginatively senses something about the patient the latter is still unaware of and conveys this to him, there will be no danger of misusing the power of suggestion, as there is when intellectual knowledge is communicated. For what the analyst surmises can be corroborated as long as it refers to something concrete. The patient's emotional reaction and a spontaneous change in his behavior will confirm or refute its validity.

This can be illustrated by a story told me by a colleague named

Gisela, who is active in the women's movement. Gisela at one time was involved with antipsychiatric groups, especially in Italy, which at first had a highly liberating effect on her. She felt stronger, more self-confident, less subject to manipulation, and had the understandable desire to share this with others as well. She worked with groups of prostitutes and women prisoners, and wherever she looked, she saw the injustice inflicted on women by a male-dominated society. She fought against the humiliation, mistreatment, and exploitation of women, and tried to win other women over to a cause she hoped would give them a sense of their own strength and worth. She reached her goal to a certain degree through her group work, but being a sensitive and sincere feminist, she saw herself confronted over and over again with situations that drove her to desperation. For years she worked to get prostitutes to organize so they would no longer be subjected to the discrimination of society and the threats of their procurers. Earlier, a prostitute knew she had to face the revenge of a procurer's mafia if she tried to break away from a tormenting and threatening relationship by taking her case to court; now, she was more or less free to do so as a result of the accomplishments of the women's groups. Yet scarcely one of these women, who had openly expressed their boundless hatred for their oppressors at the group meetings, was able to take advantage of the opportunity she now had to break free. Whenever the crucial stage was reached and it was no longer dangerous for the women to leave their male oppressors, they evinced feelings and patterns of behavior that defied normal logic, healthy common sense, and the best intentions of social psychologists. All it took was for the hated procurer, whose death his victim had so passionately desired and whom she had more than once wanted to murder so that she could finally draw a free breath, to be helpless—for example, to cry or to be sent to prison—and his victim would then go to every conceivable length to help her persecutor, would visit him in prison, and the like. Gisela was in despair. She decided that woman's slavish nature was the result of millennia of oppression and probably could never be changed.

But then, during the analysis that was part of her psychoanalytic training, Gisela came face to face with her own childhood. The more fully she became aware of the early origins of her ambivalent relationship with her father, all the more clearly did she recognize the repetition compulsion in the women with whom she had done group work. When one of these women, whom we shall call Anita, was hospitalized after attempted suicide, Gisela took her on as a patient.

Anita had been a prostitute for fifteen years, during which she had not shown any psychic symptoms. She had kept her feelings under control while adapting outwardly to her surroundings; therefore, she was able to function quite well, offering her male clientele good service without showing any signs of personal difficulties. Not until she was able to articulate her feelings of hatred in the group did her house of cards begin to collapse. Two suicide attempts accompanied her awakening. At first Gisela could not understand this. Why now? Now that Anita was finally able to sense that even as a prostitute she was respected, at least within her group, now that she could fight for her rights and admit her hatred, now of all times she was beginning, in professional language, to "decompensate." Twice in short succession she was found unconscious in her room after taking an overdose of pills. This behavior did not fit any theory, and the questions of why and why *now* gave Gisela no rest. She spent many hours of her own analysis talking about Anita, which at first made her analyst think she was running away from herself, being evasive, and exhibiting resistance. But gradually he, too, realized that Gisela was on the brink of discovering something important about the plight of women, something that was becoming especially clear to her in Anita's extreme situation but that had equal validity for her as well.

The process of discovery began when Gisela offered Anita psychoanalytic treatment that gave the latter access for the first time to the painful experiences of her childhood, which she had successfully managed to keep at a distance all her life. Now the partial freeing of her adult feelings of justifiable anger and outrage, which had occurred in the group, released her from her numbness and threatened her defenses against the pent-up feelings of rage from her early childhood. These feelings, which had never been allowed to come to the surface, were bound to other feelings that represented the real Anita. The following story came to light:

When Anita was born in 1944 her father was believed to be dead, but this later turned out to be untrue. Her mother was living with a man who had two sons of his own and who was alternately cruel and affectionate with Anita. At the beginning of her treatment she told Gisela how she had suffered because of her stepfather and how her mother, who had had to work hard in those days to provide enough food, had never protected her from him. When she was little, she often ran away to find another home with strangers; on one of these occasions, when she was only four years old, a man had mistreated and sexually abused her. The explanation for her life as a prostitute seemed clear. Although her childhood was now accessible to her consciousness, everything she said about it had the dispassionate ring of factual information in a newspaper. Anita talked about her past without the slightest agitation, sometimes even laughing over it—the same woman who in the group could fly into a rage when she spoke of the murderous thoughts she harbored toward procurers. Yet the feelings that were emerging were still separated from the experiences of her childhood. She had internalized her parents' belief that one can inflict anything on a child with impunity to such a degree that she initially did not see any point at all in being permitted to experience her childhood feelings. After she was able to do this in analysis, however, spending many hours on the couch crying over her childhood, she was able to remember something else: her real father.

Earlier in the analysis she had told Gisela that when she was four her father, who had been a prisoner of war, came home unexpectedly after being thought dead for so long; he was weak and ailing, but he showed affection toward his daughter, sang lovely songs to her, and played the accordion. This happy state of affairs lasted only two years, because he then died of cancer. For a very long time in her analysis, this idealized portrait of her real father remained intact. Here, too, her description had the ring of a factual report; the only feeling that was associated with it was one of vague sentimental devotion. But gradually this ideal construct was undermined by her genuine feelings. Anita began to remember having waited for her father all those years, hoping that he would rescue her, fantasizing, "If my daddy comes home, he'll fix Mommy and my stepfather, he'll stand up for my rights, he'll protect me, he won't let anyone hurt me like this." And now, in analysis, Anita felt the pain of her disappointment: her father had not protected her, that was nothing but a fairy tale. Rejected by her mother, he worked things out with the stepfather—Anita's worst enemy—and he, too, struck Anita if she wasn't good, if she wasn't like a little doll. These memories returned very reluctantly. Anita had to struggle against great resistance, and at first it seemed that if she gave up this illusion, she would be relinquishing the dearest thing she had in life. She doubted that she could ever bring herself to do it. But shedding her illusions actually restored her strength and finally enabled her to admit the truth she had been repressing all this time: that her father was not only interested in being affectionate with her but also masturbated on occasion while holding her on his lap, using her body for his needs. Anita kept this last secret from her conscious self so that she would not lose her idealized father, but when her dreams told her unmistakably about these experiences and made her feel outraged, grief-stricken, and anxious, she experienced a true liberation from her repetition compulsion and understood how her whole life had been dominated by it.

This woman's life as a prostitute had proved itself to be a compulsively repeated reenactment of the trauma of her early childhood. All the unconscious elements could be identified in hindsight: first there was the hope of reversing the roles, of taking revenge on the "lustful man." To be sure, Anita offered herself as a plaything to the male, the way she had as a child, but now it was in *her* power to remain in control over what happened, to disappoint the man or to satisfy him, to send him away or to show him her favor, to humiliate him or on occasion to treat him like a human being. She despised the "masochists" among her clients, yet—perhaps for this very reason—she had no trouble assuming the sadistic role with them and savoring the taste of her own power. On a conscious level she thought: Now everything is different, you can get your pleasure with me but you have to pay for it; no one can have me anymore without giving something in return. But unconsciously, the early tragedy was simply being repeated in a different form, for Anita had never been able to give up her early hope of finding a protective father. The more horrible her present life became, the more cruelly she was deceived by her procurers, the more brutally she was beaten, the less able she was to give up hoping that her love would change this man or that the next one would be her longed-for rescuer.

A person can give up conscious expectations, but attitudes deeply rooted in unconscious feelings of early childhood cannot be given up until they become conscious and have been experienced not only in the present but in relation to the past. In Anita's analysis this indeed took place when she was able, through transference, to relate to her own father the intense feelings of helpless rage and of being totally and hopelessly at the mercy of her hated and loved procurers. Added to this was her grief over the impossibility of fulfilling her earlier desires for revenge. In spite of fifteen years of victories over men, these desires could never be satisfied because the little girl she had once been and her situation in those days no longer existed.

It was this process of mourning that finally enabled Anita to renounce her lifelong hope of finding a man who would protect her. And as a result of this renunciation she broke away—without anxiety, without self-destructiveness—from the sadomasochistic relationship with her most recent procurer. At this point Anita became sure of something she had only vaguely suspected when she attempted to take her life: that the release of her genuine feelings was not compatible with the continuation of her profession. The conscious motive behind her suicide attempts had been "I can't go on working, I'm not fit for life"; the unconscious motive, however, was her suspicion that once her true self was set free, she would no longer be able to avoid feelings of humiliation, which inevitably arise when one sees oneself either as the object of another person's sexual activity or as the manipulator of the other person and his needs, not as an equal partner. It is not surprising that at the end of this process Anita was not at a loss for a new career but even had difficulty choosing among several different possibilities. After toying for a while with the idea of going into social work, she decided on the "egotistic" career of interior decorator, in which she would have more opportunity to develop her creative potential. Even as a little girl she had always wanted to have a pretty home; she had always had a great deal of taste in furnishing a place, and now she was able to turn her hobby into a career.

At the end of Anita's analysis, Gisela, her analyst, was left with many questions: What actually happens when we act as though prostitution were a profession like any other? Are we not in all good faith helping to perpetuate a great deal of denial on society's part? What kind of profession is it? Doesn't it inevitably involve the humiliation of women? And doesn't the well-intentioned struggle for social acceptance of the profession ignore the fact that prostitution is unavoidably based on denial of a natural human desire for dignity, sexual equality, and partnership? Are ideals such as equality of the sexes and sexual freedom compatible with prostitution? Doesn't the struggle for social status for prostitutes disguise the actual social injustice involved? And what about the background of the procurer? What moves a man to subjugate women, to profit from their sexual activity with other men, to humiliate, deceive, and threaten them? Isn't the procurer taking revenge on his mother by the way he treats his female victims? A man who was exploited by his mother when he was a child can unconsciously find a number of ways to reenact this exploitation in reverse. It depends on his personality and his level of education whether he will become a charming seducer or a brutal pimp; in both cases he remains a homeless drifter. He doesn't know the meaning of partnership because he doesn't know what it means to trust another person. He clings to manipulation because for him that is the only alternative to being manipulated. In order to escape this horror he must be and remain the master.

৭ 9 ৡ

The Pain of Separation and Autonomy: New Versions of the Young Child's Dependency

WHAT if a person has never had the good fortune to experience his early dependence on his parents and the accompanying separation anxiety, so that he is later unable to dissociate himself from their introjected demands? Let us assume that this person has never been in therapy or, if he has, that his therapist was not able to supply him with this missing experience, not being fortunate enough to have had it himself. What happens to such people? Usually they resort to a passive or an active reenactment of their dependency and obedience in early childhood. This is a tragic situation that we are all too ready to judge in moral terms, and we are very likely to accuse them of lacking the courage of their convictions or even of being cowards. Judgments like this do not take into account that the source of this "cowardice" can often be traced back to the very first weeks or even days of life. This can be illustrated by the figure of the seducer and his problematic nature.

Poets, composers, and painters have shown a great fascination with Don Juan, and this may be because they see aspects of their own lives in his. They feel drawn to the story and psychology of this seducer, who always needs a new woman in order to arouse hopes in her, which he must then disappoint. This man can be seen and portrayed from the moralizing perspective of his victim, the disappointed woman, or subjectively from his own perspective, providing the artist has overcome his reluctance to identify with the figure. Fellini's film *Casanova* serves as an example of the first case and his *City of Women* of the second. An author doesn't necessarily have to write in the first person in order to display his identification with the character of Don Juan. Although Kierkegaard's *Diary of a Seducer* is obviously written in this form, the titular hero is still seen from a moralizing distance. On the other hand, the story of Frédéric Moreau, presented in Flaubert's novel *Sentimental Education,* is narrated in the third person, and yet the reader senses that Flaubert is to some extent describing here, as in *Madame Bovary,* the torments of his own soul.

The seducer is loved, admired, and sought after by many women because his attitude awakens their hopes and expectations. They hope that their need for mirroring, echoing, respect, attention, and mutual understanding, which has been stored up inside·them since early childhood, will finally be fulfilled by this man. But these women not only love the seducer, they also hate him, for he turns out to be unable to fulfill their needs and soon abandons them. They feel hurt by the demeaning way he treats them because they cannot understand him. Indeed, he does not understand himself. If he could, he would not have to keep on reenacting the same drama.

I shall use Flaubert's novel to give an indication of what I have learned from the perspective of my patients about the early history of the seducer. In every case, the threatening factor in the patient's early childhood was the mother's inner sense of insecurity and resultant inflexibility; i.e., the son felt certain that if he went against his mother's wishes in any way he would be totally rejected—in other words, he would lose her. With his later female partners, he tries to nullify this childhood dependency and, by abandoning each of them in turn, to erase his early fears of being abandoned by his mother if he said no to her. The seducer bestows on women the admiration and affection he once received himself and then suddenly leaves them.

But this replacement of what has been passively suffered with a form of active behavior is not the whole picture. What is so striking in Flaubert—and he is the only writer in whom I have found this— is his probably unconscious insight that behind what pretends to be freedom lies hidden a deep and very early dependency. It is the dependency of someone who was not permitted to say no because his mother could not bear it, and who therefore refuses all his life to commit himself to his partners in the hope of making up for what was never possible with his mother—namely, to say, "I am your child but you have no right to my whole being and my whole life." Since the seducer is able to assume this attitude toward women only as an adult but not in the early relationship with his mother, his conquests cannot undo his original defeat, and since the pain of early childhood is merely concealed, not cured, by these conquests, the old wounds cannot heal. The repetition compulsion is perpetuated.

With Frédéric Moreau, Flaubert created a character who could well be described as cowardly—a man who cannot bring himself to deny women's desires and therefore must resort to lies. Frédéric's mother appears only on the periphery of the plot, but her character is developed sufficiently to make it clear that the various women in the novel represent different sides of her. Madame Arnoux symbolizes the idealized but inaccessible mother, Rosanette the naïve and demanding one, and Madame Dambreuse the cruel, humiliating mother who is at the same time seductive and love-struck. Moreau's cowardice is the tragic result of having been a narcissistically abused child. He cannot defend himself except when he is treated with obvious sadism. In every other case, especially if the woman is weak and dependent, he is completely at her mercy. He cannot escape her; he gives her the money she needs; he makes the promises she wants to hear even though he is not going to keep them. The woman's interests always take precedence over his needs. This inevitably leads to his living a lie, for someone who cannot say no at the decisive moments of his life loses his authenticity.

It may be that Moreau's situation reflects that of many men who are called seducers. The longing for love and sympathy, for giving and receiving understanding, leads the seducer, the classical Don Juan figure, to a series of women to whom he cannot openly express his disappointments because he had a mother who could not tolerate openness and he therefore had no opportunity to learn it. He is compelled to tell lies in order to spare women's feelings as he once did his mother's, and he flees from the arms of one conquest to the next. Since he cannot maintain any distance as long as a woman is helpless, he must provoke her to be cruel to him so that he can leave her in good conscience and thereby regain a measure of freedom. Yet this provocation cannot occur openly either; it comes about against his will and is painful even to him, appearing the very moment the woman discovers his insincerity. If she reacts in a loving way, he will be full of remorse and guilt feelings but will have to deceive her again at the next opportunity in order to create some semblance of freedom, i.e., of distance from the mother. He is given this opportunity if the woman reacts vengefully and cruelly to his dishonorable ways. Then he is able to abandon her, sometimes forever, and will turn to another woman, who at first responds to him like all the others, is so enchanted by his sensitivity, empathy, adaptability, and kindness that she is willing to overlook the beginning signs of insincerity at any price. But the price keeps going up, insofar as the beloved is an unconscious surrogate for the mother, who once demanded unconditional adaptation from her little boy. For no amount of even the most subtle understanding from his partner can undo the past, and the next partner will be driven to use every unconscious means she can to be cruel and unsympathetic, for she really *can't* understand what is happening and why he keeps lying to her.

Frédéric Moreau's cowardice is a tragedy, which is probably the case with all cowardice. Whether a person grows up to be honest seems to depend on how much truth the parents were able to bear and on what penalties they exacted from their child for being truthful. It was the story of Frédéric Moreau that made me realize how useless the moral categories of cowardice and bravery are and the extent to which courage really has to do with the nature of the individual's childhood.

When it was a question of expressing his political skepticism, even if he diverged sharply from prevailing views, Flaubert was able to show great courage. The keenness of his observations is virtually unmatched, and his analysis of the political, cultural, and social conformity of his day reflects his scorn for every form of lying. But it is possible that hidden behind his scorn lies the unconscious pain of the little child who had to disown his keen observations for the sake of the conformity required of him and for whom the ultimate honesty—openness toward the person closest to him—was always to remain his highest but unattainable ideal. For in order to realize his ideal he would have had to be able to be honest with his mother and be allowed to leave her when the time was ripe (whereas he in fact continued to live with her until her death). It would also have meant not always having to think first of her needs and her depressions and not having to pay for his freedom to write by becoming ill. In order to understand why Flaubert was unable to do all this, we have only to read Jean-Paul Sartre's characterization of Flaubert's mother in *The Family Idiot* or think of Moreau's ambitious, materialistic, bigoted mother. The reader of *Sentimental Education* will not be surprised to find that the son keeps his feelings from his mother and is unable either to love or to hate her. He can recapture the intense feelings of his early childhood only by transferring them to his later partners, whom he both loves and hates. Frédéric Moreau's sad fate is shared not only by Gustave Flaubert but by a great many other men.

In the final pages of the novel, Moreau tells about picking a big bouquet of flowers from his mother's garden as a boy. He intended to take the flowers to "other women," women who "sold their love for money," but at the last moment he fled from them in fear "because he thought they would make fun of him." If we consider this boyhood memory in terms of its symbolic content, we will find the key both to the psychological interpretation of *Sentimental Education* and to Flaubert's life. The flowers from his mother's garden represent the totality of feelings binding him to her: love and hatred, his longing for affection and his rebelliousness, the intensity of his inner world and his rage at being misused, his attachment to her and his need for freedom—all this had to be suppressed, could come to life only in his fictional characters, and led as well to his great wariness with women, to painful physical symptoms, and to a lifelong if unemotional attachment to his mother.

The road from the child's idealization of his parents to true, mature independence is a long one and usually passes through an area of deep conflict with the parents of the child's early years. This conflict is experienced emotionally for the first time when the child grows up and comes in contact with groups, ideologies, sexual partners, his own children, and, in certain cases, his therapist. Although these violent emotions originated in childhood, they were never allowed to be expressed then (cf. *For Your Own Good*).

Let us take a closer look at the reenactments of the early stages of dependency.

When, in puberty or adolescence, we leave the world of our parents' ideas and beliefs behind, we do not take this step in order to be alone. We join groups, we find new ideas and new models whose ways of thinking appeal to us more than those of our parents. These models may be people we already know whom we consider more clever and experienced than ourselves; they may be contemporaries whom we do not know but admire from afar, or famous people, founders of political movements, originators of major theories, or the like. Not until we have made an intellectual break with our parents are we able to profit from the rich opportunities of our new situation, to gain a broader horizon although at the same time often clinging to the security of our newfound theories. For it is virtually impossible to forgo this security during adolescence.

The nature of the initial relationship between parents and child will determine what forms the adolescent's liberation will assume in adult life and whether his or her new sense of security turns into a second, and this time permanent, prison. Since it is not usual to experience "several puberties" the way Goethe did, in postadolescence a feeling of security is generally prized more highly than freedom. Above all, it will depend on a person's earliest experiences whether he will be able to deal creatively with new theories and ultimately find his own point of view or whether he will cling anxiously to the orthodoxy of a school. If this person was raised to be absolutely obedient, without ever being able to escape his parents' watchful eyes, he will run the risk as an adult of making theories into absolutes and becoming a slave to them, even though these theories abound with words like freedom, autonomy, and progress. No theory can prevent a person from reacting to it submissively, for even the most enlightened ideas often leave our emotional life untouched. Defending liberal ideas by authoritarian, orthodox means and nurturing submissiveness and conformity in the name of intellectual progress play such a major role in our everyday life that we scarcely notice the contradiction involved here.

How can it be explained psychologically that the same person who exhibits so much acumen and critical judgment concerning his enemies at the same time retains a touching, childlike loyalty and submissiveness vis-à-vis the dictates of his own group? Anyone who knows what it means to belong to a group also knows how crucial this membership can sometimes seem. Even very brief contact with a group can give one a feeling of maternal warmth, of a good symbiosis with the mother, never experienced before, which makes one feel secure yet at the same time free and comfortable and able to express oneself satisfactorily. This is how it actually would have been had there been a good symbiosis with the mother. But since the group is only a substitute, the search for what is missing can never stop. In order for this to happen, a process of mourning would have to take place. Every form of addiction, instead of doing away with the old longing, simply perpetuates the tragedy by repeating it. A glass of whiskey or a cigarette that can be held in the hand, set aside when not needed, and immediately reached for when needed, establishes the comfortable feeling that an available mother can give. Since the real mother was not available, however (or the child would not have become addicted as an adult), the child was not permitted to experience either a good symbiosis or a liberating separation and remains dependent for the rest of his life on the image of an ideal mother he wishes for but never had. The addictive substance thus provides not only a feeling of comfort but also the torments of dependency.

When a group takes over this ersatz role, although it gives the illusion of being an ideal mother, it mercilessly requires the same adaptation to its demands that the real mother once did. Since the origins of this situation reach back to the early beginnings of life, a person will have a hard time recognizing his predicament. He does not even notice the extent of his adaptation, for he has not lost his critical faculties entirely and can still exercise them freely outside the group, even in connection with his parents as they are now. But the group, chosen in adolescence of his own free will and seemingly so promising, will end up intimidating him in the same non-verbal way his mother's expectations did during the first year of life. Just the thought of having opinions deviating completely from those prevailing in the group can evoke such strong anxiety that at first such opinions cannot even be formed. Usually the anxiety is not based on present reality but goes back to a period when it actually would have been life-threatening for the infant to risk losing love—i.e., losing the mother—by inappropriate behavior. It is this anxiety that can keep a person with such a background from freeing himself from the dictatorship of the group, even though he has outstanding intellectual gifts. The group need not be located in one specific place; it can also take the form of an ideology, a political party, or a school representing certain theories.

I have found over and over again that analysands are subject to deep fears of abandonment, even death, if they feel compelled to express views differing from those prevailing in the group to which they have given their allegiance. But the need to express oneself openly in one's own group, to be critical on occasion, can become even greater than this fear and regularly comes to the surface in analysis when the analysand becomes fully aware of the extent to which he or she had to adapt as a child to parental expectations. Frequently, although not always, the group reacts with the same rejection and hostility the parents once showed, because the defense mechanisms of the group members are threatened if one of them deviates from the required conformity. Even in such cases, however, the analysand may come to a session in high spirits and say: "Now I understand my anxiety; it wasn't cowardice. My anxiety was justified: they all looked at me with hatred in their eyes, and they ridiculed me just for saying what I was thinking and feeling—and what I am convinced some of them feel too, only they can't or won't put it into words. Although it was very painful to see that I had suddenly lost everybody's sympathy, I had the vague suspicion that there was not only loss involved here."

But the gain does not come until much later. At first the patient suffers greatly from the discovery that he has been conforming all his life for the sake of what has turned out to be merely the illusion of concern for him on the part of others. Once it becomes clear to him that he has been clinging to the smiling masks of others, he realizes the extent of his loneliness. Now that the masks have been removed on both sides, he no longer has to make an effort to behave as expected and gains more and more freedom as a result. Risking the loss of the group's approbation can activate early fears of abandonment, which are then often experienced within the protective analytic setting. In the final enactment with the analyst, the patient may also experience the trauma of being rejected as a punishment for being true to himself, something he learned all too well to avoid doing as a child. This gives him the inner strength to bear and overcome his extreme loneliness by rebelling against the analyst—for he now has the support of an empathic inner object that has gradually grown strong enough to encourage and protect the child within the patient.

This process very often bogs down at the point when the analysand succeeds in distancing himself from the system, school, party, ideology, or cult he idealized in his youth but which he unconsciously continues to use as symbols of his parents, who disappointed him. Until his disappointment—the feeling of having been abused, taken advantage of, and misled—is experienced in connection with his early childhood, the analysis will remain incomplete, and he will still be susceptible to the appeal of ideologies. I should like to illustrate this point by citing a passage written by C. G. Jung in the year 1934:

> The Aryan unconscious . . . contains explosive forces and seeds of a future yet to be born. . . . The still youthful Germanic peoples are fully capable of creating new cultural forms that still lie dormant in the darkness of the unconscious of every individual—seeds bursting with energy and capable of mighty expansion. The Jew, who is something of a nomad, has never yet created a cultural form of his own and as far as we can see never will, since all his instincts and talents require a more or less civilized nation to act as host for their development. . . . In my opinion it has been a grave error in medical psychology up till now to apply Jewish categories—which are not even binding on all Jews—indiscriminately to Germanic and Slavic Christendom. Because of this the most precious secret of the Germanic peoples— their creative and intuitive depth of soul—has been explained as a morass of banal infantilism, while my own warning voice has for decades been suspected of anti-Semitism. This suspicion emanated from Freud. He did not understand the Germanic psyche any more than did his Germanic followers. Has the formidable phenomenon of National Socialism, on which the whole world gazes with astonished eyes, taught them better? Where was that unparalleled tension and energy while as yet no National Socialism existed? Deep in the Germanic psyche, in a pit that is anything but a garbage-bin of unrealizable infantile wishes and unresolved family resentments. A movement that grips a whole nation must have matured in every individual as well. [*Collected Works* X, 165–66]

Since Jung was Swiss and therefore did not have to accommodate himself to the Nazi regime, he obviously wrote these words out of conviction. In any case, a personal, emotional involvement is unmistakable in these lines and constitutes the true significance of what might otherwise be regarded as ideological nonsense. For the affect in question goes back to the writer's childhood, although he himself is unaware of this fact. I am not referring to Jung's resentment of Freud, the Jew, who, Jung felt, did not understand his creative gifts and whose limitations as a father-substitute Jung became painfully aware of. I can scarcely believe Jung had no inkling that this confused passage had something to do with his ambivalence toward

Freud, of which he was certainly not unconscious. But he apparently did not have any idea of the extent to which early childhood feelings toward his real father were breaking through here. If he had, this passage would not have taken the form it did. Freud was the father figure of Jung's early manhood, and perhaps the former's drive theory had the same effect on Jung as the constrictions of the religious upbringing given him by his father. In the passage just cited, I can hear the lament of a child who is crying out: "You never did understand my soul, never trusted in my abilities, you wanted to confine me in the prison of your precepts and *Weltanschauung.* I always sensed this dimly without being able to say it. Now at last others are saying it, now at last liberation is at hand."

Had Jung undergone an analysis in which he was permitted to experience and accept these feelings, they would not have found expression in this unrestrained form so embarrassing to the present-day reader. But there is no point in making moralizing judgments here either. In interpreting this passage, I find it more illuminating to go beyond the disappointment the young man felt in his admired teacher and focus on the despair a highly gifted and vital child felt in relation to his father. Then these lines take on a different meaning, such as: "In my opinion, it has been a grave failing of traditional religious upbringing [= medical psychology] automatically to apply Protestant [= Jewish] categories, not even binding for all clergymen, to the child [= Germanic and Slavic Christendom]. By so doing, it has turned man's [= Germanic people's] most treasured secret, the depths of his creative, intuitive soul, into a childishly banal morass, whereas my warning voice has been suspected of sinfulness [= anti-Semitism] for decades. This suspicion originates with my father [= Freud]."

When we consider that the ideas Jung developed as a result of his friendship with Freud and his contact with the unconscious were regarded as extremely strange and threatening in his milieu, we gain further insight into the workings of the repetition compulsion. Many people whom he esteemed probably responded to his enthusiasm for National Socialism with the same distaste, at least inwardly, that others had earlier shown for the ideas of his youth. This time, however, he did not have to fear rejection, because he was espousing ideas that were now coming into ascendency.

· · ·

The unlived and therefore unresolved painful dependency of early childhood is not necessarily perpetuated in that form of submissiveness toward groups and ideologies which makes it possible for rage repressed at an early age to be abreacted onto external enemies. Various defense mechanisms can be used to reach a compromise between the necessity of sparing the feelings of one's parents and the need to express one's own feelings. A patient of mine with a strict religious upbringing, for example, was able to spare her parents by directing her newly awakened rage against God. In God, whom her parents believed in, Inge hoped to have found the strong father who would be able to endure her feelings, who was not insecure, easily offended, and ailing like her own father. She wanted to feel free to direct her disappointment, despair, and resentment at God without having to fear that this would kill Him. She read Nietzsche and appreciated his statement "God is dead." Once when she was on the couch she cried out: "The story of Eve in Paradise is outrageous! Why did God put the Tree of Knowledge right in front of her and then forbid her to eat from it?" One day she brought me "A Child of St. Mary," one of Grimm's fairy tales, which her mother had often read her and which she had been very fond of as a child.

On the edge of a large forest lived a woodcutter and his wife, and he had only one child, a girl three years old. They were, however, so poor that they no longer had their daily bread and did not know how they could feed her. One morning the woodcutter, bowed down by worry, went out into the forest to work, and as he was chopping wood, suddenly a tall and beautiful woman stood before him with a crown of shining stars upon her head and said, "I am the Virgin Mary, mother of the Christ Child; you are poor and needy; bring me your child, and I shall take her with me and shall be her mother and care for her." The woodcutter obeyed, fetched his child, and gave her over to the Virgin Mary. She took her with her to Heaven, where she fared well, ate cake, and drank sweet milk, and her clothes were of gold, and the angels played with her. When she was fourteen, the Virgin once called her and said: "Dear child, I am about to make a long journey; take charge of the keys to the thirteen doors of the Kingdom of Heaven. Twelve of these doors you may unlock and marvel at the glories within, but the thirteenth door, which this little key opens, is forbidden to you. Be careful not to unlock it, otherwise misfortune will befall you." The girl promised to be obedient, and when the

Virgin had gone, she began to look at the dwellings of the Heavenly Kingdom. Every day she unlocked one door until she had opened the twelve. In each dwelling an apostle was sitting in great glory. She delighted in all that pomp and splendor, and the angels who always accompanied her rejoiced with her. Now the forbidden door alone was left, and she felt a great desire to know what was hidden behind it and said to the angels, "I won't open it wide nor will I go in, but I'll unlock it so we may get a tiny peek through the crack." "Oh no," said the angels, "that would be a sin; the Virgin Mary has forbidden it, and some misfortune might easily befall you." Then she kept still, but the desire deep down in her heart did not keep still but gnawed and gnawed at her and left her no peace. Once when the angels had all gone out, she thought, "Now I'm quite alone and might as well look in; no one will know if I do." She searched out the key and when she had it in her hand, she couldn't help putting it in the lock, and once she'd put it in, she couldn't help turning it. Then the door flew open, and she saw the Holy Trinity sitting in fire and glory. She stopped a while, viewing everything with amazement; then she touched the glory a little with her finger, and her finger became all golden. At once she was seized with a great fear; she slammed the door and ran away. But her fear didn't leave her, do what she might, and her heart beat continually and couldn't be quieted. The gold, too, stayed on her finger, no matter how much she washed it and rubbed it.

Not long afterward the Virgin Mary returned from her journey. She called the girl to her and asked her to give back the keys of Heaven. When she handed her the bunch of keys, the Virgin looked into her eyes and said, "Didn't you open the thirteenth door, too?" "No," she replied. Then the Virgin put her hand on the girl's heart, felt it beating violently, and knew very well that she'd transgressed her command and had unlocked that door. Then she said again, "Are you sure you didn't do it?" "No," answered the girl a second time. Then the Virgin looked at the finger which from touching the Heavenly fire had become all golden and saw clearly that the girl had sinned and for a third time said, "Didn't you do it?" "No," said the girl for the third time. Then the Virgin Mary said, "You disobeyed me and, besides, you lied; you are no longer worthy to be in Heaven."

Then the girl sank into a deep sleep, and when she awoke, she was lying down here on Earth in the midst of a wilderness. She wanted to call out but was unable to utter a sound. She jumped up and wanted to run away, but wherever she turned, she was held back by dense thorn hedges which she couldn't break through. In the wasteland in which she found herself there stood an old hollow tree that had to be her dwelling. When night came, she'd crawl into it and sleep there, and when it was stormy and rainy, she'd find shelter in it. But it was a miserable life, and when she thought how fine it had been in Heaven and how the angels had played with her, she wept bitterly. Roots and berries were her only food; she searched for them as far as she could walk. In the autumn she collected the fallen nuts and leaves and carried them into her hollow tree. The nuts were her food for the winter, and when snow and ice came, she'd crawl like a poor little animal into the leaves so as not to freeze. Soon her clothes became torn, and one piece after another dropped off her body. But when the sun shone warm again, she went out and sat down before the tree, and her long hair covered her on all sides like a cloak. Thus she sat year after year, feeling the woe and the misery of the world.

Once upon a time when the trees again were fresh and green, the king of the country was hunting in the forest and was chasing a roe. And because it had fled into the thicket that surrounded that spot in the forest, he dismounted, pulled the bushes apart, and cut a path with his sword. When he finally broke through, he saw a beautiful girl sitting under the tree, and her golden hair covered her to the very tip of her toes. Amazed, he stopped and looked at her, then addressed her, saying, "Who are you? Why are you sitting here in the wasteland?" But she made no reply, for she couldn't open her mouth. Then the king continued, "Will you come with me to my palace?" Then she merely nodded a little with her head. But the king took her in his arms, put her on his horse, and rode home with her. When he reached the royal palace, he had fine clothes put on her and gave her everything in plenty, and though she was unable to speak, she was so beautiful and gracious that he began to love her with all his heart, and it wasn't long before he married her.

When about a year had passed, the queen gave birth to a son. Thereupon the next night as she was lying alone in her bed, the Virgin Mary appeared to her and said, "If you will tell the truth and confess that you unlocked the forbidden door, I will unseal your mouth and restore your power of speech; but if you persist in your sin and your stubborn denial, I will take your newborn child away with me." Then the queen was given the power to answer, but she remained obstinate and said, "No, I didn't open the forbidden door," and the Virgin Mary took the newborn child from her arms and disappeared with it. The next morning when the child was not to be found, a rumor spread among the people that the queen was an ogress and had killed her own child. She heard it all yet couldn't deny it. The king, however, was unwilling to believe it because he loved her so.

A year later the queen again gave birth to a son. In the night the Virgin Mary again came to her and said, "If you will confess that you opened the forbidden door, I shall give you back your child and free your tongue, but if you persist in your sin and deny it, I shall take this newborn child with me, too." Then the queen again said, "No, I didn't open the forbidden door." The Virgin took the child out of her arms and carried it with her to Heaven. In the morning when the second child had disappeared, the people said quite openly that the queen had swallowed it, and the king's councilors demanded she be tried. The king, however, loved her so that he didn't want to believe it and ordered his councilors not to mention the subject again on pain of death.

The following year the queen gave birth to a lovely little daughter. Then at night the Virgin Mary appeared to her for the third time and said, "Follow me." She took her by the hand and led her to Heaven and showed her there her two eldest children: they greeted her with joyous laughter and were playing with the globe of the earth. As the queen was rejoicing in all this, the Virgin said: "Is your heart not yet softened? If you admit that you opened the forbidden door, I shall give you back your two little sons." But for the third time the queen replied, "No, I didn't open the forbidden door." Then the Virgin again let her sink down to Earth and took away her third child, too.

The next morning when this became known, everybody cried out, "The queen is an ogress and must be sentenced," and the king could no longer reject his councilors' advice. Accordingly, she was tried, and because she couldn't reply and couldn't defend herself, she was condemned to die at the stake. The wood was gathered, and when she was tied to a stake and the fire began to burn round about, the hard ice of her pride melted and her heart was moved by repentance, and she thought, "If only before I die I could confess that I opened the door." Then her power of speech was restored, and she cried out in a loud voice, "Yes, Mary, I did do it." Immediately it began to rain, and the rain put out the flames, and a beam of light descended upon her, and the Virgin Mary descended with the two little sons at her side and the newborn daughter in her arms. She spoke kindly to her, "Whoever repents his sin and confesses will be forgiven," and gave her back the three children and freed her tongue and bestowed happiness upon her for the rest of her life.

As Inge was reading this fairy tale aloud to me, she suddenly flew into a rage and cried, "They kept leading their child [Inge] into temptation in order to degrade and punish her. Just the way the Virgin Mary did! What a cruel game she is playing with her foster child!" It then came out that this had been one of her parents' favorite methods of child-rearing, as recommended by an educator I have cited in *For Your Own Good* (pp. 25–27). In their zeal they intentionally kept placing Inge in situations that presented temptation in order to show her how weak she was. After we gradually gained access to the whole spectrum of her parents' child-rearing principles, her strong animosity toward God paled, and her parents, previously lumped together in her mind with God, came to life. Her first reaction toward them was one of anger, followed by grief.

Yet the patient still retained her critical ability, even in theological matters. She was able to ask questions, now in a calmer frame of mind, such as: "It says in the Bible we should not make any graven images. Why not, actually? Why is God allowed to see all our weaknesses, to read our most secret thoughts without our being able to stop Him, and to punish and persecute us for having them, while only *His* weaknesses must remain invisible? Has He no weaknesses? If God is Love, as I was taught, then He certainly should feel free to show Himself. We would learn from His love. Does He hide himself or is He hidden by those who made an image of Him, using their fathers as a model, and passed it on to us? For the Bible does offer a clearly defined image of God, if we only dare to look closely enough. His image can be pieced together from His deeds; it is the image of an irritable, hypersensitive, didactic, authoritarian father. The Bible speaks of God's omnipotence, but the Divine deeds it describes contradict this attribute; for someone who possessed omnipotence would not need to demand obedience from his child, would not feel his security threatened by false gods, and would not persecute his people for having them. Perhaps the theologians are not in a position to create an ideal image of true goodness and omnipotence differing from the character of their real fathers until they have seen through this character. And so they create an image of God based on the model they are already familiar with. Their God is like their father: insecure, authoritarian, power-hungry, vengeful, egocentric. Perhaps they could imagine other, similarly anthropomorphic images of God if they had had a different childhood."

My patient, with her anthropological interests, went on to produce fantasies of a God who perhaps once possessed the power to create the world but now confronts the sufferings of humanity with powerless suffering of His own, without having to conceal His powerlessness with commandments and authoritarian behavior. "If God really is love," said Inge, "He would manage to bestow love without setting a price on it or committing violence in its name or demanding the impossible from His children. Perhaps other peoples have such an image of God. It is unlikely that peace-loving peoples would worship a deity who had the features of the God of the Old Testament."

Before beginning her analysis Inge had read many books on anthropology, but these questions had never come to the surface, not even during the period of her hostility toward God. It was not until she experienced the parents of her early childhood that she was able to combine her knowledge and her feelings and permit herself to ask questions that once would have caused severe anxiety. The child in her, who had not been allowed to ask questions in her devout family, at first couldn't believe that the world was not falling apart as a result of her heretical ideas. For a long time she experienced this disbelief over and over again, until she finally could feel fully assured that her thoughts were not destroying either God or her parents.

The route Inge's inner development took started me thinking, too. I aked myself: Can it be that the coercive measures of "poisonous pedagogy" would have less power over us and our culture if the Judeo-Christian tradition had not lent them strong support? It is always the Isaacs whose sacrifice God demands from the Abrahams, never the other way around. It is daughter Eve who is punished for not resisting temptation and not suppressing her curiosity out of obedience to God's will. It is the pious and faithful son Job whom God the Father continues to mistrust until he has proven his faithfulness and subservience by undergoing unspeakable torments. It is Jesus who dies on the cross to fulfill the words of the Father. The Psalmists, too, never tire of extolling the importance of obedience as a condition of each and every human life. We have all grown up with this cultural heritage, but it could not have survived as long as it has if we had not been taught to accept without question the fact that a loving father has the need to torment his son, that the father cannot sense his son's love and therefore, as in the story of Job, requires proof of it.

What kind of Paradise is it in which it is forbidden—under threat of loss of love and of abandonment, of feeling guilty and ashamed—to eat from the Tree of Knowledge, i.e., to ask questions and seek answers to them? Why should it be wicked to want to know what is happening, to want to orient oneself in the world?

Who was this contradictory God/Father who had the need to create a curious Eve and at the same time forbid her to live according to her true nature?

It is conceivable that the alienated, perverse, and destructive side of present-day scientific investigation is a delayed consequence of this prohibition. If Adam is not allowed to be aware of what is before his very eyes, he will direct his curiosity to goals as far removed from himself as possible. He will conduct experiments in outer space, will play with machines, computers, monkeys' brains, or human lives in order to satisfy his curiosity but will always take anxious care not to let his gaze rest on the "Tree of Knowledge" planted right in front of him.

Thus, the pedagogical commandment "Thou shalt not be aware" actually far predates the Ten Commandments. In the Judeo-Christian tradition, it goes all the way back to the creation of Adam and Eve. Is it surprising, then, that we prefer to take upon ourselves the hell of blindness, alienation, abuse, deception, subordination, and loss of self rather than lose that place called Paradise, which offers us security, but at such a high price? Yet haven't we reached the point in world history where the "security" we have bought with our blindness is proving to be our greatest danger?

The history of human suffering is supposed to have begun with the expulsion from Paradise. But shouldn't we set this imaginary beginning even farther back in time? Can we, today, long for a Paradise whose inhabitants are ordered to accept contradictions obediently and without questioning—in other words, to remain forever in the stage of infancy? Since each of us learned as a child to overlook the contradictions in our parents, we scarcely notice similar inconsistencies later in life. If we do, then we try to incorporate them into philosophical or theological systems. The story of Paradise lost epitomizes people's longing to perceive humankind as free of suffering at the outset of existence; yet they realize, although unconsciously, that this paradisiacal freedom from suffering could not have been perfect after all, since the price that had to be paid was the loss of self.

As far as our flesh-and-blood fathers are concerned, the more they make a show of being mighty and authoritarian, the more certain they are to be insecure children inside. But to revere a God with these characteristics out of fear would be in keeping once again with the dictates of "poisonous pedagogy." If there really should be a loving God, he would not burden us with prohibitions. He would love us as we are, would not demand obedience from us, not feel threatened by criticism, not threaten us with hell, not fill us with fear, not put our loyalty to the test, not mistrust us, would let us experience and express our feelings and needs—confident that this is what we need if we are to learn the meaning of a strong and genuine love, a love that is the opposite of fulfilling one's duty and being obedient and that grows only out of the experience of being loved. A child cannot be raised to be loving—neither by being beaten nor by well-meaning words; no reprimands, sermons, explanations, good examples, threats, or prohibitions can make a child capable of love. A child who is preached to learns only to preach and a child who is beaten learns to beat others. A person can be raised to be a good citizen, a brave soldier, a devout Jew, Catholic, Protestant, or atheist, even to be a devout psychoanalyst, but not to be a vital and free human being. And only vitality and freedom, not the compulsions of child-rearing, open the wellsprings of a genuine capacity to love.

Much of what Jesus said in the course of His life and, even more, His deeds show that He did not have just this one father (God), who insisted on the observance of His commandments, on sacrifice, and was demanding, distant, invisible, and infallible, a father whose "will [must] be done." From His early days Jesus also knew another father—Joseph, who never called attention to himself, who protected and loved Mary and the child, encouraged the child, assigned him central importance, and *served* him. It must have been this modest man who made it possible for the child to distinguish what was true and to experience the meaning of love. This is why Jesus was able to see through the hypocrisy of his contemporaries. A child raised in accordance with traditional principles, who knows nothing else from the start, is not able to detect hypocrisy because he lacks a basis for comparison. Someone who knows only such an atmosphere from childhood will perceive it as normal in all situations, perhaps suffering because of it but unable to recognize it for what it is. If he has not experienced love as a child, he will long for it but will not know what love can be. Jesus did know.

There would without any doubt be more people capable of love if the Church, instead of urging its members to obey authority and expecting allegiance to Christ on these grounds, would understand the crucial significance of Joseph's attitude. He served his child because he regarded Him as the child of God. What would it be like if all of us regarded our children as children of God—which we could do, after all? In his Christmas message of 1979 in honor of the Year of the Child, Pope John Paul II said that it is the task of adults to instill ideals in their children. These words coming from a man capable of love are certainly well-intentioned. But when pedagogues, both clerical and secular, set out to instill prescribed ideals in a child, they invariably turn to the methods of "poisonous pedagogy" and at best train children to become adults who train others in turn instead of raising them to become loving human beings.

Children who are respected learn respect. Children who are cared for learn to care for those weaker than themselves. Children who are loved for what they are cannot learn intolerance. In an environment such as this they will develop their *own* ideals, which can be nothing other than humane, since they grow out of the experience of love.

I have been told more than once that someone who was able to let his true self unfold during childhood would become a martyr in our society because he would refuse to adapt to some of its norms. There is something to be said for this idea, which is often advanced as an argument in defense of traditional child-rearing practices. Parents say they want to make their child learn to adapt as early as possible so he or she will not have to suffer too much later on in school or professional life. Since we still know very little about the influence of childhood suffering on the development of personality, it would seem difficult to refute this argument. Examples from history also appear to confirm it, for there are many who were forced to die a martyr's death because they refused to accept the prevailing standards of society and instead remained loyal to the truth (and thus to themselves).

But who is it actually who is so eager to see that society's norms are observed, who persecutes and crucifies those with the temerity to think differently—if not people who have had a "proper upbringing"? They are the ones who learned as children to accept the death of their souls and do not notice it until they are confronted with the vitality of their young or adolescent children. Then they must try to stamp out this vitality, so they will not be reminded of their own loss.

In the history of art the massacre of children has been depicted over and over again. Let us take as an example King Herod's slaying of all the male children in his realm. He feels threatened by them because there may be among them the new king who will one day vie for his throne, and for this reason he brings about a bloodbath in Bethlehem by ordering every boy aged two or under to be killed. Mary and Joseph flee to Egypt in order to save their child. Their love not only saves Jesus's life, it also enables the riches of His soul to unfold, which ultimately leads to His early death. One could rightly claim that it was Jesus's authenticity that caused His death, from which a false, conformist self would have saved Him. But can a meaningful life be measured quantitatively? Would Jesus have been happier if His parents, instead of treating Him with love and respect, had raised Him from an early age to be a faithful subject of Herod or to live a long life as a scribe?

The fact that Jesus grew up with parents whose only goal was to love and respect Him can hardly be denied, not even by believing Christians, who, in accordance with religious tradition, see in Jesus the Son of God. Every year throughout the Christian world the child is honored in the celebration of Christmas, yet Christian pedagogy has never been guided by this. Even someone who assumes that Jesus owes His capacity for love, His authenticity and goodness to the grace of His Divine Father and not to the extraordinarily loving ways of Mary and Joseph might wonder why God entrusted these particular earthly parents with the task of caring for His child. It is quite astonishing that none of Christ's followers has ever raised this question, which could have led to new directions in child-rearing. The caring parents of the child Jesus have never served as models; on the contrary, religious manuals generally recommend strict disciplinary measures starting in infancy. Once it is no longer a secret that certain psychological laws are behind *this* kind of model, once enough parents become aware that preaching love will not nurture the child's ability to love, whereas respect and understanding will, then those who receive this respect and understanding in childhood will no longer be the exceptions and will not have to die a martyr's death.

If we also take Herod as a symbol of our own society, we can point to aspects of the story of Jesus that may be used as arguments either for or against traditional child-rearing practices (depending on our personal experience): on the one hand, the massacre of the innocents and, on the other, extraordinary parents, servants of their child, who in the eyes of traditional pedagogues would then of necessity have become tyrants. Society, personified in Herod, fears children's vitality and authenticity and attempts to eradicate them, but lived-out truth cannot be destroyed, not even when the officials of Church and state take it upon themselves to "administer" the truth with the intent of eliminating it. The repeated resurrection of the truth cannot be suppressed; again and again, individual human beings affirm and live it. The Church as a social institution has continually attempted to prevent this resurrection from taking place—for example, by instigating wars in the name of Christ or by encouraging parents to use strict coercive measures to deaden their children's souls (i.e., feelings) in the name of the sacred values of child-rearing (obedience, submissiveness, denial of self).

The Church's struggle (supposedly an expression of God's will) against children's vitality is renewed daily by training them to be blindly obedient to those in authority and to think of themselves as wicked; this approach is more reminiscent of Herod, with his fear of the resurrection of the truth in the child, than it is of Jesus, with His demonstrated confidence in human potentiality. The hatred rooted in the small child's reaction to this training swells to immense proportions, and the Church (in part unconsciously) abets the proliferation of evil, which, on a conscious level, it professes to oppose.

It requires no great effort to identify the apocalyptic features of our century: world wars, massacres, the specter of nuclear war, the enslavement of millions by technology and totalitarian regimes, the threat to the earth's ecological balance, the depletion of energy sources, the increase in drug addiction—the list could go on and on. Yet the same century has also brought us knowledge that is utterly new in human history and that could bring about a decisive change in our lives if its full significance was to penetrate public consciousness. I am referring to the discovery that the period of early childhood is of crucial importance for a person's emotional development. The more distinctly we come to see that the most ominous events of the present and recent past are not the products of mature rationality and the more clearly we recognize the absurdity and unpredictability of the arms race, the more urgent becomes the need to investigate the origins and nature of the human destructiveness whose helpless victims we all are.

The magnitude of destructiveness that we read about in the newspapers every day actually represents only the last chapter of long stories we are usually ignorant of. We are victims, observers, reporters, or mute witnesses of a violence whose roots we do not see, a violence that often takes us by surprise, outrages us, or simply makes us stop and think, but we lack the inner ability (i.e., parental or Divine permission) to perceive and take to heart the simple and obvious explanations that are already available.

Then God said, "Let us make man in our image and likeness to rule the fish in the sea, the birds of heaven, the cattle, all wild animals on earth, and all reptiles that crawl upon the earth." So God created man in his own image; in the image of God he created him; male and female he created them. God blessed them and said to them, "Be fruitful and increase, fill the earth and subdue it, rule over the fish in the sea, the birds of heaven, and every living thing that moves upon the earth." God also said, "I give you all plants that bear seed everywhere on earth, and every tree bearing fruit which yields seed: they shall be yours for food. . . ."

Then the Lord God formed a man from the dust of the ground and breathed into his nostrils the breath of life. Thus the man became a living creature. Then the Lord God planted a garden in Eden away to the east, and there he put the man whom he had formed. The Lord God made trees spring from the ground, all trees pleasant to look at and good for food; and in the middle of the garden he set the tree of life and the tree of the knowledge of good and evil. . . .

The Lord God took the man and put him in the garden of Eden to till it and care for it. He told the man, "You may eat from every tree in the garden, but not from the tree of the knowledge of good and evil; for on the day that you eat from it, you will certainly die." Then the Lord God said, "It is not good for the man to be alone. I will provide a partner for him." . . .

And so the Lord God put the man into a trance, and while he slept, he took one of his ribs and closed the flesh over the place. The Lord God then built up the rib, which he had taken out of the man, into a woman. He brought her to the man, and the man said:

> "Now this, at last—
> bone from my bones,
> flesh from my flesh!—
> this shall be called woman,
> for from man was this taken."

That is why a man leaves his father and mother and is united to his wife, and the two become one flesh. Now they were both naked, the man and his wife, but they had no feeling of shame towards one another.

The serpent was more crafty than any wild creature that the Lord God had made. He said to the woman, "Is it true that God has forbidden you to eat from any tree in the garden?" The woman answered the serpent, "We may eat the fruit of any tree in the garden, except for the tree in the middle of the garden; God has forbidden us either to eat or to touch the fruit of that; if we do, we shall die." The serpent said, "Of course you will not die. God knows that as soon as you eat it, your eyes will be opened and you will be like gods knowing both good and evil." When the woman saw that the fruit of the tree was good to eat, and that it was pleasing to the eye and tempting to contemplate, she took some and ate it. She also gave her husband some and he ate it. Then the eyes of both of them were opened and they discovered that they were naked; so they stitched fig-leaves together and made themselves loincloths.

The man and his wife heard the sound of the Lord God walking in the garden at the time of the evening breeze and hid from the Lord God among the trees of the garden. But the Lord God called to the man and said to him, "Where are you?" He replied, "I heard the sound as you were walking in the garden, and I was afraid because I was naked, and I hid myself." God answered, "Who told you that you were naked? Have you eaten from the tree which I forbade you?" The man said, "The woman you gave me for a companion, she gave me fruit from the tree and I ate it." Then the Lord God said to the woman, "What is this that you have done?" The woman said, "The serpent tricked me, and I ate." Then the Lord God said to the serpent:

"Because you have done this you are accursed
more than all cattle and all wild creatures.
On your belly you shall crawl, and dust you shall eat
I will put enmity between you and the woman,
between your brood and hers.
They shall strike at your head,
and you shall strike at their heel."

To the woman he said:

"I will increase your labour and your groaning,
and in labour you shall bear children.
You shall be eager for your husband,
and he shall be your master."

And to the man he said:

"Because you have listened to your wife
and have eaten from the tree which I forbade you,
accursed shall be the ground on your account.
all the days of your life.

With labour you shall win your food from it
all the days of your life.
It will grow thorns and thistles for you,
none but wild plants for you to eat.
You shall gain your bread by the sweat of your brow
until you return to the ground;
for from it you were taken.
Dust you are, to dust you shall return."

The man called his wife Eve because she was the mother of all who live. The Lord God made tunics of skins for Adam and his wife and clothed them. He said, "The man has become like one of us, knowing good and evil; what if he now reaches out his hand and takes fruit from the tree of life also, eats it and lives forever?" So the Lord God drove him out of the Garden of Eden to till the ground from which he had been taken. He cast him out, and to the east of the Garden of Eden he stationed the cherubim and a sword whirling and flashing to guard the way to the tree of life. [from the Book of Genesis]

Why Is the Truth So Scandalous?

❀

Galileo Galilei, Italian scientist, born in Pisa February 2, 1564, died in Arcetri near Florence January 8, 1642; was appointed professor of mathematics at Pisa in 1589, at Padua in 1592; called back to Pisa in 1619, he was also named court mathematician at the Grand Duke's court in Florence. Galileo's greatest talents were in the area of practical physics and applied mathematics.

His contribution to the history of science . . . lies fundamentally in his having completely liberated physics from its dependence on a priori philosophical principles, which had dominated it up to that point, basing it on observation instead of speculation; likewise, he did not explain natural phenomena philosophically or theologically as manifestations of God's will but in terms of natural laws. In so doing he laid the foundation for modern experimental science, which resulted, however, in sharp disagreement with prevailing church doctrine, culminating in open conflict over the question of the Copernican system. Expressing his agreement with this system in 1597 in a letter to Kepler, he defended it publicly in his treatise on sunspots (1613), which led the Inquisition to initiate proceedings against him. The first trial ended in 1616 with a condemnation of the two propositions—that the sun is the center of the solar system and that the earth moves—as *absurd, philosophically false, theologically heretical and erroneous* [author's italics], and silence was imposed on Galileo. After publishing his theories again in 1632 in his treatise on the Ptolemaic and Copernican systems, he was brought to trial a second time in 1633 and forced to recant under threat of torture. The assertion attributed to him, "eppur si muove" (nevertheless it does move) is legendary. In addition, the church condemned him to house arrest, first in the residence of the Archbishop of Siena, later in his own villa in Arcetri, where he went blind in 1637. The Church's condemnation of the writings of Copernicus was not rescinded until 1835.

—*Der grosse Brockhaus* (1954)

‹§ 10 ›»

The Loneliness of the Explorer

I N his lecture "The Aetiology of Hysteria," published in 1896,
Freud reports with great clarity, directness, and persuasiveness
(at least for the reader of today) that in all eighteen cases of hysterical illness treated by him (six men and twelve women) he discovered in the course of the analytic work repression of sexual abuse
by an adult or by an older sibling who had in turn previously been
abused by adults. None of the eighteen patients was aware of this
fact when treatment began, and Freud contends that their symptoms would not have appeared if these early memories had remained conscious. He is describing facts whose emergence came as
a surprise even to him, and as a curious scientist of integrity he could
hardly ignore this evidence; he seeks his audience's understanding in
spite of the moral indignation he feels himself. Sometimes one has
the impression that he is trying to convince himself as well as his
audience, because the facts in question strike him as monstrous. How
was someone at the turn of the century who had learned to regard all
adults as respected authority figures and who could not yet have any
inkling of the knowledge we have today of ambivalence, the crucial
importance of early childhood experiences, and the power of the
repetition compulsion in the adult's unconscious come to terms with
such a discovery? Understandably, he was horrified and was inclined to pass moral judgment, something we as analysts of adults
who abuse their children can perhaps not avoid until we have been
able to experience with them the inner distress that goes with these
acts. But Freud obviously had no knowledge at that point of the
later ramifications of his finding, and he therefore had no choice but
to consider these adults perverse. Since they were parents and
therefore had to be respected at any cost, Freud was continually
tempted not to believe what he discovered about his patients.

One can sense in "The Aetiology of Hysteria" the brilliant explorer's struggle to free himself from the commandments that dominated his upbringing. The audience Freud is addressing, with which he partly identifies, might want to say, "What must not be, cannot be." And the researcher replies, "But I have found it to be so." He knows that every possible objection will be raised to what he is saying. Some will say sexual seduction of children is *so rare* that it cannot possibly be the cause of hysterical illnesses, which occur so frequently. Others will claim the opposite, saying that sexual abuse, particularly among the lower classes, is found *so frequently* that there would have to be a much greater incidence of hysteria than there is, especially in that milieu; but it is known to be the case that a much higher percentage of this kind of illness occurs among the privileged classes. Freud answers this potential objection with a point that strikes me as still valid today: that the upper classes, thanks to their level of education and their often one-sided intellectual development, are better able to generate defenses against their traumas, and it is precisely these defenses (repression, splitting off of the feeling connected with the recollected content, and denial by means of idealization) that cause neurosis. The objections to his trauma theory adduced by Freud in 1896 can still be encountered in the same contradictory form today, although the narcissistic cathexis of the child by the adult, in which sexual and aggressive abuse play a major role, can no longer be denied in view of all we know now. Before Freud felt compelled to conceal his finding behind the drive theory, he wrote the following passage:

> All the singular conditions under which the ill-matched pair conduct their love-relations—on the one hand the adult, who cannot escape his share in the mutual dependence necessarily entailed by a sexual relationship, and who is yet armed with complete authority and the right to punish, and can exchange the one role for the other to the uninhibited satisfaction of his moods, and on the other hand the child, who in his helplessness is at the mercy of this arbitrary will, who is prematurely aroused to every kind of sensibility and exposed to every sort of disappointment, and whose performance of the sexual activities assigned to him is often interrupted by his imperfect control of his natural needs—all these grotesque and yet tragic incongruities reveal themselves as stamped upon the later development of the individual and of his neurosis, in countless permanent effects which

deserve to be traced in the greatest detail. Where the relation is between two children, the character of the sexual scenes is none the less of the same repulsive sort, since every such relationship between children postulates a previous seduction of one of them by an adult. The psychical consequences of these child-relations are quite extraordinarily far-reaching; the two individuals remain linked by an invisible bond throughout the whole of their lives.

Sometimes it is the accidental circumstances of these infantile sexual scenes which in later years acquire a determining power over the symptoms of the neurosis. Thus, in one of my cases the circumstance that the child was required to stimulate the genitals of a grown-up woman with his foot was enough to fixate his neurotic attention for years on to his legs and to their function, and finally to produce a hysterical paraplegia. [S.E., III, 215]

In these few words Freud sums up the situation of the child as it has existed unchanged for millennia, at least in our culture. The link between parents' need for erotic fulfillment and their right to use and punish the child is such an inherent feature of our culture that until recently its legitimacy had been questioned by very few.

Now, however, the psychoanalytic method has brought us face to face with the consequences of this phenomenon—with repression and the related loss of vitality that occurs in neurosis. This revelation has apparently severely strained the limits of what people can accept. The shock, confusion, and dismay it caused could be mastered (warded off) only by denying the facts or, if this was no longer possible, by constructing various theories. The more complicated, incomprehensible, and rigid these theories, the better guarantee they provided that the actually very obvious but painful situation remained concealed.

There is a striking divergence in the ways the public reacts to news and information. In a single evening readers can find all manner of shocking events reported in the newspaper without being shaken out of their accustomed tranquillity. There may be an account of a father who stabbed his wife and three children to death and then took his own life. This man was considered a conscientious employee, and there had been nothing unusual about his previous behavior. Depending on their level of education and orientation, our newspaper readers may think, "The man was simply a born psychopath, even though he was able to cover it up until now." Or,

"The housing shortage and the stress of his job drove the man to murder his wife and children." The same newspaper may carry a report about the trial of a terrorist, during which the young man, accused of multiple homicide, delivered an hour-long ideological speech. There is also an interview with his mother, who claims convincingly that her son had never caused any trouble all through his childhood and adolescence, until he went to college. Then readers come to the "obvious" conclusion that the "bad influence" of the other students, who were raised too permissively, made this man become a terrorist. Continuing to leaf through the paper, they may now find another item about the rising suicide rate in a "luxury" prison, where each prisoner is isolated in his own cell. This might cause them to exclaim: "That goes to show you how spoiled people are nowadays! Their high standard of living makes them even more dissatisfied, and it may be that a permissive upbringing is responsible for all the acts of violence being committed by today's young people." Explanations such as these comfort readers and reinforce their value system. The events in question have no personal significance for them. They would basically *rather not know* how it is possible for a loving father suddenly to murder his three children, how an obedient son can so easily turn into a terrorist, why a prisoner in isolation commits suicide. For who can guarantee that their form of adjustment, successful thus far, does not have its dangerous shadow side, too, and that they will always manage to keep it at a distance? Understanding for someone else's unconscious presupposes a familiarity with our own. How can we understand drug addiction, delinquency, or the outbreak of mental illness if the unconscious portion of our own and the other person's psyche is ignored?

In "The Aetiology of Hysteria" Freud is struggling with this resistance on the part of the public. He knows that he has hit upon a truth that concerns everyone, i.e., the consequences of childhood trauma for later life (which is not to be equated with causal determinism), and at the same time he knows that the overwhelming majority of people will oppose him precisely because he is telling the truth.

The content of Freud's discoveries can be so widely denied because most people ignore their unconscious, all the more so if they are dominated by it in some fateful way. After all, we all have a perfect right to consider our dreams insignificant and to deny the existence of our unconscious. This gives rise to the paradoxical situation in which the newspaper readers described above can react to even the most incomprehensible, bizarre human behavior without amazement and are willing to accept the most absurd reasons given for this behavior without any sign of emotion as long as they personally are left out of the picture. Yet they will react with anger or scorn if someone points out the unconscious motives for the incomprehensible behavior, for if they took these explanations seriously, the complicated defense mechanisms so essential to them would be threatened.

Freud's drive theory accommodates these defense mechanisms by locating the origins of neurosis in infantile sexual fantasies and conflicts, thus preserving the required idealization of the parents. This was something one could understand and—in view of the dominance of "poisonous pedagogy" in 1897—even accept. But the empirical findings that led Freud to his trauma theory could not be made to fit the drive theory, even though he seems to have tried to do so for the rest of his life. The sexually (and non-sexually) abused child, whom Freud described in 1896 and then abandoned in 1897, is quite logically no longer to be found in his later drive theory, for the vocabulary of "poisonous pedagogy" and an eye for the reality of the victimized child are mutually exclusive. An analyst who knows the harm that can unconsciously be done to children will not, like most parents or educators, attempt to cover up the abuse of power by dismissing his or her patient's vague, halting recollections as infantile fantasies. Of course, a child may have a rich fantasy life, but this always serves the purpose of helping him cope with reality. For the sake of survival he will usually make beloved attachment figures seem better than they are and never denigrate them.

The man who went down in history as the discoverer of the Oedipus complex wrote these words in 1896:

> The general doubt about the reliability of the psycho-analytic method can be appraised and removed only when a complete presentation of its technique and results is available. Doubts about the genuineness of the infantile sexual scenes can, however, be deprived of their force here and now by more than one argument. In the first place, the behaviour of patients while they are reproducing these infantile

experiences is in every respect incompatible with the assumption that the scenes are anything else than a reality which is being felt with distress and reproduced with the greatest reluctance. Before they come for analysis the patients know nothing about these scenes. They are indignant as a rule if we warn them that such scenes are going to emerge. Only the strongest compulsion of the treatment can induce them to embark on a reproduction of them. While they are recalling these infantile experiences to consciousness, they suffer under the most violent sensations, of which they are ashamed and which they try to conceal; and, even after they have gone through them once more in such a convincing manner, they still attempt to withhold belief from them, by emphasizing the fact that, unlike what happens in the case of other forgotten material, they have no feeling of remembering the scenes.

This latter piece of behaviour seems to provide conclusive proof. Why should patients assure me so emphatically of their unbelief, if what they want to discredit is something which—from whatever motive—they themselves have invented?

It is less easy to refute the idea that the doctor forces reminiscences of this sort on the patient, that he influences him by suggestion to imagine and reproduce them. Nevertheless it appears to me equally untenable. I have never yet succeeded in forcing on a patient a scene I was expecting to find, in such a way that he seemed to be living through it with all the appropriate feelings. Perhaps others may be more successful in this.

There are, however, a whole number of other things that vouch for the reality of infantile sexual scenes. In the first place there is the uniformity which they exhibit in certain details, which is a necessary consequence if the preconditions of these experiences are always of the same kind, but which would otherwise lead us to believe that there were secret understandings between the various patients. In the second place, patients sometimes describe as harmless events whose significance they obviously do not understand, since they would be bound otherwise to be horrified by them. Or again, they mention details, without laying any stress on them, which only someone of experience in life can understand and appreciate as subtle traits of reality. [pp. 204–5]

Was it Freud's "naïveté," as he himself later thought, or was it brilliant intuition that led him to write a passage like this, whose meaning is so unmistakable?

. . .

Every religion has its taboos, which must be accepted by its followers if they do not want to be rejected by the community of believers. This excludes any further development within the body of the faithful, but it cannot prevent individuals from attacking specific taboos from time to time; in so doing they abandon familiar ground and become the founders of new creeds, having been unable to change or enrich the old one. Others are now able to choose among different faiths, providing they were not too strictly conditioned to believe only in their own as a child.

But what happens when a great scientific discovery, relevant for everyone, is made the exclusive property of one school of thought and is surrounded by dogmas and taboos? A paradoxical situation then arises in which the original discovery, which might have been the starting point for further findings and for a substantial heightening of consciousness stagnates because the dogmas that have become entrenched in the meantime would be threatened by new findings.

It seems to me that this is the situation in which psychoanalysis finds itself today. The ramifications of Freud's recognition that early childhood suffering is preserved in the adult's unconscious have by no means been fully explored. Even the first obvious conclusion to be drawn from it represented a dangerous threat to an established taboo. What Freud learned about his patients through hypnosis and his subsequent use of the method of free association seemed to point inescapably to the fact that as children they had been sexually abused by their parents or other family members or by their care givers. In order for Freud to take his patients' accounts seriously in the face of resistance from the public, he would have had to be free from the strictures of the patriarchal family, from the demands of the Fourth Commandment, and from the guilt feelings caused by his introjected parents. Since that kind of freedom was totally impossible at the time, perhaps Freud had no choice but to interpret what his patients told him as fantasies and to construct a theory that would spare adults from reproach and would allow him to trace his patients' symptoms back to the repression of their own infantile sexual wishes.

In a letter to Wilhelm Fliess dated September 21, 1897, Freud gives the reasons that led him to renounce his trauma theory. He refers to the realization of the unexpected frequency of hysteria, in every case of which the same thing applied, though it was hardly credible that perverted acts against children were so general. (Perversion would have to be immeasurably more frequent than hysteria, as the illness can only arise where the events have accumulated and one of the factors which weaken defence is present.) [*The Origins of Psychoanalysis*, pp. 215–16]

As fate would have it, the methods Freud developed and handed on to future generations as a heuristic tool enable us to recognize a multitude of facts that seemed highly improbable to him in his day. The greater part of a century has passed since he wrote the lines just cited. During this time, very different types of patients from many countries have been analyzed and have had the opportunity to express openly in analysis their desires, fantasies, and thoughts. On the basis of these analyses, we know how frequently one's own children can be the cause of sexual arousal; we also know that in those cases where such desires can be acknowledged and openly expressed, sexual abuse does not occur. The tendency for adults to use their children as best they can to meet all their needs is so widespread and so taken for granted in world history that most people do not refer to this form of sexual abuse as a perversion; it is simply one of the many ways adults exercise power over their children.

There were several motives, personal ones among them, that moved Freud to abandon his trauma theory. In the above letter to Fliess he enumerated all those he was conscious of, and he subsequently replaced the earlier theory with that of the Oedipus complex, thus enabling people to close their eyes to or minimize what was no doubt an unwelcome and offensive truth for them, much in the same way the Church for a long time treated the discoveries of Galileo and Copernicus. But once a truth has been stated, it cannot disappear from sight entirely; sooner or later it will prevail, even if it is retracted by the person who discovered it.

Freud tried all his life to salvage his theory pertaining to the sexual origin of the neuroses of his day—by camouflaging the real situation with theories that diverted attention from the actions of the adult to the fantasies of the child, thus making his findings accepable to a generation molded by "poisonous pedagagy," i.e., also to himself. It goes without saying that I do not regard sexual trauma as the only possible origin of neurosis, as claimed by Freud's trauma theory of 1896, for there are, as we know, countless other ways children can be mistreated and at the same time deprived of their voice and their awareness. But sexual abuse, with its role in the formation of psychic disturbances, needs our special attention because it has been silenced, ignored, or denied for so long.

In spite of the high price he paid, Freud still could not prevent those people who have applied his psychoanalytic methods over the past eighty-some years from seeing connections (in such areas as family therapy, analysis of children, treatment of schizophrenia, and psychohistory) that confirm at least partially the validity of his original insights—even if, or perhaps because, no theory has yet been developed to explain them. Freud wrote in 1896:

> If we have the perseverance to press on with the analysis into early childhood, as far back as a human memory is capable of reaching, we invariably bring the patient to reproduce experiences which, on account both of their peculiar features and of their relations to the symptoms of his later illness, must be regarded as the aetiology of his neurosis for which we have been looking. These *infantile* experiences are once more *sexual* in content, but they are of a far more uniform kind than the scenes at puberty that had been discovered earlier. It is now no longer a question of sexual topics having been aroused by some sense impression or other, but of sexual experiences affecting the subject's own body—of *sexual intercourse* (in the wider sense). You will admit that the *importance* of such scenes needs no further proof; to this may now be added that, in every instance, you will be able to discover in the details of the scenes the *determining* factors which you may have found lacking in the other scenes—the scenes which occurred later and were reproduced earlier.
>
> I therefore put forward the thesis that at the bottom of every case of hysteria there are *one or more occurrences of premature sexual experience*, occurrences which belong to the earliest years of childhood but which can be reproduced through the work of psycho-analysis in spite of the intervening decades. I believe that this is an important finding, the discovery of a *caput Nili* in neuropathology . . . [*S.E.*, III, pp. 202–3]

And several pages later we read:

> Lastly, the findings of my analysis are in a position to speak for themselves. In all eighteen cases (cases of pure hysteria and hysteria combined with obsessions, and comprising six men and twelve women)

I have, as I have said, come to learn of sexual experiences of this kind in childhood. I can divide my cases into three groups, according to the origin of the sexual stimulation. In the first group it is a question of assaults—of single, or at any rate isolated, instances of abuse, mostly practised on female children, by adults who were strangers, and who, incidentally, knew how to avoid inflicting gross, mechanical injury. In these assaults there was no question of the child's consent, and the first effect of the experience was preponderantly one of fright. The second group consists of the much more numerous cases in which some adult looking after the child—a nursery maid or governess or tutor, or, unhappily all too often, a close relative—has initiated the child into sexual intercourse and has maintained a regular love relationship with it—a love relationship, moreover, with its mental side developed—which has often lasted for years. The third group, finally, contains child-relationships proper—sexual relations between two children of different sexes, mostly a brother and sister, which are often prolonged beyond puberty and which have the most far-reaching consequences for the pair. In most of my cases I found that two or more of these aetiologies were in operation together; in a few instances the accumulation of sexual experiences coming from different quarters was truly amazing. You will easily understand this peculiar feature of my observations, however, when you consider that the patients I was treating were all cases of severe neurotic illness which threatened to make life impossible.

Where there had been a relation between two children I was sometimes able to prove that the boy—who, here too, played the part of the aggressor—had previously been seduced by an adult of the female sex, and that afterwards, under the pressure of his prematurely awakened libido and compelled by his memory, he tried to repeat with the little girl exactly the same practices that he had learned from the adult woman, without making any modification of his own in the character of the sexual activity.

In view of this, I am inclined to suppose that children cannot find their way to acts of sexual aggression unless they have been seduced previously. The foundation for a neurosis would accordingly always be laid in childhood by adults, and the children themselves would transfer to one another the disposition to fall ill of hysteria later. [pp. 207–9]

What might it have meant in practical terms if Freud had remained true to this insight? If we picture his readers, the women of the bourgeoisie of that day, with their elegant long dresses that hid their ankles, and the men with their stiff white collars and faultlessly cut suits (for it can hardly be supposed that his books were read by the working class), it is not hard to imagine the outrage and indignation that would have greeted the facts presented above. The indignation would not have been directed against this form of child abuse per se but against the man who dared to speak about it. For most of these refined people were firmly convinced from an early age that only fine, noble, valiant, and edifying deeds (subjects) ought to be talked about publicly and that what they as adults did behind closed doors in their elegant bedrooms very definitely had no place in print. Satisfying sexual desires with children was nothing bad in their eyes as long as silence was preserved, for they were convinced that no harm would be done to the children unless the matter was discussed with them. Therefore, the acts they performed were shrouded in silence, as if children were dolls, for they firmly believed a doll would never know or tell what had been done to it. In order to ensure discretion, children were not sexually enlightened; their erotic activities—such as touching their genitals or masturbating—and any show of interest in sexual matters were forbidden. At the same time, they were raised in the spirit of the Fourth Commandment, and their entire life was dominated by the principle of respect for their parents. Children thus had to come to terms, without anyone to help them, with the irreconcilable contradiction that it was filthy and depraved to touch their own genitals but that it was also wrong of them not to allow an adult to play with their body. Even to ask questions about this was dangerous. Freud's case history of Dora shows the endless obstacles a woman who has grown up in this atmosphere has to contend with if she wants to resolve the discrepancy between what has been passed on to her on a conscious level and what she has perceived half-consciously, for she can no longer live with this discrepancy. The earliest traumas cannot be consciously recalled but are manifested in destructive and self-destructive behavior, symptoms, fantasies, and dreams; they contradict the idealized image of the parents, which must be preserved for many reasons. Accordingly, people like Dora do everything in their power to avoid pain by preventing their trauma from becoming conscious. In a letter to Fliess dated April 28, 1897, Freud describes how one of his new patients deals with this conflict:

Yesterday I started treatment of a new case, a young woman, whom for lack of time I should have liked to have frightened off. She had a brother who died insane, and her chief symptom—insomnia—dates from the time she heard the carriage driving away from the house taking him to the asylum. Since then she has been terrified of carriage drives and convinced that an accident was going to happen. Years later, while she was out driving, the horses shied and she took the opportunity to jump from the carriage and break a leg. Today she came and said she had been thinking over the treatment and had found an obstacle. "What is it?" "I can paint myself as black as necessary, but I must spare other people. You must allow me to mention no names." "Names don't matter. What you mean is your relationship with the people concerned. We can't draw a veil over that." "What I mean is that earlier the treatment would have been easier for me than now. Earlier I didn't suspect it, but now the criminal nature of certain things has become clear to me, and I can't make up my mind to talk about them." "On the contrary, I should say that a mature woman becomes more tolerant in sexual matters." "Yes, there you're right. When I consider that the most excellent and high-principled men are guilty of these things, I'm compelled to think it's an illness, a kind of madness, and I have to excuse them." "Then let us speak plainly. In my analyses I find it's the closest relatives, fathers or brothers, who are the guilty men." "It has nothing to do with my brother." "So it was your father, then."

Then it came out that when she was between the ages of eight and twelve her allegedly otherwise admirable and high-principled father used regularly to take her into his bed and practise external ejaculation (making wet) with her. Even at the time she felt anxiety. A six-year-older sister to whom she talked about it later admitted that she had had the same experiences with her father. A cousin told her that at the age of fifteen she had had to resist the advances of her grandfather. Naturally she did not find it incredible when I told her that similar and worse things must have happened to her in infancy. In other respects hers is a quite ordinary hysteria with usual symptoms. [*The Origins of Psychoanalysis*, pp. 195–96]

Just a few months later, in September 1897, Freud distanced himself from his trauma theory, which no one, not even his collaborator Josef Breuer, was able to accept, and then found the "solution" in infantile sexuality and the Oedipus complex—in other words, in his drive theory.

ᨄ 11 ᨃ

Is There Such a Thing as
"Infantile Sexuality"?

I T was a long time before I could finally take seriously the doubts about the drive theory that had kept troubling me ever since the days of my training as an analyst and could finally stop feeling obligated to regard it as the cornerstone of psychoanalysis, but I had to take this step if I was to remain loyal to my basic principle of learning from my patients instead of trying to make them fit my theories. What I have found out about "infantile sexuality" in the analyses I have conducted myself and in those I have supervised may be summed up as follows:

1. Some, though by no means all, of the anxiety, bewilderment, and uncertainty present in every patient's childhood was of a sexual nature. But now I no longer interpret such difficulties the way I was taught to—as a defense against the child's own sexual desires—but in part as reactions to adults' sexual desires, of which the child was the object. As I have already indicated, in order to survive, a little child needs love, care, attention, and tenderness from the adult. He will do anything in order to get them and to keep them. If he senses that his closest and most important attachment figure's interest in him has a (conscious or unconscious) sexual content—which is frequently the case, since the parents of our patients often are sexually unfulfilled—this will make him insecure, sometimes frightened, and in extreme cases totally disoriented. Nevertheless, he will still make every effort to satisfy the adult's desires or at least not to frustrate them to any great extent, because he doesn't want to offend the adult and thus run the risk of rejection.

2. One of the inescapable laws governing a child's existence is determined by *what parents need from their child*, and sexuality is no exception here. Children will produce pseudo-sexual feelings in

order to be a satisfactory partner for the frustrated parent and not
to be deprived of the parent's attention (Pierre Boudier has done an
illuminating study of this problem in the children of psychotic
mothers.)

3. Genuine sexual maturity coincides with physical maturation
in puberty. What Freud describes as "infantile sexuality" during
the first to fifth years of life is in my view made up of many different
elements, which I shall enumerate here:

a. *Autoeroticism*, or interest in one's own body and self.

b. Healthy and intense *curiosity*, not yet suppressed by means of
false and evasive information, on the part of the young child, who
is interested in everything around him and who also reacts strongly
to differences between the sexes and to the "primal scene" (parental
sexual intercourse).

c. Intense *jealousy* of the intimacy shared by the two parents,
from which the child is excluded (the Oedipal triangle).

d. The little boy's pleasure at his *ability to manipulate his penis*
and his *fear* that adults may put a stop to his pleasure (fear of
castration, which was often threatened in the nineteenth century).

e. The little girl's *envy of* little boys, especially if adults explain
sexual characteristics in terms of "having one" and "not having one"
and exaggerate the importance of masculinity (penis envy).

f. The strength and *intensity of children's physical sensations* in
general, including those in the oral and anal areas (the view that
sensations in these areas are of a sexual nature is one imposed on the
child from outside).

g. *The (power) struggle* that normally takes place *during toilet
training*, which can lead to so-called anal fixation and actually says
more about the attempt to deprive the child of power than it does
about his or her sensuous drives and desires.

h. The constant *adjustment to adult desires* (which can also be
expressed in its negative form as defiance) and the complete readi-
ness to respond to them.

Freud attributes the decline of sexual interest during the latency
period to repression of the Oedipus complex. There may, however,
be other reasons for this change. If we regard small children, not
as subjects, not as instigators, but as objects of adults' sexual desires,
then other considerations immediately come to mind: adults are
more likely to make sexual advances toward their younger children

than toward their older ones. Young children live in much closer contact with their parents, often sharing the same bedroom. They are also much more attractive and sexually stimulating in their first years than when they start school. In addition, adults can rely more on a young child's discretion than an older one's, and until recently people were convinced—indeed, some still are—that what happens to very little children has no consequences at all and will never be divulged to a third party.

4. It is quite natural for children to awaken sexual desire in the adult, because they tend to be beautiful, cuddly, affectionate, and because they admire the adult so much, probably more than anyone else does. If adults have a satisfying sex life with another adult, they have no need to act upon the desires aroused by the child or to ward them off. But if they feel themselves humiliated and not taken seriously by their partner, if their own needs were never allowed to unfold or mature, or if they were themselves seduced and violated as children, then these adults will show a strong tendency to impose their sexual needs on the child.

5. The desires experienced by an adult as sexual are often of a narcissistic nature. In another connection (in *The Drama of the Gifted Child*), I investigated the narcissistic origins of sexual perversions in some detail. I would not be surprised if the most extreme cases of explicit pedophilia were to reveal a completely nonsexual etiology (questions of power vs. powerlessness, for instance).

6. It has been my experience that a therapist makes much more therapeutic progress if he or she tries to understand patients' sexual problems as a result of sexual abuse by adults. I do not interpret the seductive behavior of a so-called hysterical patient as an expression of her sexual desires but as an *unconscious message* concerning an event she has completely forgotten, which can be approached only by way of this reenactment. I believe that in her active role the patient will repeatedly demonstrate that which once—or more than once—happened to her but which she cannot remember because it was too traumatic to retain on a conscious level without the aid of an empathic support figure. Instead, she reenacts the unconscious childhood trauma that caused her illness (cf. the stories of Anita and of Klaus Thomas's art student).

The story of early abuse need not be presented in a hysterical, seductive form. What has been passively endured is frequently transformed into active behavior, but this is not the only defense mechanism we encounter. Frigidity, insomnia, restlessness, or addiction can also result, and there may be no sign of the hysterical patient's typical theatricality, which represents a more obvious reenactment of her sexual abuse, though under a different guise.

The six points I have just cited, which conflict sharply with Freud's theory of infantile sexuality, are not part of the theoretical equipment I have always worked with. They gradually emerged from my practical work with patients, from numerous observations and dreams, and, ultimately, from the discovery that this approach helps patients to understand themselves and their fate better than does the search for their infantile sexuality, a concept they are usually willing to accept but one that does nothing to make them feel they are truly understood. When I communicate this new approach of mine to other psychoanalysts, I am often confronted with the question, already mentioned, of why this has to be regarded as so radically different, why there is not room for both interpretations, namely, assigning a significant role to sexual traumatization as well as to sexual desire during childhood. If my theses were based solely on abstract theoretical considerations, then presumably it would be an easy matter to put things together and take them apart again arbitrarily, for the "psychic apparatus" as an intellectual construct can be described any way one pleases. But I have no use for such abstractions. The ideas I have developed here are based on concrete experiences, which are not new but which did not take on meaning for me until I began to see them in relation to the hidden but ubiquitous exercise of power over children by adults. From this perspective I understand the concept of "infantile sexuality" as an expression of a pedagogical way of thinking that overlooks the actual imbalance of power.

Since children need to idealize their parents in order to survive and since their upbringing forbids them to notice, become aware of, or articulate the wrong done to them, but since, on the other hand, children's feelings are very strong and intense, it should come as no surprise that the theory of infantile sexuality has prevailed as long as it has. Yet we *should* be surprised that, whereas it is now so easy for many people to take for granted the absurd idea that a child wants to have sexual relations with a grownup, in all of psychoanalytic theory there is very rarely any mention of the effect a child has on sexually unfulfilled parents. Furthermore, the question is rarely raised of what it means for little children, during a display of affection, suddenly to become confused when they see in their mother's or father's eyes a sexual need they would like to respond to but cannot.

Encountering this look alone causes only a very mild form of disorientation, but a whole gamut of incomprehensible and frightening sexual contacts between child and adult—up to and including rape—occurs much more frequently than people like to admit.

In *The Restoration of the Self*, Heinz Kohut explains the difference between the types of neurosis encountered in our day and in Freud's by pointing out that, as children, today's patients were deprived of physical contact with their parents, whereas the previous generation suffered from sexual overstimulation in childhood. The distinction ignores the evidence of the clinical material, from which Kohut's examples are also taken and which demonstrates again and again that sexual stimulation can be followed by displays of rage or indifference, as the case may be. Yet Kohut's concept of the self-object is particularly helpful in explaining this combination if we give due weight to the widespread phenomenon that children are very often used as substitutes for the self-objects their parents lacked.

It is a known fact that fathers sometimes rape their daughters, and recently more cases have been reported than ever, because nowadays daughters have more opportunity to reveal what was formerly kept secret, providing the trauma occurred at a relatively late age and can still be recalled (cf. my Afterword of 1984). These rapes often have nothing to do with so-called incest love but merely provide fathers, as an Italian newspaper once put it, with "the cheapest possible way of getting their pleasure."

When I speak of unconscious trauma, I do not mean that one specific event will inevitably cause neurosis. The pathogenic factor is the entire atmosphere of early childhood, which comes to light in the transference and countertransference. It is not necessarily emotional deprivation that leads to psychic disturbances but above all narcissistic wounds—including sexual abuse. These wounds occur at that time of life when the child is most helpless and are concealed by subsequent repression. While this repression ensures parents that their secret will be safe, the child's lack of conscious knowledge blocks access to his or her feelings and vitality. Not being able to talk about or even *know* about these wounds is what later leads to pathological developments.

Virginia Woolf, who suffered from repeated psychotic episodes from the time she was twelve, committed suicide at the age of fifty-nine. Her biographer, Quentin Bell, reports that she suffered from "a cancer of the mind, a corruption of the spirit" and "heard the voices of insanity." He writes: "I do not know enough about Virginia's mental illnesses to say whether this adolescent trauma was in any way connected with them" (p. 44). Yet on the preceding page he tells in detail about the way the two little girls, Virginia and her sister Vanessa, were used for years by their much older half-brother George for his sexual "skirmishes." Not without empathy Bell says:

> To the sisters it simply appeared that their loving brother was transformed before their eyes into a monster, a tyrant against whom they had no defence, for how could they speak out or take any action against a treachery so covert that it was half unknown even to the traitor? Trained as they were to preserve a condition of ignorant purity they must at first have been unaware that affection was turning to concupiscence, and were warned only by their growing sense of disgust. To this, and to their intense shyness, we may ascribe Vanessa's and Virginia's long reticence on the subject. George was always demonstratively emotional, lavish and irresponsible in his endearments and his embraces; it would have taken a very knowing eye to perceive that his caresses went perhaps further than was proper in even the most loving of brothers, and the bedtime pettings may have seemed no more than a normal extension of his daytime devotion. It would have been hard for his half-sisters to know at what point to draw a line, to voice objections, to risk evoking a painful and embarrassing scandal: harder still to find someone to whom they could speak at all. Stella, Leslie, the aunts—all would have been bewildered, horrified, indignant and incredulous.
>
> Their only course seemed to be one of silent evasion; but even this was denied them; they must join in praising their persecutor, for his advances were conducted to an accompaniment of enthusiastic applause in which the girls could hear the repeated hope that "dear George" would not find them ungrateful. [p. 43]

These sexual games continued over a number of years until Virginia was eleven.

In her "loving" environment, there was not a soul in whom Virginia could have confided without fearing that she herself would be blamed, since her half-brother was already grown up and would be defended by the other adults. Perhaps she could have overcome her hesitancy if another half-brother had not already done something similar when she was six. In a letter to Ethyl Smyth dated January 12, 1941 (the year of Woolf's death!), Virginia writes: "I still shiver with shame at the memory of my half-brother, standing me on a ledge, aged about 6 or so, exploring my private parts" (p. 44). A document that was discovered later (Monk's House Papers) revealed that the half-brother referred to here was not George but Gerald.

It has been my experience that in the late stages of patients' analysis, memories often come to the surface of being fondled as a child by an uncle or a stranger, not infrequently a priest. The patient did not dare to resist these advances or even tell anyone what happened. From the perspective of the drive theory, the obvious thing to do would be to sound the patient out about the pleasurable feelings supposedly experienced at the time. Patients often accept this approach without resistance because they are so used to not being understood. Yet the case of Virginia Woolf shows how completely such drive interpretations can ignore the child's very real distress and loneliness. It also frequently turns out that the remembered "uncle" was a screen memory. Only when this experience has been relived and given emphatic attention by the analyst can the even earlier repressed memory of a similar experience with the father or older brother emerge. The recollection is often accompanied by numerous dreams with similar content and by experiences in the transference. Again and again in the transference and in relationships with present-day partners the need then arises to have privacy, one's own carefully guarded space (cf. the title of one of Woolf's books: *A Room of One's Own*), to stop letting oneself be used in all possible kinds of ways, to be able to say no, to experience oneself as a separate person. Suspicion also emerges of the other person's intentions, combined with a great fear of losing the loved person if one doesn't place oneself entirely at the other's disposal. During this stage of analysis, patients often dream, for example, that for the first time they are finally able to bring themselves to close the bathroom door. It becomes clear that they never would have dared to do this during puberty and that the father was always free to enter the bathroom whenever he pleased. To shut oneself in would have been a sign of a lack of trust and would have meant offending him. One patient dreamed that he again saw the narrow passages of his earlier dreams but this time was no longer willing to squeeze through the small openings and bend down in order to enter the next room. Now he avoided these passages and discovered large new rooms. Another patient dreamed that she discovered a room in her apartment that could be locked securely and that belonged *only to her* from then on. Dreams like this have a symbolic character, for they represent freeing the self from someone else's power, but very often they also bring actual early situations to light (as in the dream about the bathroom), which of course had real, as well as symbolic, significance for the self.

The need to terminate one's entanglement with someone else's desires and experience oneself as a separate person is often (although not always) connected with the coming to consciousness and emotional reliving of the experience of having been sexually abused as a child. The discovery of one's own inner rooms in the dream corresponds to the discovery of the self, which is no longer the instrument of the other person and only now really becomes free. Very often chronic insomnia or frigidity disappears at this point. Although Woolf's biographer reports that she "felt that George had spoilt her life before it had fairly begun," the link between this fact and her "mysterious" psychosis remains a riddle to him. Woolf's husband, Leonard, the owner of the Hogarth Press, was the famous publisher of Freud's works in England. Perhaps this acquaintance with Freud could have saved the life of his wife, the gifted writer, if Freud had not abandoned his seduction theory. Perhaps she would have received understanding and therefore help from him or from his followers.

Serge Lebovici once spoke in a lecture about three cases of insomnia in small boys, all of which could be traced back to seduction by the mother. The children fell asleep during the session as soon as he was able to re-create the situation between mother and child in such a way that the child was no longer afraid of losing the person he loved if he simply was to fall asleep and pay no further heed to his mother. In order to give himself over trustingly to sleep, an infant, during the symbiotic stage, must be assured of a good symbiosis, and at a later stage a child must feel assured that his self will not be lost during sleep. Sexually stimulated children cannot develop this essential feeling of trust; their center is located outside themselves, and they are always ready to comply when something is expected of them; they are restless, overly excited, homeless in a sense, and without the right to "a room of their own."

Psychoanalytic terminology uses the word "seduction" for quite different phenomena, which I should like to keep separate here. That is why I prefer to speak of the sexual abuse of the child, which includes both flagrant and subtle forms of mistreatment. The word "seduction" reinforces the wishful thinking of the adult, who assumes that the child shares his or her desires; these projections are absent in the word "abuse." In his story *The Stoker* (which later became the first chapter of the novel *Amerika*), Franz Kafka describes the abuse of a child's body as experienced from the child's point of view, not as interpreted by adult theory.

> And once she [the servant Johanna] called him "Karl" and, while he was still dumbfounded at this unusual familiarity, led him into her room, sighing and grimacing, and locked the door. Then she flung her arms round his neck, almost choking him, and while urging him to take off her clothes, she really took off his and laid him on her bed, as if she would never give him up to anyone and would tend and cherish him to the end of time. "Oh, Karl, my Karl!" she cried; it was as if her eyes were devouring him, while his eyes saw nothing at all and he felt uncomfortable in all the warm bedclothes which she seemed to have piled up for him alone. Then she lay down by him and wanted some secret from him, but he could tell her none, and she showed anger, either in jest or in earnest, shook him, listened to his heart, offered her breast that he might listen to hers in turn, but could not bring him to do it, pressed her naked belly against his body, felt with her hand between his legs, so disgustingly that his head and neck started up from the pillows, then thrust her body several times against him—it was as if she were a part of himself, and for that reason, perhaps, he was seized with a terrible feeling of yearning. [*Amerika*, p. 29]

We have psychoanalysis to thank for the discovery of defense mechanisms, one of which is projection. Indeed, if the analyst were unaware of this mechanism, he would be totally unable to work with transference, which is of central significance in the analytic process. But we have not yet perceived all the implications of this discovery. If we do not want to be "poisonous pedagogues" and attribute the "sin" of projection to the child alone, we must realize that parents also project onto their children. The younger the child, the stronger the parents' projection, for the child is not yet able to show them the absurdity of their projections. Parents who beat their children very often see the image of *their* parents in the infant they are beating.

What happens to small children, perhaps even infants, if they become the object of projections, something that can make life difficult even for an experienced analyst? This will place a heavy burden on them for the rest of their life, especially if the parents are latently or manifestly psychotic. Perhaps it was the tragic nature of this irreversible situation that made Freud turn his attention from it and develop a method of treatment within the framework of his drive theory and structural model that restricted itself to seeing only the child's and patient's projections. Insofar as they are present, they can in fact be done away with in the course of treatment, but this will have no effect on the underlying *cause* of the disturbance.

Heroard, the physician at the French court when Louis XIII was a little boy, describes in his memoirs the games adults played with the prince. Activities that had to be concealed in the Victorian Age still took place then in complete and good-humored openness. I shall quote here a lengthy passage from *Centuries of Childhood* by Philippe Ariès, who draws upon these memoirs:

> One of the unwritten laws of contemporary morality, the strictest and best respected of all, requires adults to avoid any reference, above all any humorous reference, to sexual matters in the presence of children. This notion was entirely foreign to the society of old. The modern reader of the diary in which Henri IV's physician, Heroard, recorded the details of the young Louis XIII's life is astonished by the liberties which people took with children, by the coarseness of the jokes they made, and by the indecency of gestures made in public which shocked nobody and which were regarded as perfectly natural. No other document can give us a better idea of the non-existence of the modern idea of childhood at the beginning of the seventeenth century.
>
> Louis XIII was not yet one year old: "He laughed uproariously when his nanny waggled his cock with her fingers." An amusing trick

which the child soon copied. Calling a page, "he shouted 'Hey, there!' and pulled up his robe, showing him his cock."

He was one year old: "In high spirits," notes Heroard, "he made everybody kiss his cock." This amused them all. Similarly everyone considered his behaviour towards two visitors, a certain de Bonières and his daughter, highly amusing: "He laughed at him, lifted up his robe and showed him his cock, but even more so to his daughter, for then, holding it and giving his little laugh, he shook the whole of his body up and down." They thought this so funny that the child took care to repeat a gesture which had been such a success; in the presence of a "little lady," "he lifted up his coat, and showed her his cock with such fervour that he was quite beside himself. He lay on his back to show it to her."

When he was just over a year old he was engaged to the Infanta of Spain; his attendants explained to him what this meant, and he understood them fairly well. "They asked him: 'Where is the Infanta's darling?' He put his hand on his cock."

During his first three years nobody showed any reluctance or saw any harm in jokingly touching the child's sexual parts. "The Marquise [de Verneuil] often put her hand under his coat; he got his nanny to lay him on her bed where she played with him, putting her hand under his coat." "Mme de Verneuil wanted to play with him and took hold of his nipples; he pushed her away, saying: 'Let go, let go, go away.' He would not allow the Marquise to touch his nipples, because his nanny had told him: 'Monsieur, never let anybody touch your nipples, or your cock, or they will cut it off.' He remembered this." Again: "When he got up, he would not take his shirt and said: 'Not my shirt, I want to give you all some milk from my cock.' We held out our hands, and he pretended to give us all some milk, saying: 'Pss, pss,' and only then agreeing to take his shirt."

It was a common joke, repeated time and again, to say to him: "Monsieur, you haven't got a cock." Then "he replied: 'Hey, here it is!'—laughing and lifting it up with one finger." These jokes were not limited to the servants, or to brainless youths, or to women of easy virtue such as the King's mistress. The Queen, his mother, made the same sort of joke: "The Queen, touching his cock, said: 'Son, I am holding your spout.'" Even more astonishing is this passage: "He was undressed and Madame too [his sister], and they were placed naked in bed with the King, where they kissed and twittered and gave great amusement to the King. The King asked him: 'Son, where is the Infanta's bundle?' He showed it to him, saying: 'There is no bone in it, Papa.' Then, as it was slightly distended, he added: 'There is now, there is sometimes.' "

The Court was amused, in fact, to see his first erections: "Waking up at eight o'clock, he called Mlle Bethouzay and said to her: 'Zezai, my cock is like a drawbridge; see how it goes up and down.' And he raised it and lowered it."

By the age of four, "he was taken to the Queen's apartments, where Mme de Guise showed him the Queen's bed and said to him: 'Monsieur, this is where you were made.' He replied: 'With Mamma?' "
"He asked his nanny's husband: 'What is that?' 'That,' came the reply, 'is one of my silk stockings.' 'And those?' [after the manner of parlour-game questions] 'Those are my breeches.' 'What are they made of?' 'Velvet.' 'And that?' 'That is a cod-piece.' 'What is inside?' 'I don't know, Monsieur.' 'Why, a cock. Who is it for?' 'I don't know, Monsieur.' 'Why, for Madame Doundoun [his nanny].' "

"He stood between the legs of Mme de Montglat [his governess, a very dignified, highly respectable woman, who however did not seem to be put out—any more than Heroard was—by all these jokes which we would consider insufferable today]. The King said: 'Look at Madame de Montglat's son: she has just given birth.' He went straight away and stood between the Queen's legs."

When he was between five and six, people stopped talking about his sexual parts, while he started talking more about other people's. Mlle Mercier, one of his chambermaids who had stayed up late the night before, was still in bed one morning, next to his bed (his servants, who were sometimes married, slept in his bedroom and do not appear to have allowed his presence to embarrass them). "He played with her, toyed with her toes and the upper part of her legs, and told his nanny to go and get some birch twigs so that he could beat her, which he did. . . . His nanny asked him: 'What have you seen of Mercier's?' He replied calmly: 'I have seen her arse.' 'What else have you seen?' He replied calmly and without laughing that he had seen her private." On another occasion, "after playing with Mlle Mercier, he called me [Heroard] and told me that Mercier had a private as big as that (showing me his two fists) and that there was water inside."

After 1608 this kind of joke disappeared: he had become a little man—attaining the fateful age of seven—and at this age he had to be taught decency in language and behaviour. When he was asked how children were born, he would reply, like Molière's Agnès, "through the ear." Mme de Montglat scolded him when he "showed his cock to the little Ventelet girl." And if, when he awoke in the morning, he was still put in Mme de Montglat's bed between her and her husband, Heroard waxed indignant and noted in the margin of his diary: *insignis impudentia*. The boy of ten was forced to behave with a modesty which nobody had thought of expecting of the boy of five. Education scarcely began before the age of seven; moreover, these tardy scruples of decency are to be attributed to the beginnings of a reformation of manners, a sign of the religious and moral restoration which took place in the seventeenth century. It was as if education was held to be of no value before the approach of manhood.

By the time he was fourteen, however, Louis XIII had nothing more to learn, for it was at the age of fourteen years two months that he was put almost by force into his wife's bed. After the ceremony he "retired and had supper in bed at a quarter to seven. M. de Gramont and a few young lords told him some broad stories to encourage him. He asked for his slippers and put on his robe and went to the Queen's bedchamber at eight o'clock, where he was put to bed beside the Queen his wife, in the presence of the Queen his mother; at a quarter past ten he returned after sleeping for about an hour and performing twice, according to what he told us; he arrived with his cock all red."

The marriage of a boy of fourteen was perhaps becoming something of a rare occurrence. The marriage of a girl of thirteen was still very common.

There is no reason to believe that the moral climate was any different in other families, whether of nobles or commoners; the practice of associating children with the sexual ribaldries of adults formed part of contemporary manners. In Pascal's family, Jacqueline Pascal at the age of twelve was writing a poem about the Queen's pregnancy.

Thomas Platter, in his memoirs of life as a medical student at the end of the sixteenth century, writes: "I once met a child who played this trick [knotting a girl's aiguillette when she married, so that her husband became impotent] on his parents' maidservant. She begged him to break the spell by undoing the aiguillette. He agreed and the bridegroom, recovering his potency, was immediately cured." Père de Dainville, the historian of the Society of Jesus and of humanist pedagogics, also writes: "The respect due to children was then [in the sixteenth century] completely unknown. Everything was permitted in their presence: coarse language, scabrous actions and situations; they had heard everything and seen everything."

This lack of reserve with regard to children surprises us: we raise our eyebrows at the outspoken talk but even more at the bold gestures, the physical contacts, about which it is easy to imagine what a modern psycho-analyst would say. The psycho-analyst would be wrong. The attitude to sex, and doubtless sex itself, varies according to environment, and consequently according to period and mentality. Nowadays the physical contacts described by Heroard would strike us as bordering on sexual perversion and nobody would dare to indulge in them publicly. This was not the case at the beginning of the seventeenth century. There is an engraving of 1511 depicting a holy family: St Anne's behaviour strikes us as extremely odd—she is pushing the child's thighs apart as if she wanted to get at its privy parts and tickle them. It would be a mistake to see this as a piece of ribaldry.

The practice of playing with children's privy parts formed part of a widespread tradition, which is still operative in Moslem circles. These have remained aloof not only from scientific progress but also from the great moral reformation, at first Christian, later secular, which disciplined eighteenth-century and particularly nineteenth-century society in England and France. Thus in Moslem society we find features which strike us as peculiar but which the worthy Heroard would not have found so surprising. Witness this passage from a novel entitled *The Statue of Salt*. The author is a Tunisian Jew, Albert Memmi, and his book is a curious document on traditional Tunisian society and the mentality of the young people who are semi-Westernized. The hero of the novel is describing a scene in the tram taking him to school in Tunis:

In front of me were a Moslem and his son, a tiny little boy with a miniature tarboosh and henna on his hands; on my left a Djerban grocer on his way to market, with a basket between his legs and a pencil behind his ear. The Djerban, affected by the warmth and peace inside the tram, stirred in his seat. He smiled at the child, who smiled back with his eyes and looked at his father. The father, grateful and flattered, reassured him and smiled at the Djerban. "How old are you?" the grocer asked the child. "Two and a half," replied the father. "Has the cat got your tongue?" the grocer asked the child. "No," replied the father, "he hasn't been circumcised yet, but he will be soon." "Ah!" said the grocer. He had found something to talk about to the child. "Will you sell me your little animal?" "No!" said the child angrily. He obviously knew what the grocer meant, and the same offer had already been made to him. I too [the Jewish child] was familiar with this scene. I had taken part in it in my time, provoked by other people, with the same feelings of shame and desire, revulsion and inquisitive complicity. The child's eyes shone with the pleasure of incipient virility [a modern feeling, attributed to the child by the educated Memmi, who is aware of recent discoveries as to early sexual awakening in children; in former times people believed that before puberty children had no sexual feelings] and also revulsion at this monstrous provocation. He looked at his father. His father smiled: *it was a permissible game* [Ariès's italics]. Our neighbours watched the *traditional scene* with complaisant approval. "I'll give you ten francs for it," said the Djerban. "No," said the child. "Come now, sell me your little . . ." the Djerban went on. "No! No!" "I'll give you fifty francs for it." "No!" "I'll go as high as I can: a thousand francs!" "No!" The Djerban assumed an expression of greediness. "And I'll throw in a bag of sweets as well!" "No! No!" "You still say no? That's your last word?" the Djerban shouted, pretending to be angry. "You still say no?" he repeated. "No!" Thereupon the grown-up threw himself upon the child, a terrible expression on his face, his hand brutally rummaging inside the child's fly. The child tried to fight him off with his fists. The father roared with laughter, the Djerban was convulsed with amusement, while our neighbours smiled broadly.

This twentieth-century scene surely enables us to understand better the seventeenth century before the moral reformation. [pp. 100–5]

No one at that time seems to have taken offense at the fact that adults could use the prince's sexual organ as a plaything. We mustn't forget here that these same adults would claim the right of privacy in regard to this area of their own body (cf. the expression "private parts"). It is not customary in our culture for people to expose themselves and allow others to take hold of their sexual organs in public. That can be done only with a child. If this happened to a prince, it will surely have been no different for a middle-class or peasant child, although no doctors happened to include this in their memoirs. In any case, no one gave a thought to what was happening in the soul of a little child mistreated in this way, who was denied respect in that very area in which adults placed special emphasis upon receiving it themselves. Probably in later life he will find no other way of dealing with this treatment than by mistreating others. If it happens, however, that a child has the eye of a Hieronymus Bosch, who observed the performance of Black Masses and the actions of perverse monks and also became the plaything of numerous servants and others who were milling about, then he will be able to depict these episodes later in his paintings.

If we assume that there is nothing exceptional about the above events in Louis XIII's childhcod and that similar games took place in the Victorian Age, only in secret and in the dark, then we realize what subject matter Freud had to deal with when he began to confront the unconscious. It is also understandable that in view of his discoveries he considered the directions taken by Jung and Adler to be an evasion of extremely uncomfortable hidden truths that quite naturally elicited powerful denial on the part of the general public. Only Freud had the courage to recognize the importance of sexuality, repressed as it was in the darkest reaches of forgotten childhood. But then, after discovering the prevalence of sexual abuse of children, he distanced himself from his findings and came to see the child as a source of sexual (and aggressive) desires directed at the adult. As a result, parents' sex play with their children could continue under cover of darkness.

Psychoanalysis, by focusing on the treatment of the patient's drive conflicts, concerns itself only with the last act of a lengthy drama. It is not acceptable in terms of the Fourth Commandment, however, to become familiar with the earlier acts. For this reason, classical psychoanalysis remained unaware of, or at least displayed no interest in, the childhood of Laius—in other words, in the prologue to the childhood of Oedipus.

Laius, son of Labdacus, of the line of Cadmus, was king of Thebes. For many years he had been married to Jocasta, daughter of Menoeceus, a noble of that city, yet she had borne him no children. Because he longed so deeply for an heir, he questioned the oracle of Apollo at Delphi and was given this answer: "Laius, son of Labdacus, you desire a child. Well then, you shall have a son. But Fate has decreed that you shall lose your life at his hands. This is the will of Zeus, son of Cronus, who heard the curse of Pelops, whom you once robbed of his son." Laius had committed this wrong in his youth, when he had been forced to flee from his own country, had taken refuge with King Pelops, and then repaid the kindness of his host with rank ingratitude. For at the Nemean games he had carried off Chrysippus, Pelops' beautiful son.

Since Laius was well aware of what he had done, he believed the oracle and lived apart from his wife for a long time. But the great love they had for each other drove them into each other's arms again in spite of the warning they had received, and in due time Jocasta bore her husband a son. When the child was before their eyes, they remembered the utterance of the oracle, and in an effort to escape the decree of Fate, decided to expose the newborn infant in the mountainous region of Cithaeron, his ankles pierced and bound with a thong. But the shepherd who had been chosen to carry out this cruel command had pity on the innocent boy and handed him over to a fellow herdsman who, on the slopes of those same mountains, pastured the sheep of Polybus, king of Corinth. Then he went home and pretended to have done as he had been told. The king and his wife Jocasta were certain the child must have died of hunger and thirst or been torn to pieces by wild beasts, and that the oracle, therefore, could not possibly be fulfilled. They eased their conscience with the thought that, by sacrificing the child, they had saved him from murdering his father, and resumed the course of their days with lighter hearts.

In the meantime the shepherd of Polybus loosed the bonds of the child he had accepted, not knowing who he was or whence he came, and because his ankles showed wounds, he called the boy Oedipus, or Swollen-Foot. Then he took him to his master, the king of Corinth, who had compassion on the foundling and bade his wife Merope rear him as if he were her own son, and the court and the entire country did, indeed, regard him as such. He grew into young manhood as a prince, never doubting that he was the son and heir of King Polybus, who had no other children. But chance shattered his joyful self-assurance. Once at a banquet, a citizen of Corinth who bore him a grudge from sheer envy, grew heated with wine and called to Oedipus, who was reclining on the couch opposite him, that he was not the king's true son. The youth was so deeply disturbed by this taunt that he could hardly wait for the end of the feast. All that day he kept his doubts to himself, but the next morning he confronted the king and queen and asked for the truth. Polybus and his wife were indignant at the miscreant who had allowed such words to slip from him, and tried to quiet the youth with evasive replies. He was calmed by the love which shone through all they said, but from that time on suspicion gnawed at his heart, for the words of his enemy had made a deep impression on him. He resolved to leave the palace secretly, and without the knowledge of his foster parents he set out for the oracle of Delphi, hoping to hear the sun-god give the lie to what he had been told. Phoebus Apollo did not deign to reply to his question. Instead he revealed a new and far more terrible misfortune than the one Oedipus feared. "You will slay your father," said the oracle. "You will wed your own mother and leave loathsome descendants behind in the world." When Oedipus heard this, he was struck with horror, and since he still regarded Polybus and Merope as his father and mother, he did not dare return home, for fear that Fate might guide his hand against the king, and the gods afflict him with madness so wild that he would wickedly wed his mother.

He left the oracle and took the road to Boeotia. While he was still between Delphi and the city of Daulia he came to a crossroads and saw a chariot rolling toward him. In it sat an old man he had never seen, and with him were a herald, a charioteer, and two servants. The charioteer and the old man impatiently crowded the wayfarer from the narrow path. Oedipus, who was quick to anger, lunged out at the charioteer, and at that the old man brandished his goad at the insolent youth and brought it down on his head. This roused Oedipus to senseless rage. For the first time he used the great strength the gods had given him, lifted the staff he carried on his journey, and struck the old man so that he toppled backwards from the chariot. A fight ensued, and the youth had to defend his life against three assailants. But he was younger and stronger than they. Two he killed. One escaped and ran away, and Oedipus continued on his journey.

He did not dream that he had done anything but take revenge on some common Phocian or Boeotian who had tried to harm him. For there had been nothing about the old man to show that he was a dignitary or of noble birth. In reality he was Laius, king of Thebes, his father, who had been bound on a journey to the Pythian oracle. And so Fate fulfilled the prophecy given to both father and son, the prophecy both had so zealously sought to evade. Damasistratus, a man from Plataea, found the bodies lying on the ground, was moved to pity, and buried them. Hundreds of years later, travellers could still see the monument: a heap of stones, lying in the fork of the road.

Not long after this, a fearful monster appeared before the gates of Thebes, a winged sphinx, whose forepart was that of a maiden while the hindpart had the shape of a lion. She was one of the daughters of Typhon and Echidna, the serpent-nymph whose fruitful womb had borne so many monsters, and a sister to Cerberus, the hound of Hades, to the Lernean Hydra, and the fire-spewing Chimaera. This sphinx settled on a cliff and asked the people of Thebes all sorts of riddles the Muses had taught her. If a man could not hit upon the answer, she tore him to pieces and devoured him. This affliction came upon the city just as the people were mourning their king, who had been slain on a journey—no one knew by whom. Creon, Queen Jocasta's brother, had become ruler in his stead, and the sphinx grew so bold that she consumed his own son, to whom she had posed a riddle he could not solve. This last blow decided King Creon to proclaim that whoever freed the city of the monster should receive the realm in reward and his sister Jocasta to wife. At the very moment the crier was calling out these words, Oedipus entered the city of Thebes. Both the danger and the prize challenged him, and besides he did not place too high a value upon a life so shadowed by gloomy prophecy. He climbed the cliff where the sphinx had taken up her abode and offered to solve a riddle. The monster was determined to confront this bold stranger with one she considered quite impossible to guess. She said: "In the morning it goes on four feet, at noon on two, and in the evening on three. Of all creatures living, it is the only one that changes the number of its feet, yet just when it walks on the most feet, its speed and strength are at their lowest ebb."

Oedipus smiled when he heard this riddle, which did not seem at all difficult to him. "It is Man," he replied. "In the morning of his life, when he is a weak and helpless child, he crawls on his two hands and two feet. At the noon of his life he has grown strong and walks on his two feet, but when he is old and the evening of his life is come, he needs support and takes a staff for a third foot." This was the correct answer, and the sphinx was so ashamed of her defeat and so enraged that she threw herself from the cliff and died on the instant. Creon kept his promise. He gave Oedipus the kingdom of Thebes and married him to Jocasta, who was his mother. Through the years she bore him four children: first the twin boys Eteocles and Polynices, and then two daughters, the elder of whom was Antigone, and the younger Ismene. But these four were not only his children but also his sisters and brothers.

For many years the dreadful secret remained hidden, and Oedipus, who was a good and just king, though he had his faults, ruled Thebes together with Jocasta and was loved and honored by his subjects. But in due time the gods sent a plague upon the land which wrought havoc among the people and against which no remedy could prevail. The Thebans regarded this pestilence as a punishment and sought protection from their king who, they believed, was a favorite of the immortals. Men and women, the aged and the children, came to the palace in a long procession led by priests with olive branches in their hands, seated themselves all about and on the steps of the altar standing before the palace, and waited for their king to appear. When Oedipus heard their clamor, he came out and asked its cause, and why the entire city fumed with the smoke of offerings and resounded with lament. The eldest among the priests answered in behalf of all: "You can see for yourself, O master," he said, "what wretchedness we are forced to endure. The hills and the fields are burned with drought and heat; the plague is raging in our homes. The city cannot lift its head through the waves of blood and destruction. And so we have come to take refuge with you, our beloved king. Once before you freed us from the tyranny of the Asker of Riddles. Surely this did not come to pass without the help of the gods. And so we put our trust in you, believing that either through gods or men you will find help for us again."

"My poor children," Oedipus replied, "I know the cause of your prayers. I know that you are wasting with disease. But my heart is sadder than yours, for I do not mourn this one or that one, but the entire city. To me your coming is no sudden awakening, as though I had slept! I have brooded over your distress and cast about for some cure, and I think I have found it at last. For I have sent my own brother-in-law Creon to Delphi, to the oracle of Apollo, to ask by what deed or what other means the city can be set free!"

Even as Oedipus spoke, Creon appeared in the throng and reported the oracle to the king before all the people. But it was not very consoling. "The god bade us thrust out an evil the land is harboring," said Creon, "and not to cherish that for which no purification can atone. The murder of King Laius weighs as bloodguilt upon the land."

Oedipus, who did not guess that the old man he had killed was the very one for whose sake the wrath of the gods was visited upon his subjects, had them tell the story of the murder, but still his spirit was blind to the truth. He declared that he regarded it as his duty to deal with this matter himself, and dismissed the assembled people. Then he had proclaimed throughout the land that anyone who knew of the murderer of King Laius should report all he had learned; that if one dwelling in another land knew anything, the city of Thebes would give him thanks and reward for his information; but that he who kept silence to shield a friend, or to hide his complicity, should be excluded from all religious services, from the sacrificial feast, and even from intercourse with his fellow citizens. As for the murderer himself, he cursed him with awful imprecations and called down on him misery and need for all the days of his life, and in the end utter destruction. He was not to escape disaster, even if he were hiding in the palace itself. In addition to all this, Oedipus dispatched two messengers to the blind seer Tiresias, who almost matched Apollo in his power to probe the unknown and behold the unseen. Soon after, the aged seer came before the king and the assembly of the pople. A boy led him by the hand. Oedipus told him of the misfortune which had fallen on the country and begged him to use his gift of prophecy to help find the murderer of King Laius.

But Tiresias broke into lament and, stretching his hands out toward the king as if to ward off some terrible thing, he exclaimed: "Awful is the knowledge that brings sadness to him who knows! Let me go home! O king, bear your burden and let me bear mine!" These veiled words only made Oedipus more and more insistent, and the people themselves fell on their knees to beg the seer to speak. When he refused to make his meaning clear, Oedipus grew angry and taunted Tiresias with being the confidant or perhaps even the helper of the murderer, saying that only the old man's blindness kept him from thinking that he himself had committed the crime. This accusation loosened the prophet's tongue. "Oedipus," he cried, "obey the orders you yourself proclaimed! Do not speak to me, do not speak to any one of your people. It is you who are the evil that taints the city. Yes, it is you who murdered the king and live in guilty union with those dear to you!"

And still the mind of Oedipus was closed to the truth. He called the soothsayer a knave and a trickster and accused both him and Creon of plotting against the throne, of weaving a network of lies in order to drive him, who had liberated the city, from power. But Tiresias replied by calling him—unambiguously now—the slayer of his father and the husband of his mother, and then groped for his little guide's hand and went away in anger. Meantime Creon had heard of the accusation launched against him and hastened to confront Oedipus. A violent quarrel broke out between them, and Jocasta's attempts to calm them were of no avail. They parted unreconciled and rankling with bitterness and hatred.

Jocasta herself was blinder than the king himself; hardly had she heard that Tiresias had pointed him out as the slayer of Laius, when she protested against the seer and his vaunted powers. "It just goes to show," she said scornfully, "how little these prophets know! Take an example: An oracle once told my first husband Laius that he would die at the hands of his son. But actually he was killed by robbers, at a forking of the road, and our only son was tied by the feet and exposed in a waste mountain region when he was only three days old. That is how oracles are fulfilled!"

The queen laughed mockingly, but her words had a very different effect from that she had intended. "At a crossroads?" Oedipus asked, his heart shaken with fear. "Did you say that Laius fell at a crossroads? How old was he then? How did he look?"

Jocasta answered readily, unaware of her husband's agitation. "He was tall, and his hair was just turning white. He was not unlike you."

And now Oedipus was seized with real terror. It was as if a flash of lightning had split the darkness of his mind. "It is not Tiresias who is blind!" he cried. "He sees, he knows!" And though in his soul he recognized the truth, he asked question after question, hoping for answers which would prove his discovery a mistake. But the replies only established it more firmly, and at last he learned that a servant had escaped, come home, and told of the murder; that when Oedipus ascended the throne, this man had begged to be sent as far as possible from the city, to the farthest pastures of the king. Now he was summoned, but just as he arrived, a messenger from Corinth entered the palace to announce to Oedipus the death of Polybus, his father, and to call him to the vacant throne.

When she heard this, the queen said triumphantly: "O divine oracle, where are the truths you utter! The father Oedipus was supposed to slay has just died peacefully of old age." But King Oedipus, who had greater reverence for the gods, thought otherwise. He wanted to believe that Polybus was his father, yet could not bring himself to think that an oracle might be false. And he hesitated to go to Corinth for still another reason. There was the second part of the oracle to consider! Merope, his mother, was living, and Fate might drive him into marriage with her. What doubts he still had were soon dispelled by the messenger, the very herdsman who, many years ago on Mount Cithaeron, had accepted the infant from a servant of Laius and loosed the thongs which bound his pierced feet. It was an easy matter for him to prove that Oedipus, though heir to the throne of Corinth, had been only the foster son of Polybus. And when the king of Thebes now asked for the servant who had delivered him to the herdsman, he discovered that it was he who had escaped death when King Laius was murdered and had been tending the king's cattle at the borders of the realm.

When Jocasta heard this, she left her husband and the assembled people with loud wails of despair. Oedipus, who still was trying to evade the inevitable, explained her going in this way: "She is afraid," he said to the people. "She is a proud woman and fears that I may turn out to be of humble birth. As for me, I regard myself as the son of Good Fortune, and I am not ashamed of a family tree such as that." And now the herdsman was brought, and the messenger from Corinth at once recognized him as the servant who had put the child into his hands. The old man paled with terror and stammered denials, but when Oedipus had him fettered and threatened him, he told the truth: that Oedipus was the son of Laius and Jocasta, that the oracle predicting he would slay his father had caused them to expose the child, but that he, out of pity, had saved his life.

And now everything was revealed in awful clarity. Oedipus fled from the great hall and ran through the palace asking for a sword to strike from the face of the earth the monster who was both his mother and his wife. But there was no one to answer him, for all scattered before this apparition of madness and rage. At last he reached his bedchamber, smashed the locked door, and broke into the room. He was halted by the sight which met his eyes. High above the bed hung Jocasta, her hair framing her face in tangled strands, a rope tightened about her throat. For a long time Oedipus stared at the corpse, and grief rendered him speechless. But then he cried aloud and lowered the rope until the body touched the floor. From her robe he tore the golden clasps, clutched them in his hand, raised them high, and bidding his eyes never more see what he did or suffered, pierced the balls until a stream of blood gushed from the sockets. He asked the servants to open the gates and lead him out to the people of Thebes, that they might see the slayer of his father, the husband of his mother, a monster on earth, one hated by the gods. They did his bidding, but his subjects, who had loved and revered their ruler for so long, felt only compassion for him. Even Creon, whom he had accused unjustly, did not make mock of him or rejoice in his misfortune. He hurried to remove from the sight of the populace this man laden with the curse of the gods, and put him in the care of his children. Oedipus was moved by so much kindness. He made his brother-in-law keeper of the throne for his young sons, requested that his ill-omened mother be buried, and put his orphaned daughters under the protection of the new ruler. For himself he demanded exile from the country he had tainted with his twofold crime. He wanted to live or die, according to the will of the gods, on Mount Cithaeron, where his parents had exposed him so long ago. Then he called for his daughters, whose voices he yearned to hear one last time, and laid his hand on their heads. He blessed Creon for all the undeserved love he had shown him, and fervently prayed that—under their new king—the people of Thebes would enjoy the favor of the gods he himself had been denied.

Creon led him back into the palace, and now Oedipus, whom many thousands had obeyed, whose glory as the liberator of Thebes had spread over the world, this man who had solved the most difficult of riddles and found the key to his own life's enigma all too late, prepared to go through the gates of his city like a blind beggar, and set out on the journey to the very borders of his realm. [Schwab, *Gods and Heroes*, pp. 230–40] ef# 12 ﷽

Oedipus: The "Guilty" Victim

I n Sophocles' tragedy, Oedipus punishes himself by putting out his eyes. Even though he had no way of recognizing Laius as his father; even though Laius had tried to kill his infant son and was responsible for this lack of recognition, even though Laius was the one who provoked Oedipus' anger when their paths crossed; even though Oedipus did not desire Jocasta but became her husband thanks to his cleverness in solving the sphinx's riddle, thus rescuing Thebes; and even though Jocasta, his mother, could have recognized her son by his swollen feet—to this very day no one seems to have objected to the fact that Oedipus was assigned all the blame. It has always been taken for granted that children are responsible for what was done to them, and it has been essential that when children grow up, they not be aware of the true nature of their past. In return, they are given the right to treat their own children in the same fashion. It was actually quite consistent for Oedipus to blind himself when he began to suspect the cruel game the gods had been playing with him. Because the gods fear human beings who can see, Oedipus had to sacrifice his sight to avoid being banished or destroyed by the gods and his fellow humans. His blindness saves his life, because it serves to pacify and reconcile the gods.

The limitations of the concept of the Oedipus complex are being noticed increasingly, even in the psychoanalytic literature, and are being discussed with growing openness. The following considerations can no longer be ignored:

1. The most prominent aspect of this theory (the struggle against the rival, the father, for the primary object, the mother) is so obviously tailored to fit *male* development that much of what has been written in this context about female sexuality does not ring true and

ef

inevitably leads to misunderstanding and misinterpretation of female development.

2. The changing nature of contemporary family life and our expanding knowledge about various child-rearing methods very different from our own are shedding more and more light upon the connection between the Oedipus complex and the patriarchal system.

3. The awakening interest analysts are taking in narcissistic needs such as respect, mirroring, being understood and taken seriously is making it clear that a large portion of those desires previously thought to be connected with drives can be more fully understood within a different context. Traumatizations resulting from the frustration of narcissistic needs often lead to feelings that can now be understood and described much more adequately than with the word "Oedipal."

4. We can no longer deny the fact that many people, numerous analysts among them, do not experience real improvement or freedom from symptoms until their second analysis. Possibly they are unable to turn their full attention to their self until they have "graduated" from the Freudian theory encountered in their first analysis.

5. No matter how completely most psychoanalysts closed their eyes to the truth about parents, sooner or later the younger ones among them could gain crucial knowledge from therapists treating psychotics or from family therapists about the sexual violence directed against children—knowledge that can no longer be denied by applying the Oedipal interpretation, which regards parents as the objects of their children's sexual fantasies.

In view of these considerations, familiar to analysts, one might ask oneself why Freud's concept of the Oedipus complex has survived so long and why it not only plays a central role in analytic training but also is treated—or at least was for a long time—as an essential component of analytic thought at conferences and in professional publications. There are several important reasons for this:

When Freud developed his theory of the Oedipus complex in the late nineteenth century, he was way ahead of his time. It should not be forgotten that the discovery that a four-to-five-year-old can be buffeted by strong feelings, that he can suffer from jealousy, ambivalence, and fear of losing love, and that the repression of all these feelings produces neurosis, was a revolutionary one for those days. When we consider that many people today, some eighty years later, are still oblivious to the richness of the child's inner world and that very few biographies reach back to the childhood of their subject, we can appreciate how pioneering Freud's theory was at that time. Since it understandably aroused a great deal of resistance, which is always mobilized to combat unconscious content, it is also understandable that for a long time psychoanalysts interpreted any criticism of the Oedipus complex as a sign of defensiveness and resistance.

Although such interpretations did help to protect Freud's valuable discovery from uncomprehending attack, they also became inflexible with the passage of time by attributing absolute validity to what was actually a historically delimited combination of truth and error, making it into an instrument of power. When an initiate of psychoanalysis was unable, with the best will in the world, to discover in himself the desire to have sexual relations with his mother, he then had to accept the explanation that he had repressed his desire so totally because it was a forbidden one. It is not surprising that many training analysts tried to stifle their doubts in order not to lose hope of finding release through psychoanalysis and to preserve their valued membership in the psychoanalytic club. When people give up the truth as they see it for the sake of an ideology, however, they then, regardless of the reasons that made them do it, defend the ideology from attack by the next generation with every means at their disposal. If they did not, they would be forced to face the tragic dimensions of their own loss. Yet now, in the 1980s, it is no longer possible to reduce the feelings and repressed content of childhood to a mere matter of drives without considerable distortion. It is also difficult, within the Oedipal framework, to account for a child's ambivalence toward *both* parents, although the attempt to do so is made repeatedly.

The authoritarian tradition of "poisonous pedagogy" has also contributed to reinforcing the theory of the Oedipus complex. It has always been the goal of parents and pedagogues to divert a child's attention from the motives for their own behavior to the supposedly bad and sinful motives behind the child's desires and to convince the child to be grateful for the way he or she has been raised. It must have been Freud's unconscious dependence on this tradition that caused him to formulate the Oedipus complex, a theory that, in a new form, once again assigned all guilt to the child; this freed Freud from the painful isolation in which he found himself as a result of the discoveries he made in 1896 concerning parents' sexual abuse of their children. Shocking as people of that day found the idea of a child with sexual desires, this was still far more acceptable to the contemporary power structure, whose motives were disguised and buttressed by established methods of child-rearing, than was the whole truth about what adults do with their children, also in the area of sexuality. The Oedipus theory made it possible to continue to treat the child, now seen as having sexual desires, as the object of adults' didactic (or therapeutic) efforts.

An analysis aimed at working through the Oedipus complex, like raising a child to be unaware, serves to mask the abuse and mistreatment of children on the part of the adults who have control over them. When the child's guilt or Oedipus' conflict becomes the center of attention, no one thinks to ask *why* Oedipus' father, King Laius, had his son's feet pierced immediately after his birth and then had him left in the wilderness to die. A good upbringing in Freud's day strongly discouraged questioning parental motives, and his theory is in full accord with this type of upbringing.

As a result of the more relaxed attitude toward child-rearing since World War II, parents today no longer possess the privileges of totalitarian rule, and children who grow up in a somewhat freer atmosphere are better able to see through their parents' manipulative methods. Many training analysts, themselves victims of "poisonous pedagogy" without ever realizing it, may well feel threatened by the relatively greater freedom enjoyed by the younger generation and think they must therefore further reinforce the grip of the theories they religiously adhere to. One of the bulwarks of psychoanalytic training is the Oedipus complex, which it is just as inappropriate for a training candidate to question as it is for a Jesuit novice to doubt the Creed. Only someone who has reached an advanced age is entitled to raise such questions. Heinz Kohut, for one, admits that many of the patients he treated successfully showed no signs of Oedipal problems, and Jan Bastiaans, for many years president of the Dutch Psychoanalytic Association, determined during the course of his experiments with LSD that when early childhood traumas are reactivated under the influence of this drug, feelings of abandonment and deep humiliation and other psychic wounds regularly come to the surface, but never the torments of the Oedipal conflict. On the basis of my own experience with patients, sexual abuse of the child frequently seems to play a role in these traumas as well. As I have already indicated above, the feelings Freud associated with the Oedipus complex can be conceptualized much more precisely today than was possible in his time, thanks to our improved understanding of narcissistic needs. If it is nonetheless still considered obligatory to reduce everything to the level of drives, then we must conclude that the Oedipus complex does not owe its survival to experiential data but to the entrenched power of the psychoanalytic societies, whose goal it is to uphold the defense mechanisms of generations of fathers.

Various associations are linked to the word "Oedipal." Just because we doubt that a four-year-old boy desires to have sexual intercourse with his mother, this by no means implies we do not acknowledge that the child has feelings stemming from his position in the family triangle. Jealousy, powerlessness, hopeless rivalry with the adult male, who impresses on the child the latter's lack of power, feelings of inadequacy, a desire for closeness, confusion arising from stimulation—all this is part of the so-called Oedipal phase from ages three to five, a period when children's beauty is in full flower and they are often a prime sexual object for adults and older siblings. Children have just learned to speak clearly by this age; they are graceful in their movements, admire their parents, are attached to them, do not yet display mistrust or criticism, and are thus ideal, available objects. If the parents' emotional life is stunted because access to their own childhood has been cut off, they will have difficulty understanding and responding to the abundant and intense feelings of their children. For many people, sexual excitement is the only possible form of emotional communication other than rage. A large number of parents unabashedly reveal their sexual needs to their children and receive from them the ersatz satisfaction they require. Between parents' overt violation of the child and their unconscious (because repressed) expectations lies a whole spectrum of parental attitudes that inevitably produce in the child feelings of bewilderment and inadequacy, disorientation, stress, powerlessness, and overstimulation. If we assume the ubiquity of the Oedipus complex, we mask this situation, and outright sexual manipulation will be misconstrued as a response to the child's own sexual desires.

Parents influenced by the theories of Wilhelm Reich, Freud's disciple, were actually convinced that they had to help their children express their infantile sexuality, which was understood in a genital sense. The belief that a child must learn obedience at a very early age and that his or her will must be broken while still in diapers enabled our parents and grandparents to conceal from themselves their urge for domination. The Oedipus complex lends itself to performing a similar service for the younger generation, because it is based on the same mechanism, namely, the splitting off of one's own impulses and their projection onto the child. Unfortunately, it is well-meaning parents in particular who are thrown into confusion by this theory. The child now becomes the bearer of sexuality, of what was once forbidden, taboo, and therefore "dirty" in the parents' eyes, even though their attitude, stemming from early childhood, is concealed (i.e., remains unconscious) behind a façade of intellectual tolerance.

I shall illustrate what I mean by this with an example. A book on sex education by Helmut Kentler includes the report of a father who is a member of "Commune 2":

> It is evening, both children are in bed. I am stroking Nessim and also stroke his penis. Grischa: "I want a penis too." I try to tell her that she has a vagina that can be stroked. Grisha persists, "I want a penis to wee-wee with." I recall a conversation with the psychoanalyst Hans Kilian in which we discussed the hypothetical possibility of men no longer needing to regard the penis as their exclusive property. I say, "Grischa, you can have Nasser's [Nessim's] penis. You can stroke his penis." Grischa accepts this idea immediately, tries to stroke Nasser's penis. Nessim resists at first, probably fearing an aggressive attack on his penis by Grischa. I tell her she must stroke his penis very gently. Nasser now agrees to it but wants to stroke Grischa's vagina in return. Grischa resists just the way Nasser did a moment ago. I tell him he must stroke her vagina very gently too. The two of them are now in agreement but argue over who is to go first. Nasser agrees to let Grischa stroke his penis first. Dispute over how often she may stroke it. She wants to do it "very many times," counts on her fingers. Nasser

wants it to be just once. I say something conciliatory. Grischa strokes Nasser's penis very tenderly with one finger, then Nasser strokes Grischa's vagina just as tenderly. Then they try to have intercourse. [*Sexualerziehung* (Sex Education), p. 137]

It is interesting that in his pedagogical zeal the narrator totally overlooks the significance of his own observations, i.e., that *both* children reject the passive role here (Grischa resists just the way Nessim did a moment earlier), each experiencing the other's form of affectionateness as an attack.

At least two attitudes can be detected on the part of the narrator. His apparent, conscious attitude reflects his no doubt sincere and well-intentioned attempt to spare his children the repressive, anti-sexual upbringing that caused so much harm in earlier generations. This adult owes his knowledge about the subject to reading psycho-analytic literature and to his own boyhood experiences. But much earlier, during his first years of life, he had internalized his parents' lack of confidence in the creative capacities of the child along with the belief that the child must be taught everything by the parents (even sensual pleasure). In this way, the passion to instruct on the part of "poisonous pedagogues" of yore has been able to creep into the attitudes of many contemporary parents, who sometimes are com-pelled, like their own parents, to try to teach their children "correct" feelings and manipulate them "for their own good." There may be very different motives, conscious and unconscious, that cause adults to manipulate their children in sexual matters in the name of a permissive upbringing—with the result, in the case just cited, that the two children finally attempt coitus—but these motives can scarcely be deciphered without knowledge of the parents' childhood. At the same time, readers already sensitive to pedagogical vocabu-lary will be able to read between the lines in the scene described above. They will wonder why children should be encouraged to attempt coitus. Won't the children then sense they are being mis-used to fulfill someone else's needs? Why shouldn't children who have known parental love and tenderness be able to experience this tenderness, along with their awakening sexuality, on their own when they reach puberty and to discover their own forms of pleas-ure? Aren't we impeding their process of discovery when we para-doxically believe *we* are the ones who can and must teach our children how to enjoy sexuality? As long as the introjects active within us remain unconscious, we will duplicate the same old pedagogical patterns, only in a different form. Because we have been taught from an early age "not to be aware" and because the effects of this upbringing are so pervasive we cannot stop raising our children in a manipulative fashion until we become sensitive to these unconscious attitudes within ourselves.

In contrast to a strict authoritarian upbringing—which places emphasis on unconditional obedience, on being hard and unfeeling, etc., and whose philosophy as well as methods have a destructive effect on the child's soul—the philosophy of a so-called permissive or antiauthoritarian upbringing is altogether humane and well-meaning. It is more difficult to detect in this form of child-rearing the hostility toward children harbored in the traditional unconscious compulsions, but this hostility lives on in the zeal of an adult who is more concerned and familiar with his ideology than with the real-life child. Only from this perspective can I understand someone writing that children must be "taught" to rebel, to have an antiauthoritarian attitude, and to enjoy sexuality. If children have been accustomed from the start to having their world respected, they will have no trouble later in life recognizing disrespect directed against them in any form (including authoritarian behavior) and will rebel against it on their own. If, on the other hand, they have had a certain attitude drilled into them on ideological grounds, they will not be aware of it later when something else is drilled into them in the name of a different ideology. And children who have experienced tenderness do not need to be taught to be tender in sexual matters; they will be that way as a matter of course.

As far as I can tell, the approach to sex education advocated in the passage cited above is already out of fashion, because little by little parents became aware that they were allowing themselves to be manipulated by ideologies. I try to use concrete examples in dealing with the subject of confusion on the part of parents, who are sometimes just as much the captives of the pedagogical misconceptions of ideologues and theorists as are their children. The folly of the pedagogical principles of a Dr. Schreber (a famous ninteenth-century author of child-rearing manuals about whose severely disturbed son Freud wrote an essay, cf. p. 198) was not at all obvious to his generation, not even to Freud. Similarly, since we are not conscious of the traces of "poisonous pedagogy" still present in our own attitudes and vocabulary, we can sometimes be deceived even today by pedagogical advice based on the drive theory, finding it altogether appropriate and correct. For this reason, not only concerned parents but even child therapists can become confused by the theory of the Oedipus complex, and their capacity to empathize can be impaired by it.

A children's analyst once requested a supervisory session with me, during which she told me she was treating a four-year-old boy who had suddenly begun to develop phobias and who reacted with particular panic to men with a certain kind of haircut. What was causing her a good deal of difficulty in the treatment was the way the little boy had started to harass her sexually, reaching roughly under her dress, pressing himself against her, and making her feel as though she were being assaulted by a sexually aroused man. The therapist told me she had presented this case in a seminar and had received varying responses. A few colleagues saw the boy's behavior as Oedipal, which fitted in with his rejection of certain men. Others were of the opinion that the child had "not yet reached the Oedipal phase." These interpretations were of no use to their colleague; she blamed herself for feeling offended and somehow threatened every time the boy attacked her instead of being able to preserve her analytic detachment.

In my eyes, this feeling of hers was a definite clue, and I asked myself what trauma the boy could be trying to express. The therapist left my office with this question in mind as a working hypothesis. After a few days she called to report that a conversation with the child's parents had brought the following facts to light: When the mother had to remain hospitalized for two weeks following surgery, the father took over the care of the boy, whom he loved very much and liked to play with. He didn't want to entrust his son to anyone else, not even temporarily, and so he took the boy with him everywhere, even when he went out to taverns with his friends. When these friends came to see him, they occasionally played sex games with his son, inserting their finger into his anus and playing with his penis. The father seemed genuinely convinced that such sex play was part of a progressive upbringing, but during his conversation with the analyst, it came out that as a child he had been subjected to various abuses of a sexual nature himself.

After the analyst was able to set aside the constraints of her theoretical training, she realized on her own, without the need of further supervisory sessions, that for a long time the boy had been trying to tell her in play therapy, by means of his reenactments, what had happened to him on those evenings. As soon as she was ready to listen, the boy then told her verbally as well how "the men reached under the ladies' dresses and were 'told off' by them." From then on, the reenactment, which the therapist had found so threatening and which was meant to provoke her to "tell him off," was no longer necessary.

Every aspect of this story was based on real events, yet at the same time it served as a summation of details already familiar to me from other cases and opened my eyes to a broad spectrum of sexual abuses of children once I was prepared to stop warding off the information it provided. Suddenly my ears were also opened to hear that there are parents who are never able to get out of debt and therefore "rent out" their children for sex games, firmly convinced that this will not hurt the child while he or she is still so young. I have been told by the person in charge of a telephone distress line that the threat of subjecting children to these games if they disobey is sometimes used by young parents as a form of discipline. Sexual abuse figures prominently in the documentation of psychological mistreatment published by this distress line. For instance, children are forced to watch various kinds of sexual activity because this is supposed to intensify the adults' pleasure. Possibly parents are taking revenge in this way for traumatic experiences suffered in their own childhood.

Those still burdened with the baggage of the drive theory who hear about these things will minimize the extent of the harm involved. They will be able to convince themselves that the child experienced pleasure during the mistreatment and will think the only problem was how the conflict between the id and the superego was resolved. If they decide to do away with this baggage, however, because they can no longer overlook the way it serves to disguise the use of force, then their interest will turn from so-called infantile sexuality to sexuality per se as one of the possible forms in which the victimizer exercises power over the victim. This phenomenon is by no means limited to parent-child relations but is commonly observed between siblings as well. In therapy, my colleague's four-year-old patient immediately assumed the active role of the aggressor as a way of describing to her situations in which he had been the victim (and spectator). Older siblings who mistreat and abuse younger ones likewise use active means to tell what happened to them earlier. This will continue to be the case as long as the child or adult has to keep quiet about the wrong done to him or her. In order to experience oneself as victim, one needs the ear of a supportive person. If no one is available, the wrong will be inflicted on someone else, giving rise to guilt feelings, which in turn interfere with the disclosure of the truth. This is why people cling to their guilt feelings, for they lend an illusion of power ("I did wrong, but I could have done differently"). To realize consciously one's status as victim also means to sense the same boundless powerlessness of a child who has been subjected without warning to an outburst of rage or to sexual manipulation by someone the child loves who suddenly acts in a strange manner. For this reason, patients need therapists and analysts who will stand by them and support them as they suffer the pains of their powerlessness; they do not need people who, acting as spokesmen for prevailing societal norms, try to talk them out of their vague awareness of their earliest experiences. If therapists are true advocates of their patients and not servile representatives of society, they will not attempt to conceal the way sexuality can be used to exercise power over those weaker than oneself.

Young adults often report that their small children evince a strong interest in the difference between the sexes, and they regard this as a corroboration of Freudian theory. Is it conceivable for a normal, lively child *not* to be interested in something so obvious? After Adam and Eve ate the apple from the Tree of Knowledge, they became aware for the first time that they were sexual beings and felt ashamed. Not even psychoanalytic theory has been able to set us free from this pattern of linking knowledge, sexuality, and shame. Why shouldn't a child show interest in the fact that there are two sexes, in the physical differences between mother, father, and siblings, in how children come into the world, in how the child gets inside the mother's body, in the physical bond between mother and father, etc.? For the adult, these questions are already associated with sexual experience, but for the child they are not. Children ask their questions without embarrassment; embarrassment arises only when they see it in the eyes of adults who were raised according to

the principles of "poisonous pedagogy." The association of knowledge with guilt and shame, inculcated by these principles, makes it
difficult for parents to see children's questions for what they really
are: an expression of healthy curiosity, interest, and openness. A
sexually abused child no longer has this freedom to ask questions
spontaneously. Whatever we put into a child's soul we naturally will
find there, but if we become conscious of what we are doing, we
then have the chance to free ourselves from the constrictions of our
past.

In the beginning, children are the mute receivers of our projections. Unable to defend themselves against them, unable to give
them back to us or interpret them for us, they are able only to serve
as their bearers. This would seem to prove that the world, humankind, and society must always be the way we experienced them in
our past. But this is not necessarily the case. If young adults are ever
actually able to free their sexuality from the narcissistic power
struggle and from the influence of "poisonous pedagogy" and enjoy
it for its own sake, they will not have the need to project their sexual
conflicts onto their child. Once children are allowed to be more than
bearers of parental projections, they can become an inexhaustible
source for their parents of undistorted knowledge about human
nature. Sensuality, pleasure in one's own body, pleasure in the affection shown by another person, the need to express oneself, to be
heard, seen, understood, and respected, not to have to suppress
anger and rage and to be allowed to voice other feelings as well,
such as grief, fear, envy, and jealousy—all this is part of human
nature, even at a very early age.

In training to be analysts we learn to regard Freudian drive
theory as a great revolution. It is said that Freud offended society by
depriving people of the "illusion" of the innocent child, but this
statement contains two false premises. First, a child's innocence is
real, not an illusion, and second, the reality of this innocence has
practically never been accepted (thanks to the influence of religion
and pedagogy). Until recently, there was scarcely a pedagogue to
be found who did not believe it was his or her task to teach children
morality. Among the few exceptions was Janusz Korczak, a pioneering nonconformist who in 1928 wrote these words, which even today
still strike us as unorthodox:

Children are forbidden to criticize, they are not permitted to notice our mistakes, passions, or absurdities. We appear before them in the garb of perfection. Under threat of our wrath, we protect the secrets of the ruling clan, the caste of initiates called to higher tasks. Only a child can be stripped naked and pilloried without a second thought.

The game we play with children is a game with a marked deck of cards; we win against the low cards of childhood with the aces of adulthood. Cheaters that we are, we shuffle the cards in such a way that we deal ourselves everything good and valuable in order to take advantage of their weaknesses. What about our ne'er-do-wells and happy-go-lucky types, the pleasure-seeking gourmets, the dumbbells, lazy-bones, scoundrels, adventurers, those with no conscience, the swindlers, drunkards, and thieves; what about our acts of violence and our crimes, those that are public knowledge and those that go undetected; how many quarrels, underhanded deeds, and scenes of jealousy are we responsible for, how much slander and blackmail, how many wounding words and dishonorable actions; how many family tragedies, whose victims are the children, are enacted in secret? And we dare to make accusations?

Are we so biassed that we mistake the displays of affection we force on children for genuine love? Don't we understand that it is we who are seeking children's affection when we draw them to us, we who run to them when we are at a loss, that in moments of impotent pain and boundless loneliness we seek protection and shelter with them and burden them with our suffering and our yearning? [*Das Recht des Kindes auf Achtung* (The Child's Right to Be Respected), pp. 21–23]

Let us hope it won't take three hundred years for "poisonous pedagogy," our most powerful inner voice of authority, to promulgate this empirical (by no means "illusional") knowledge that the child is innocent. That is how long it took the Church finally to accept the mathematical proofs for the Copernican system, but today we are living in different times. In any case, it would be of benefit for patients suffering from depression if their therapists could give up the concept of the guilty child.

The physician Janusz Korczak was a keen observer; without the aid of theories, he lived for thirty years among lower-class children who came to his Children's Home having been neglected and often subjected to severe mistreatment. He must have been treated well in childhood in order not to have to ward off what he saw, i.e., not to explain the children's misery in terms of their guilt and obscure the tragic truth with the aid of "poisonous pedagogy." So completely have we internalized the values of "poisonous pedagogy" that even today someone who insists on the innocence of the child runs the risk of being accused of being "naïve" or "sentimental" or of "romanticizing."

The image of the innocent child that Freud was supposedly the first to alter had in fact always been, even for Rousseau, merely a theoretical construct no one took seriously. For in practice it was assumed that wickedness had to be driven out of children and that they had to be taught to be good. As proof of children's wickedness, it was often pointed out, for example, that they liked to torture animals; what was not mentioned, however, was where they had learned how to torture and what drove them to it.

The situation is similar with regard to sexuality. Since children have always been ideal bearers of all the split-off, unacceptable aspects of the adult, why not also bearers of sexual desires, especially in the puritanical times around the turn of the century when sexuality was taboo? To ascribe to children what one is ashamed of in oneself or would like to be rid of is by no means new and is in keeping with the way traditional power structures operate. Even though children can (and must!) have sexual fantasies and desires as a substitute for their often unfulfilled needs for closeness, care, and affection, or as a defense mechanism against the memory of traumas, why should this be irreconcilable with a child's innocence? What is actually taboo in our society is to notice that adults have the right to put the child to whatever use they please if it satisfies their needs, to utilize the child as an outlet for abreacting humiliation they once suffered themselves. As long as adults are not conscious of their past, there is no other alternative for them, and they feel justified in behaving this way as long as the child is seen as a cruel (Melanie Klein) and lustful (Freud) creature in need of taming and control by adults.

The concept of the innocent child goes back in history no farther than Rousseau's rosy visions and in puritanical times served to disguise the child's function as scapegoat. But the idea of the pure parents who have the task of raising the inexperienced child—a creature especially susceptible to the temptations of the devil (i.e., of spontaneous feelings)—in such a way that he or she will "turn toward the good" has a history that goes back thousands of years. It was Freud who questioned this shibboleth with the discovery that completely isolated him from his contemporaries. But not until he propounded his drive theory did he win followers, who even today still see Freud's great and courageous achievement to lie in this second phase of his thinking. Yet Freud's theory of infantile sexuality did not essentially alter traditional attitudes toward the child; it only turned out to be a late reinforcement of the puritanical view.

If Freud had continued to believe his patients, he might have shaken, challenged, and even changed these attitudes. The drive theory, with which he replaced the trauma theory, could only prolong society's sleep, which had already lasted for thousands of years, and prevent people from becoming aware.

﮳ 13 ﮲

Sexual Abuse of the Child:
The Story of the Wolf-Man

THE general public tends to doubt the prevalence of sexual abuse of children by older siblings and adults and to deny its lasting effects, because the necessary repression of what one knew as a young child blocks any later insight into this subject. Furthermore, it is not in the best interest of adults, once they are in a position to take over the active role themselves, to uncover the motives behind their actions. But most important, the principles of "poisonous pedagogy" insist that parents' actions toward their children be regarded exclusively as loving and beneficial and that children be denied the right to protest.

Freud's case history of the Wolf-Man, entitled "From the History of an Infantile Neurosis," demonstrates to the reader who is sensitive to the language of "poisonous pedagogy" the way a great innovator, laboring under the burden of the pedagogical principles he has internalized, pits his own intellect against what he knows to be true. Even though the implications of his knowledge are buried, they do not disappear from sight entirely; since there are tombstones with names written on them, it is impossible to withhold the whole story from future generations. For example, Freud does not dispute the "seduction" of the Wolf-Man by his sister, although he greatly minimizes its significance.

In this chapter, I shall present the story of the Wolf-Man in order to show how my hypothesis about the crucial importance of a trauma repressed at a very early age—which here, as in most cases, remains hidden behind a screen memory—can be verified with the aid of later biographical data. The nature of the enactments produced by the Wolf-Man's repetition compulsion tells us that it was not his witnessing of the primal scene or his drive conflicts that made him ill but rather the abuse he suffered at a very early age and was unable to articulate all his life because he had no one he could confide in. In order to make this clear, I must first make a digression here.

Freud describes the Wolf-Man's problematic attitude toward money as follows:

> He had become very rich through legacies from his father and uncle; it was obvious that he attached great importance to being taken for rich, and he was liable to feel very much hurt if he was undervalued in this respect. But he had no idea how much he possessed, what his expenditure was, or what balance was left over. It was hard to say whether he ought to be called a miser or a spendthrift. He behaved now in this way and now in that, but never in a way that seemed to show any consistent intention. Some striking traits, which I shall further discuss below, might have led one to regard him as a hardened plutocrat, who considered his wealth as his greatest personal advantage, and who would never for a moment allow emotional interests to weigh against pecuniary ones. Yet he did not value other people by their wealth, and, on the contrary, showed himself on many occasions unassuming, helpful, and charitable. Money, in fact, had been withdrawn from his conscious control, and meant for him something quite different. . . .
>
> He himself was puzzled by his behaviour in another connection. After his father's death the property that was left was divided between him and his mother. His mother administered it, and, as he himself admitted, met his pecuniary claims irreproachably and liberally. Yet every discussion of money matters that took place between them used to end with the most violent reproaches on his side, to the effect that she did not love him, that she was trying to economize at his expense, and that she would probably rather see him dead so as to have sole control over the money. His mother used them to protest her disinterestedness with tears, and he would thereupon grow ashamed of himself and declare with justice that he thought nothing of the sort of her. But he was sure to repeat the same scene at the first opportunity. [*S.E.*, XVII, pp. 73–74]

It should be obvious that a child who was abused at a very early age in order to fulfill an adult's or older sibling's needs will be left for the rest of his life with the feeling that he had to give too much of himself. Naturally, this will also express itself in the person's attitude toward money as well as toward his feces. Even though his underlying feeling is a message concerning a real event, he is not able to make the proper connection unless someone helps him to experience the emotional content of this event and its significance for him. Since, on the contrary, he is repeatedly told that, according to the expectations of those who are raising him, he is not giving enough, is not emptying his bowels at the right time or in the right quantity, the feeling that too much is being demanded of him combines with a bad conscience and eventually results in the unbearable conviction that he is a bad person for always feeling exploited "without cause" and for not being glad to give away all that he has and is. The average layperson will surely have no trouble believing that sexual abuse of a child will lead to problems in his or her later sex life. This connection is not so obvious, however, to an orthodox analyst who has become practiced in tracing all the patient's difficulties back to infantile sexual desires.

The consequences of sexual abuse, however, are not restricted to problems in one's sexual life; they impair the development of the self and of an autonomous personality. There are several reasons why this is so:

1. To have one's helplessness and total dependency taken advantage of by the person one loves, by one's mother or father, at a very early age soon produces *an interlinking of love and hate.*

2. Because anger toward the loved person cannot be expressed for fear of losing that person and therefore cannot be lived out, ambivalence, the interlinking of love and hate, remains *an important characteristic of later object relationships.* Many people, for instance, cannot even imagine that love is possible at all without suffering and sacrifice, without fear of being abused, without being hurt and humiliated.

3. Since the fact of abuse must be repressed for the sake of survival, all knowledge that would threaten to undo this repression must be warded off by every possible means, which ultimately results in *an impoverishment of the personality* and a loss of vital roots, manifested, for example, in depression.

4. The consequences of a trauma are not eliminated by repressing it but are actually reinforced. The inability to remember the trauma, to articulate it (i.e., to be able to communicate these earlier feelings to a supportive person who *believes* you), creates the need to articulate it in *the repetition compulsion.*

5. The unremembered plight of *being at someone else's mercy*

and being abused by a loved object is perpetuated either in a passive or an active role, or alternately in each.

6. One of the simplest and completely unnoticed forms of perpetuation of the active role is *abuse of one's children* for one's own needs, which are all the more urgent and uncontrollable the more deeply repressed the original trauma.

I can imagine that this last point will bewilder many readers, who will angrily ask: Is the affection I show my child wrong, too? Is the love I have for my child also to be forbidden me? Of course this is not what I mean. Physical attraction and affection are always a part of love, and this has nothing to do with abuse. But parents who have had to repress the fact of having been abused and who have never consciously relived it can become very confused in this regard where their children are concerned. They will either suppress their genuine feelings of affection for fear of seducing their child or they will unconsciously do the same to the child that was done to them, without having any idea of how much harm they are causing, since they themselves always had to distance themselves from their suffering. How can these parents be helped? There is probably no possibility of curing their compulsion to repeat without extensive therapy. It is indeed difficult for people who as children were the property of their parents to realize when they are treating their own children like *their* property. Nevertheless, I see some hope if people become sensitive to the question, if they become conscious of these connections. This assumes that a person can at least admit that his or her parents were not gods or angels but often deprived and emotionally very isolated people for whom their child was the sole permissible object for the discharge of their affect; these parents, moreover, found justification for their behavior in various ideologies, including pedagogy and, not least of all, even psychoanalysis with its theory of "infantile sexuality." But let us return to the example at hand—the Wolf-Man.

Freud's second analysis of the patient he made famous ended in 1920, again with an apparent cure; then, in 1926, the Wolf-Man developed paranoia. He went to Freud, who was unable to take his case at that time but referred him to his pupil, Ruth Mack-Brunswick, who was able to help him considerably. Muriel Gardiner, one of Mack-Brunswick's other analysands—an "analytic sister" of the Wolf-Man, so to speak—published a book in 1971 that contained, along with Freud's and Mack-Brunswick's presentations of the case, an autobiographical sketch by the Wolf-Man. Mack-Brunswick describes in detail her patient's problems with money and his distrust of doctors, dentists, and tailors, culminating in a deluded and paranoid belief that his nose had been mutilated by the dermatologist Dr. X. She correctly suspected that aggression directed against Freud lay behind these delusions of persecution. Since she interpreted them as an expression of the patient's "passive homosexual desires," which had been disappointed by Freud, she did not need to defend her teacher against her patient's reproaches and was able to help him express his rage, which brought about an improvement. She herself was surprised at his recovery, because she found what she considered a necessary prerequisite for the healing process to be missing in the patient, namely, full acceptance of his "desire for castration" and of his "homosexual desire to take the woman's role in sexual intercourse with his father." She says:

> But the only way out was through the acceptance of his own castration: either this, or the actual retracing of his childish steps to the scene which was pathogenic for his feminine attitude to the father. He now realized that all his ideas of grandeur and fear of the father and, above all, his feeling of irreparable injury by the father were but cloaks for his passivity. And once these disguises were revealed, the passivity itself, whose unacceptability has necessitated the delusion, became intolerable. What appeared to be a choice between acceptance or refusal of the feminine role was in reality no choice at all: had the patient been capable of assuming the feminine role and admitting his passivity to the full, he could have spared himself this illness, which was based on the mechanisms of defence against such a role. [*The Wolf-Man by the Wolf-Man*, p. 292]

Thus, the trauma of his mistreatment is interpreted in terms of a "passive attitude," and "acceptance of his own castration" is urged. Although I regard such theories as doing violence to the patient, I can see that in this specific case they were of benefit to the Wolf-Man. For if the analyst had been able to recognize that the Wolf-Man had several *real* reasons for reproaching Freud, both as a person and in his role as father figure in the transference, she would have attempted, consciously or unconsciously, to protect her idealized mentor from these reproaches, as the following passage indicates:

The patient's statement that no doctor or dentist ever seemed to treat him properly is superficially to some extent justified. But when one examines the circumstances surrounding the long line of the patient's medical and dental experiences, one is forced to the conclusion that he himself demanded and facilitated bad treatment on the part of his attendants. Distrust was a prime condition of treatment. The normal individual breaks off treatment when he becomes dissatisfied with his physician; he certainly does not permit himself to be operated upon by someone whom he regards as his enemy. The passive nature of our patient makes every breach with a father-substitute difficult: his first attempt is to placate the assumed enemy. This attitude will be recalled from the earlier analysis, where his gesture of turning toward the analyst meant: Be good to me. This same gesture, with the identical content, occurred in the course of the analysis with me.

Professor X. was, of course, the chief persecutor; the patient had at once remarked that X. was an obvious substitute for Freud. In regard to Freud himself, the persecution was less evident. The patient blamed Freud for the loss of his fortune in Russia, but laughed at the idea that Freud's advice could have been intentionally malicious. It was necessary for him to seek out an indifferent but equally symbolic persecutor, to whom he could consciously and wholeheartedly ascribe the most vicious motives. There were, in addition, various minor persons by whom the patient considered himself imposed on, badly treated, and sometimes cheated. It is worthy of note that in just those relations where he probably really was imposed on, he was entirely unsuspecting. [pp. 298–99]

Even if the financial advice Freud gave the Wolf-Man was well-intentioned, of which there can be no doubt, it may be that it had catastrophic consequences for his patient. Such things happen every day, for advice cannot anticipate the future, which no one knows, and errors cannot be avoided. If, however, the analyst giving advice is also a father figure, he must allow the child in his patient the right to be disappointed, which under certain circumstances can lead to an eruption of uncontrollable narcissistic rage. This outburst will take place if the oversized, idealized father, imagined until now to be all-powerful and all-knowing, is unmasked and seen to be powerless or even simply shows his human limitations before the patient can bear to face them. The Wolf-Man still should have had the right to express his rage, even if Freud had understood him better, had not done violence to him with theories and interpretations, had not humiliated and misled him by raising money for him after he had lost his entire fortune in the Russian Revolution, and had not made him fear being abandoned. I have included all these points in one sentence, because for me they are four equally valid examples of unintentional cruelty, regardless of whether this was caused by Freud's own illness or by his theories.

It would be presumptuous and unfair of me to reproach Freud for not understanding his patient as well then as he might today. But this does not alter the fact that the Wolf-Man was not able, either with Freud or with Freud's faithful disciples, to experience and fully express his disappointment with his analyst or his childhood rage associated with his parents and sister. Just as, in childhood, he was exclusively among people who revered his wealthy and powerful parents and to whom he could therefore never pour out his heart, so too, throughout his entire later life, he moved in circles which felt grateful devotion to Freud and in which he was valued and "courted"—but also misused—only because of his celebrated connection with the great master.

My belief that Freud's interpretation did violence to his patient does not derive from Karin Obholzer's book, which records the conversations between an attractive young woman and an eighty-eight-year-old, well-bred, thoroughly compliant old man (the Wolf-Man) but from my study of Freud's presentation of the Wolf-Man's case and a comparison of this with the latter's childhood memoirs. There are passages in Freud's case history that ascribe childhood feelings and conditions to the patient that were without a doubt true for Freud himself but that make him seem oblivious to the plight of his patient. Thus, Freud thinks the importance of the primal scene for the Wolf-Man lies in its association with the possible birth of a younger sibling, an occurrence that was not part of the Wolf-Man's experience but one that did happen seven times in Freud's life. When Freud states that his patient had been given good reason to hope he would never have a younger brother or sister, this could easily be a case of projective identification on the part of the analyst. Nor can it be taken for granted that the aristocratic Russian landowners let their child sleep in their bedroom, something that was demonstrably true of Freud's parents.

In the Wolf-Man's memoirs there is a description of the paternal grandfather and his sons, which I see as shedding important light on the child's situation:

> When Uncle Nicholas decided to marry, my grandfather got the incredible idea of competing with him and taking away the bride he had chosen. She was not to marry Uncle Nicholas but his father! So actually a situation arose similar to that in Dostoevsky's *The Brothers Karamazov*. The chosen bride, however, preferred—just as in Dostoevsky's novel—the son to the father, and married Uncle Nicholas. Thereupon his father became very angry and disinherited him. . . . My grandfather was, in his time, one of the richest landowners in southern Russia. [p. 14]

If we read this passage carefully, it will come as no surprise that the grandfather's most gifted son, the Wolf-Man's beloved Uncle Peter, developed a chronic psychosis in adolescence and that the Wolf-Man's father presumably took his own life after a number of depressive episodes. The story of Uncle Peter shows the Wolf-Man's family background so clearly that I shall quote from it extensively— as an antidote to Freud's interpretations based on the drive theory.

> My favorite uncle was always Uncle Peter, the youngest of the four brothers. I was terribly happy whenever I heard that he was coming to visit us. He would always come to me, or call me into his room, and play with me as though he were my age. He invented all sorts of tricks and jokes which simply delighted me and which I found the greatest fun.
>
> According to my mother, Uncle Peter had always been a sort of "sunny boy," with a consistently gay and happy disposition, and therefore a most welcome guest at all kinds of parties and social affairs. After high school he studied at the Petrovsky Academy in Moscow, at that time a very famous College of Agriculture. Sociable as he was, Uncle Peter made many friends at college, whom he would then invite to our estate during the summer. . . .
>
> Soon, strangely enough, Uncle Peter, this jolly fellow, began to show signs of most peculiar behavior and to express himself no less strangely. At first his brothers were simply amused, as they did not take his changed behavior seriously and considered it merely harmless whims. But soon they, too, realized that this was a serious matter. The famous Russian psychiatrist Korsakoff was consulted, who, alas, diagnosed this as the beginning of a genuine paranoia. So Uncle Peter was confined in a closed institution. However, as he had a large estate in the Crimea, his brothers finally arranged for him to be taken there

where he lived many years as a hermit. Although Uncle Peter had studied agriculture, he later wished to devote himself exclusively to historical research. All these plans, of course, came to nothing, because of his delusions of persecution. . . .

Uncle Peter's family and friends accepted his eccentricities at first from the comic side, and were much amused by his idea that any unmarried female was spreading out her net to catch him and was hell-bent on getting him to marry her. Every time he was introduced to a young lady there was great excitement, since he immediately became suspicious of marriage plans and malicious machinations. But when he started complaining that everybody was jeering at him, that the pigeons watched and mimicked all his movements, and when he started telling all kinds of absurd stories, everybody saw that this was a case of mental illness. He was allowed to live on his estate in the Crimea in complete isolation from the outside world. It was said that cows, pigs, and other domestic animals were the only company he tolerated and permitted to share his living quarters. It was easy to imagine what these quarters must have looked like.

Shortly after we learned of Uncle Peter's death Therese sent me an article which had appeared in a Munich magazine under the title "A Millionaire Gnawed by Rats." Since all contact between Uncle Peter and his surroundings had been cut off, his death had not been immediately discovered. Only after it had been noticed that the food delivered to his house had not been touched for several days was it suspected that something unusual must have happened. So the body was found only some days after death had occurred. In the meantime rats had set upon the cadaver and had started gnawing. [pp.13–14, 81]

Uncle Peter wants to study history (his own history?) and is prevented from doing so by his illness. He is suspicious of women, is made fun of because of it, and when he says that the pigeons are mimicking him, he is confined to his estate for reasons of insanity.

We can only surmise what the Wolf-Man's father must have transmitted unconsciously to his only son of his no doubt burdensome relationship with his own parents, for Freud never explored this question. For him, as for most people, love for a child automatically excluded cruelty, and he focused all his attention on investigating the significance of the primal scene, which unquestionably played a more important role in little Sigmund's living arrangements than it did in the Wolf-Man's.

We know that the pseudonym of Freud's famous patient comes

from a dream he had as a child, which is recorded by Freud as follows:

> "I dreamt that it was night and that I was lying in my bed. (My bed stood with its foot towards the window; in front of the window there was a row of old walnut trees. I know it was winter when I had the dream, and night-time.) Suddenly the window opened of its own accord, and I was terrified to see that some white wolves were sitting on the big walnut tree in front of the window. There were six or seven of them. The wolves were quite white, and looked more like foxes or sheep-dogs, for they had big tails like foxes and they had their ears pricked like dogs when they pay attention to something. In great terror, evidently of being eaten up by the wolves, I screamed and woke up." [p. 173]

In the picture the patient drew of the wolves in the tree he shows five wolves, not "six or seven," staring at the child.

In his analysis many determinants of this dream emerge: the frightening story of the tailor and the wolves, told him by his maternal grandfather; the very real danger of wolves in the Russian countryside in those days; the fairy tales "Little Red Riding-Hood" and "The Wolf and the Seven Kids"; the terror his sister was always able to awaken in her little brother by showing him the picture of a wolf walking on its hind legs, etc. It seems to me that we can find another determinant of this dream if we consider the child's specific, individual situation more carefully. The grandfather ("Father Karamasov") and his four sons were all father figures who, the boy felt, were keeping their eye on him, i.e., constantly staring at him in the dream. Was the unwavering, uncanny gaze of the five wolves actually the mysterious, incomprehensible, and possibly homosexually tinged gaze of his own father, multiplied by five? (The cruel legendary grandfather and his four sons also add up to the number five.) This question can never be satisfactorily answered, lacking the analytic setting. I have presented these ideas here to demonstrate, with the use of material familiar to many analysts, how the drive theory in my opinion obscures obvious connections and how this obfuscation prevents the patient's key traumatic experiences from coming to the surface during analysis.

As a training analyst, I often had occasion to read the case presentations of colleagues who were applying for membership in the Psychoanalytic Association. I noticed that their attempts to meet the demands of the psychoanalytic institutes—that is, to concentrate exclusively on what occurred in the transference and countertransference and to explain this in terms of whatever theory happened to be in fashion at the moment (e.g., drive theory, structural model, ego psychology, the concepts of Melanie Klein, Kohut, Kernberg, etc.)—were claiming so much of the authors' attention that in many cases their patients' childhood was virtually ignored. What happened in the transference was interpreted in each case in terms of one particular concept. In the discussions, various alternative views were presented, depending on the theory being defended. Thus, the patient's behavior—his protracted silence, for instance—could be interpreted as defiant aggression, as "passive homosexual seductiveness," as "the desire to be penetrated by the analyst" (with interpretations), as "the need to spoil the analyst's pleasure in his work," as distrust, rivalry, etc. In these discussions I often had the impression that much of what was being said might be true, but since it did not take the patient's early childhood into consideration, it had no biographical relevance. To be sure, whether the patient is regarded as passively homosexual or as openly defiant depends not only on the analyst's theory but also on the feelings arising in the transference and countertransference. But these feelings cannot be put to productive use in working with the patient if they appear in a vacuum; they must be understood in the context of the patient's childhood. Then, everything the patient says or does will no longer be seen simply as part of the here and now but—to the extent this information is taken seriously—as links in a chain of compulsive repetitions, the logic of which can often be grasped with the aid of a few facts about the patient's early history. When it is discovered, for example, that the silent patient mentioned above grew up with a mother who was interned in a concentration camp as a child and never spoke of it or with a father who committed atrocities in the Vietnam War and, similarly, never spoke of it, then the analyst is in a position to realize that his patient's silence is the only way he can convey an earlier situation he has not yet been able to express in words. It is a situation to which he has been subjected all his life and to which he must first subject his analyst before he himself can consciously confront this feeling of standing before a wall of silence.

I hope this example of the silent patient makes it clear that nothing is to be gained by quizzing patients. What is important is to ask questions along with them, to encourage them to ask and not be deaf and blind to the verbal and nonverbal information they have already given. A well-trained child who later enters analysis will be able to communicate only a very small part, perhaps as little as ten percent, of his trauma. If we are intent on playing the judge by trying to determine the legitimacy of his complaints and to point out his exaggerations ("But your father wasn't *always* cruel"), then we will deprive him of even that ten percent. For then the patient will be just as afraid of us as he is of his internalized object or of his so-called superego. If we permit him instead to see in us an advocate, whose concern is not to defend and protect the father but to stand by the patient, then our imagination and empathy will help him experience his early feelings of abandonment, loneliness, anxiety, powerlessness, and rage without having to protect his parents from them, because with our aid he will realize that feelings do not kill.

Perhaps he will never be able to give voice to the remaining ninety percent of his complaints, because a child's suffering surpasses the imagination of any adult. But at least he will be more likely to get closer to the unconscious trauma if the analyst relinquishes his or her judgmental role.

In Freud's presentation of the Wolf-Man's case history we find the following passage:

When the news of his sister's death arrived, so the patient told me, he felt hardly a trace of grief. He had to force himself to show signs of sorrow, and was able quite coolly to rejoice at having now become the sole heir to the property. He had already been suffering from his recent illness for several years when this occurred. But I must confess that this one piece of information made me for a long time uncertain in my diagnostic judgement of the case. It was to be assumed, no doubt, that his grief over the loss of the most dearly loved member of his family would meet with an inhibition in its expression, as a result of the continued operation of his jealousy of her and of the added presence of his incestuous love for her which had now become unconscious. But I could not do without some substitute for the missing outbursts of grief. And this was at last found in another expression of feeling which had remained inexplicable to the patient. A few months after his sister's death he himself made a journey in the neighbourhood in which she had died. There he sought out the burial-place of a great poet, who was at that time his ideal, and shed bitter tears upon his grave. This reaction seemed strange to him himself, for he knew that more than two generations had passed by since the death of the poet he admired. He only understood it when he remembered that his father had been in the habit of comparing his dead sister's works with the great poet's. He gave me another indication of the correct way of interpreting the homage which he ostensibly paid to the poet, by a mistake in his story which I was able to detect at this point. He had repeatedly specified before that his sister had shot herself; but he was now obliged to make a correction and say that she had taken poison. The poet, however, had been shot in a duel. [pp. 167–68]

Since the patient had been sexually abused, tormented, threatened, and dominated by his older sister from earliest childhood and later learned that his beloved father preferred her to him, perhaps his lack of grief at her suicide was the expression of his true self. He was glad that he was now the "sole heir" to the fortune, i.e., to his parents' love as well. The fact that this feeling was ambivalent, since the Wolf-Man was also attached to his sister in some respects, does not mean it did not exist. Yet the passage indicates, among other things, how greatly Freud's interpretive work was influenced by his pedagogical way of thinking and by his own childhood (he had five sisters before his brother Alexander, his junior by ten years, was born). To substantiate this thesis fully would require writing a new book about the Wolf-Man that would point out in some detail the traces of "poisonous pedagogy" in Freud's approach. I do not see this as my task, even though it might be educationally useful to investigate Freud's pedagogical attitudes, which mirrored the values of his society.

All I wanted to do here was to use a well-known example to show how someone can spend all his life reenacting a severe childhood trauma (sexual abuse) in all kinds of situations and can even unconsciously lead several analysts of high repute to misuse him repeatedly for their own purposes. In his case history of the Wolf-Man, Freud reports:

The patient suddenly called to mind the fact that, when he was still very small, "on the first estate," his sister had seduced him into sexual practices. First came a recollection that in the lavatory, which the children used frequently to visit together, she had made this proposal: "Let's show our bottoms," and had proceeded from words to deeds. Subsequently the more essential part of the seduction came to light, with full particulars as to time and place. It was in spring, at a time when his father was away; the children were in one room playing on the floor, while their mother was working in the next. His sister had taken hold of his penis and played with it, at the same time telling him incomprehensible stories about his Nanya, as though by way of explanation. His Nanya, she said, used to do the same thing with all kinds of people—for instance, with the gardener: she used to stand him on his head, and then take hold of his genitals. [p. 164]

When we keep in mind that the boy actually didn't spend much time with his parents but grew up with his sister and their nurse and that he was afraid of the English governess, we can understand that his sister's behavior, along with the story she made up about the nurse, robbed him with a single blow of the one and only person to whom he could have communicated his feelings of fear and powerlessness. He might have dealt successfully with his sister's power over him if his relationship with the nurse had been left intact. But the idea that the person closest to him did "even worse things" with men than his sister did with him led to the child's sudden psychic loneliness (in the midst of people who "loved" him but had no understanding of his fears) and to the eruption of his infantile neurosis.

The Wolf-Man found himself in the same situation later when he became the object of the needs of his analysts and his analytic sister and again, finally, as a man of nearly ninety, when he gave the young journalist Karin Obholzer the opportunity to use him as a witness against psychoanalysis. The fact that he had been victimized by his sister was still influencing his relationships with women when he was an old man. In his conversations with Obholzer he mentions several times that he is trying in vain to stop seeing a woman whose friendship he finds he cannot do without. As a result, he is putting up with a number of things he actually doesn't like at all. We can also assume that it never occurred to him to refuse Muriel Gardiner's wish to make public his memoirs together with the two case histories because he was grateful to her for her long years of selfless support. Similarly, he felt obliged to answer Obholzer's questions because in his loneliness he didn't want to lose the concern and interest the young woman showed him. The Wolf-Man never learned, either in childhood or in his analyses, that one can resist the demands made by a person one loves without perishing as a result. Moreover, a child who has been abused at an all too early age will not even be fully aware of being abused in later life. He may suspect it but will quickly doubt his own suspicions and feel guilty for having them. Still, we can assume that the Wolf-Man's harmful training did not begin in infancy, for he had an affectionate nurse and therefore as a child was probably able to become aware of a number of things. This is why his memory of being abused by his sister remained conscious, but he couldn't know, on the other hand, in what way his nurse, previous to this, had in all probability abused him in infancy for her own needs. Presumably he later had to reenact unconsciously *this portion* of his repressed trauma in his repetition compulsion by repeatedly allowing himself to be manipulated by other people, being suspicious of these people, and developing symptoms; yet it was impossible for him ever to see through the symptoms or make a break with those who were manipulating him. This is just the way it is for an infant, who is also unable to forbid adults to abuse his body; he cannot even perceive in himself the wish to do so, for he loves the person who is doing it to him and is totally dependent on him or her.

Taking the Wolf-Man's entire life history into account, I would therefore surmise that his sister's so-called seduction of him, which was not repressed, was preceded by earlier sexual manipulation by his nurse, unremembered by the patient and therefore reenacted with numerous people throughout his life. This hypothesis is by no means intended to disparage the Wolf-Man's benefactors. He probably did not make it at all easy for them to see through the reenactments produced by his repetition compulsion.

⊷§ 14 §⊷

Nonsexual Taboos

A LTHOUGH we encounter sexual abuse of children much more frequently in our practice of psychoanalysis than one likes to admit (among other reasons because patients' parents did not have a satisfying sex life), this is by no means the only topic children are kept in the dark about. The members of every generation experience, in addition to the universally binding taboos of their society, specific ones that have to do with the historical point at which they happen to be children. The former type of taboo, restricted to a geographical area and described by ethnologists, can easily be observed by every visitor to a foreign culture. The unconscious prohibitions of a Christian culture, for instance, are much more easily detected by a Mohammedan than by a Christian, and vice versa. But a given generation's taboos (whatever is internalized in childhood as being forbidden) peculiar to a certain time are almost impossible to unearth within a society, not even on the analyst's couch, as long as that analyst belongs to the same generation and society as his or her patient. Josef Breuer's sudden retreat from the patient Anna O., who shocked him with the sexual nature of her pathology, is a striking example of this. But Breuer was not a psychoanalyst. Today, should an analyst feel threatened by the associations or enactments of his patients, he would not run away but would either be incapable of hearing what his patients were saying or would take refuge in theoretical interpretations. Once, when talking to a large group of colleagues, I encountered this tragic, unintentional need to ignore what the patient says, which might also be called unconscious resistance on the part of analysts. This meeting resulted in a valuable deepening of my understanding of taboos restricted to a specific time. I shall have to go into some detail to illustrate what I mean.

In 1979 I met with two sizable groups of professional colleagues to discuss *The Drama of the Gifted Child*. The discussions were held in two different cities not far from each other but separated by the border between Germany and Switzerland. In both groups I was questioned about the problem of assigning guilt, and in order to make my point, I mentioned the dramatic case of Adolf Hitler's childhood, which I was writing about at the time (cf. *For Your Own Good*). The Swiss audience reacted quite calmly; it was obvious to most of them that I had chosen an example of extreme destructiveness to try to explain how it could happen that an ordinary child with no noticeable peculiarities came to harbor a hatred of such destructive dimensions. No doubt my listeners had difficulty relinquishing the familiar concept of a "born psychopath" and instead identifying with someone they considered a monster; they would have preferred to retain their belief that Hitler was the devil personified and had nothing in common with normal human beings, but they were still perfectly able to follow my presentation. There was an entirely different reaction from the group I talked with in a city in southern Germany. When I asked my audience in the course of the discussion if they would like me to use the example of Hitler's childhood to show how a person can under certain circumstances develop into such a great hater, I was greeted with silence at first. Finally, a few participants said they would rather not hear about it. Then some others, mostly women, indicated that they *did* want to hear about it, and the subject could no longer be avoided.

First someone voiced the opinion that a historical phenomenon like National Socialism could not be explained by the life story of a single individual. Somewhat amazed, I tried to make clear that this had not been my intention, that what interested me was simply the question of how it had come about in this particular case that a person could become possessed by hatred of such enormous proportions. Moreover, I said, I knew of no better way to show that the hatred which a child is not allowed to express in childhood is fundamentally insatiable, remaining unsatisfied all his life in spite of later opportunities for abreaction (which were unlimited for Hitler, in view of his power). Once we understand this, we can also see why even the most intense acting out of feelings may sometimes (in group therapy, for instance) bring temporary relief but does not ultimately free a person from his or her childhood traumas. If, on the other hand, feelings associated with the child's first attachment figures can be *experienced*, they will no longer need to be abreacted in the repetition compulsion with substitute objects. Paradoxical as it may sound, if the impotent hatred of early childhood can be experienced, destructive and self-destructive behavior will come to an end. This can be observed again and again with adolescents. The case of Adolf Hitler vividly demonstrates the fundamental difference between experiencing, which is therapeutically so crucial, and the addictive, destructive acting out associated with the repetition compulsion. It also shows how little the adult's power is able to compensate for his powerlessness as a child if he was never allowed to experience the latter consciously. This is what I wanted to demonstrate on the evening in question.

But the assumptions on which my thinking was based turned out not to be as obvious for the others as I had expected. Doubt was expressed, for instance, that Hitler was in fact a hater. How could I respond to that? I was speaking with people who were a decisive twenty years younger than I, who in view of their own personal history had an excuse not to share my knowledge. And so I searched my mind for evidence, recalling a passage from *Mein Kampf* that I wanted to cite, but I decided not to. It seemed senseless to pursue the argument, although I didn't yet understand why I felt this way. It was as though I were suddenly facing a wall.

In conversations following the meeting, several young colleagues told me they had been expecting me to talk about feelings (as if hatred were not a feeling). Others, already familiar with my work, said it was too bad we didn't get to talk about psychoanalytic problems (as if the dynamics of hatred were not a psychoanalytic problem). It was apparent that with the mere mention of Hitler I had touched upon a taboo, had summoned up a complex of feelings connected with tabooed experiences. Any intellectual argument would do, as long as it was able to prevent these feelings from breaking through.

From feelings of my own that came to the surface, I began to understand what was at work here. At first I felt like someone who had abused her hosts' hospitality, who had referred to a subject everyone wanted to avoid. If a young man at the turn of the century, around the time when Freud's *Interpretation of Dreams* appeared, had talked to his parents at the dinner table about sexuality, in all seriousness and in a way free of all obscenity, the uncomfortable atmosphere would have made him feel as though he had behaved indecently, the way I felt now. That evening I had experienced firsthand how true it is that sexuality is no longer taboo for us, that we as analysts are willing to speak without ado, even in a group, about any and all sexual problems, but not about the specific person Adolf Hitler. Will we ever be capable of understanding what happens to the hatred we felt in childhood if we shut ourselves off from our immediate historical past? It is of little use to make demands in this regard. What is required to break down taboos is the support of a therapist who is not under the sway of these taboos because he or she has already worked them through.

I am glad that as a result of this evening in Germany I made a discovery that gave me a better understanding of that country's younger generation. My colleagues transmitted to me *their* feelings as children of standing before a wall when they tried to ask questions that activated deep resistance on the part of their parents. What they must have heard or sensed in response was: "One doesn't ask such questions, they're stupid, and even if you think you know a thing or two, you still can't grasp what happened. In fact, everything was entirely different from the way you see it now. Do you have any idea of what Hitler did for us? Can you even pretend to pass judgment? It's presumptuous to talk about things you never saw and never experienced. You can't possibly understand them."

Children sense that resistance is hidden behind these answers and will stop asking questions. If they should continue to ask nonetheless, they will be so confused by the arguments given that they will finally become ashamed and will feel guilty. They will feel they are being indecent for mentioning the subject again and, as a result, will respect their parents' silent resistance. Thus, the children's impulse to question will be stifled although it will not be completely destroyed. Many psychosomatic and neurotic illnesses whose treatment I have supervised took an unexpected turn when we included the parents' experiences in World War II in our considerations and interpretations.

It was as though the children were using the enactments of their illness as a way of searching for the answers their parents withheld by keeping silent. Their desperate, lonely search often took the form of a sexual perversion that could not be understood by means of classical psychoanalytic interpretations. These cases involved patients who were their parents' first-born right after the war, i.e., at a time when the parents' horrifying experiences were already a thing of the past. Because these experiences were not discussed, the first-born child became the sole helpless receiver of these split-off, threatening contents. The parents unconsciously passed their unmastered personal history on to their child at a tender age, often simply by way of glances. Later, in analysis, these children may present many sexual problems and make it difficult for the analyst to think in terms of anything else. If it should occur to him, however, to ask his patients what their parents must have gone through during the war, he will at first encounter the greatest resistance, but the way will be paved to work through the forbidden topic. Every analyst who has already had this experience realizes what a radical turn the analysis can then take.

The ability to identify with these people who had been children soon after the war—something I owe in part to the group discussion I have just described as well as to sessions with my own patients— also helped me later to understand some of the reactions to my book *For Your Own Good.* After the German edition appeared, I was told that many critics wanted to review the book but did not consider themselves qualified to deal with the Hitler chapter and felt they would first have to study the period in question much more thoroughly. As a result, that chapter, which I consider the central one of the book, was (with a few important exceptions) mentioned only cursorily in the reviews, even in the best and more original ones. When this section of the book *was* referred to, it was obvious that the reviewers were very anxious not to say the wrong thing and were only giving an accurate account of the author's ideas, without risking taking a position of their own.* All their comments made clear that there was a taboo, internalized at an early age, that prevented them from asking questions about the kind of person Hitler was or from wanting to know anything concrete about the

---

* (1984) In contrast, the first major American review I received of *For Your Own Good* was devoted primarily to the Hitler chapter (see Ashley Montagu in *Psychology Today,* May 1983).

subject. The danger zones that had to be avoided at all costs were their parents' feelings of guilt and shame, along with bewilderment and disillusion at their complicity in the catastrophe unleashed by Hitler. The mechanisms of child-rearing apply here, too: it is not only beatings and sexual abuse that are passed on to one's children but guilt feelings as well. If someone has been made to feel guilty from childhood for everything done to him by his parents, how is he to endure the resulting confusion without the help of his own children, whom he can make feel guilty in turn? Every analyst knows that genuine guilt cannot be deduced from the fact that someone has guilt feelings, for pedagogical principles permit parents to raise their children to have them from an early age.

How senseless these guilt feelings are is something I felt very keenly that unforgettable evening in southern Germany. The parents of my colleagues had been mistakenly led to see in Hitler the great fatherly redeemer they had dreamed of since childhood. When he disappointed them and they then felt ashamed of their hopes, they delegated their feelings to their children, who, now in 1979 in their thirties, were the adults sitting before me. When I mentioned the subject of Hitler, they reacted like their parents, who had not been able to tolerate their children's questions. *I* was now the child who had to experience the parental feelings of guilt and shame he or she had never been able to comprehend. My audience delegated to me their childhood feelings, and at the same time saw in me a judge who wanted to condemn their parents. This is why they felt compelled to defend their parents to me.

It is no easy matter to deal with this phenomenon, but that does not mean we can avoid addressing it, for a growing number of people are coming to therapists' offices and clinics who were once war children and who have never had the opportunity of sharing the fears, bewilderment, and pain of their childhood with anyone or even of talking about these emotions. I have used the German taboo behind their silence as an example here because I am familiar with it through my work with patients and colleagues, but I assume other countries have their own taboos that are different for every generation and that it could be the specific task of psychoanalysis to uncover.

There is much to learn from the analyses of these former war children that can also be applied to other patients. What has been written in numerous studies about mothers in the Third Reich who were victims of persecution and about their children is undoubtedly also valid for the mothers of psychotics or of borderline cases. The difference is that we know more about the histories of mothers who were in concentration camps; we can understand them better because their fate was a collective one. But we often know nothing of the individual fate of the mothers of schizophrenics, especially if we go along with our patients' idealization of their childhood. Nevertheless, we cannot help taking an interest in the traumatic experiences both of patients and their parents, and I find that this could be the most fruitful aspect of psychoanalysis. When patient and analyst together look into the former's past, with its national, religious, and familial taboos, then the patient senses that the analyst is truly concerned and not intent on proving the worth of his analytic training, thereby continuing to idealize his teachers (parents).

The specific ways parents unconsciously communicated their war experiences to their children by their silence depends on what their position or rank was, what they lived through, and the perspective from which they experienced the Third Reich and the war. It is also decisive how old the child was at the time of Germany's surrender. There are a great number of children born during the war whose first years were filled with the horrors of the bombings and who have been able to remember this period as adults because there was a supportive person who lived through it with them. If the most difficult and bewildering period for the parents, however, happens to fall in the first, nonverbal stage of the children's lives, when they normally have very intense feelings and are supposed to repress them, the children will have to live with the effects of repression in later life and pay a high price for it. Now, let's imagine that a patient who had these childhood experiences and never shared them with anyone enters analysis and that his analyst keeps waiting for a chance to apply drive interpretation to this case. The patient will then feel he is being ignored and misunderstood and will develop a narcissistic rage, which in turn gives the analyst grounds for seeing him as destructive or incurable. Thus, the patient's pathogenic trauma is repeated, a trauma whose origin does not lie in external events but in having been left alone with his questions and his pain.

If all the citizens of Germany, both West and East, under a certain age were to cry out: "Let bygones be bygones! We don't want to be eternally reminded of the persecution of the Jews. After all, we weren't born until after the war and we didn't experience any of it. We're no longer interested in the Third Reich, we have other problems now . . .," we could understand this sentiment all too well and someone who is not an analyst could let it go at that. But someone who has analyzed or supervised the analysis of postwar children and gained insight into their unconscious will know it is an illusion to think that these bygones can be bygones. The greater the refusal to face the past, the more incomprehensible its neurotic and psychotic manifestations in the next generation. This is true for the children of both the persecutors and the victims.

Claudine Vegh's book of conversations with the children of some of these victims brings to light a ban of silence imposed on a large group of today's parents, whose own parents had been deported during the war. The author talked individually and at length with several people who had been persecuted by the Nazis as children. The result turns out to be a series of monologues by people who talked about the extreme traumas of their childhood for the first time in thirty-five years. Most of them had never told their spouse or even their mother anything about their experiences.

The degree of actual danger, of cruelty, fear, and isolation undergone by these people, was so great that no one can blame them for trying all their lives to forget the horrors of that time when they had no one to give them support and sympathy. Yet their own children can never understand the reason for this silence even though they sense its effects on their parents' behavior from the very beginning. Sometimes the children develop symptoms as a way of seeking access to their parents' innermost selves, where childhood feelings, and with them the wellsprings of vitality, often remain locked up for decades.

It is significant that in spite of great resistance, the survivors whom Vegh asked for an interview all—with the exception of one person, a psychotherapist—agreed to talk to this woman, who had had a similar fate as a child, and that all of them reported they had noticed a distinct feeling of relief the day following their interview. This therapeutic effect can be attributed not only to the lifting of the ban of silence but also to the fortunate circumstance that by listening empathically Vegh offered them the kind of support they needed to approach their trauma and feel its pain without becoming traumatized anew, something that can easily happen in analysis when a survivor goes to great lengths to break his or her protective silence and is then confronted with interpretations based on the drive theory (cf. p. 232). Similarly, when a survivor appears in court to testify against a war criminal, there is not a therapeutic effect but rather a renewed traumatizing one because he or she cannot sense any sympathy in this cold atmosphere. As analysts, we can change neither society nor our patients' past or parents, but we can avoid retraumatizing our patients, and beyond that, we can assume the supportive role required if they are to discover the significance of their trauma.

In his afterword to Claudine Vegh's book, Bruno Bettelheim writes:

> Why are the victims in the position of not being able to speak about what happened to them in those days; why is it still dreadfully difficult for them, even twenty or thirty years later, to tell what they experienced as children? And why is it so important that these things be discussed? I am of the opinion that these two questions are closely related. For something one cannot talk about also cannot be buried, finds no resting place. If one doesn't refer to it, the wounds continue to fester from generation to generation. It is as Raphaël says: "The world must realize that these deportations have branded us even into the third generation. It is dreadful. . . ."
>
> In case there should still be any doubt that these terrible events have also branded the next generation, they will be dispelled by a book that appeared recently in the United States (Helen Epstein, *Children of the Holocaust*, New York, 1979). The author's parents are both survivors of German death camps. Her life has been shaped and marred by her parents' fate and by their inability to talk about it, and this in spite of the fact that she was born in the United States and grew up there. Unlike those whose words we hear in her book, Helen Epstein was never dragged from her home, never forcibly separated from her parents, and never had to go into hiding to stay alive. Her parents took great pains to raise their children in such a way that they would feel secure, which they in fact were in New York. And yet, as the child of survivors of the death camps, Helen Epstein was heavily burdened by her parents' past and the effect it had on the

present. As an adult, she wanted to learn once and for all whether her plight was an exception or whether others whose parents had a similar background shared her experience. She sought these people out and had conversations with them. They too had grown up in relative security just like Helen Epstein. And yet she discovered that they all, each in a different way, had been deeply affected by the harsh fate their parents had undergone in the past. They all had suffered from their parents' inability to be open about their experiences and the marks left by them.

Helen Epstein describes the consequences the parents' unspoken pain had for their children with the image of an iron box she made for herself and carried around hidden deep within her. The box turned her life into a torment: "For years it lay there in an iron box, buried so deeply within me that I was never able to find out what it really was. I only knew I was carrying some sort of hazardous explosive material around with me, more secret than sexual matters and more dangerous than ghosts and phantoms. Ghosts have a shape and a name. But what was in my iron box had neither the one nor the other. Whatever it was living inside me was so powerful that words dissolved before they could describe it."

By denial, whether of facts or feelings, a person becomes alienated from oneself. To use Helen Epstein's image, the facts and feelings are put inside a box that is carefully locked forever. No matter how hard someone tries to get rid of it, this can't be done; the box remains as a foreign object in a life that is controlled by it.

An unacknowledged trauma is like a wound that never heals over and may start to bleed again at any time. In a supportive environment the wound can become visible and finally heal completely.

When we treat patients whose parents were either persecutors or their victims and who later concealed the most dramatic aspects of their life under a ban of silence, we are faced with a difficult task, but at the same time we have the opportunity to expand the boundaries of present-day psychoanalysis, providing we keep the following requirements in mind:

1. To be sensitive to the child's narcissistic needs for echoing, mirroring, understanding, respect, and support, and to the ensuing traumatizations if these needs are not met.

2. To have understanding, proceeding from the foregoing sensitivity, for the reactive significance of the child's narcissistic rage.

3. To know that even unintentional cruelty hurts and that the

patient must experience in analysis the anger and pain of his or her early childhood in order to be set free, even though as an adult the patient knows that the parents were victims as well.

4. To realize that children will pay for their parents' silence with pathological symptoms.

5. To recognize that grief leads to reconciliation, whereas guilt feelings are divisive.

6. To make the conscious decision not to assume a judgmental role, which would be colored by the moral precepts of our own upbringing.

7. To identify the patient's taboos, peculiar to his or her country and family.

It is not analysts' freedom from trauma but rather their ability to experience and articulate it that makes them sensitive to the problems of their patients. They can be more supportive in helping a patient experience his or her childhood traumas if they no longer need to fear the traumas of their own childhood or puberty.

❧ 15 ❧

The Father of Psychoanalysis

I F children are always led by the hand and thus prevented from finding their own way, they will gradually stop making discoveries for themselves. There are fathers who in their own way love their children very much, protect them, and would like to introduce them to their intellectual world, becoming so obsessed with this idea that they can scarcely imagine that their children, whom they regard as an extension of themselves, could see the world any differently than they do. This overly protective atmosphere severely jeopardizes a child's vitality and capacity for development. He is grateful to his father for so much (for life, for love, for the knowledge imparted to him) and at first gladly refrains from doing anything that might hurt him. But if his urge to express himself is great enough, he will either become mentally ill or be forced to hurt his father. The consequences of the latter step will depend on the father's degree of maturity.

We cannot hold it against Sigmund Freud that he tried to bestow so much on his wonderful, beloved child, psychoanalysis: his theories about psychic mechanisms, the Oedipus complex, his drive theory, and, finally, his structural model. The child, however, has long since grown up, has made discoveries of his own, and can no longer go through life holding his father's or grandfather's hand and seeing the world with their eyes. Freud might not have impeded the development of psychoanalysis by overloading it with content relevant predominantly to his own day if he had bequeathed his followers the freedom to make use of his instruments to discover what was true for *their* patients and *their* time. But as we know, Freud was no exception as a father. Like most fathers of his day, he imposed severe restrictions on his "sons," with the result that the most gifted of them were left with the choice of allowing themselves to be constricted by the contents of his theories or— if, like Jung and Adler, they were unwilling to do this—of making a complete break with the master. By doing the latter, they sacrificed in their own systems the advantages afforded by Freud to explore a patient's early childhood with the aid of transference and countertransference. In Freud's lifetime, then, there were either loyal followers or renegades. Not until after his death did analysts like Balint, Winnicott, Kohut, and others make discoveries of their own by using his methods and yet remain within the fold. Without the psychoanalytic method, their new insights about early childhood would not have been possible. But could these insights have been reached while Freud was still alive?

If my analogy is of some value, then one could also say that a father cannot both sire a brilliant child and try to guide his every footstep without detriment to the child's creative powers. No one can bestow on humankind a method with the vision and explosive force of psychoanalysis and at the same time prescribe what use is to be made of it. Once brought into the world, it leads a life of its own and has unlimited possibilities for development if no longer held back by its father.

The psychoanalytic approach cannot renounce its attempt to unmask dishonesty without renouncing itself. But if it remains true to its central task and refuses to stop uncovering, understanding, and making visible the way things really are, it will never content itself with a rigid system for the very reason that such systems are hiding places for dishonesty in its various guises.

We cannot reproach Freud for not knowing what we know today or for giving up his trauma theory in favor of the Oedipus complex, although I personally am sorry he did the latter, for I have found confirmation of his earlier findings in nearly all the cases I have analyzed or supervised. The effects of the abuse of power can easily be identified in the childhood of every patient, and its narcissistic significance is being recognized increasingly. Yet the sexual components of abuse still are the most difficult to uncover, and we know it is the fact of concealment that isolates the child, leaving him alone with his secret and thus making him ill. But without being analyzed himself, how could Freud have lived with the consequences of his original discovery?

It would be interesting to try to imagine what attitude Freud would have toward his various teachings if he were alive now. Perhaps he would choose not to reissue some of his works, in particular the case study of Schreber. If he were a young man today, possibly he would no longer be happy with his structural theory, which he developed in later life. We might wonder if it wouldn't seem strange to him that drive interpretations he considered appropriate eighty years ago are sometimes being passed on in the very same form, or if it wouldn't surprise him that after half a century the truths of his day (for example, regarding male and female sexuality) are being handed down unexamined as though we had not learned a great deal to add to them. But all this is pure speculation, mixed with hope and idealization. Many analysts would still like to see in Freud the farsighted, tolerant—in short, perfect—father, not subject to historical limitations, and would prefer to deny the fact that even a genius is a child of his times. But perfection would not be human and would therefore certainly not provide the right soil for psychoanalytic discoveries. Wouldn't it be an unavoidable step in an analyst's maturation process to give up the strong idealization of Freud and work through the ensuing grief? How are we to develop the ability to make discoveries of our own if we retain our deeply concealed, childlike obedience toward him?

My speculations about Freud's willingness to revise his position are probably purely illusory. It is possible that the father of psychoanalysis, like most fathers, would not be able to transcend his own situation; perhaps he would adhere to his drive theory and the Oedipus complex today the same way he did then and consider all those who didn't go along with him as renegades or enemies. This would be painful but it would not alter the fact that some of us are not willing to live and work with blinders on for the sake of being regarded as our father's loyal children. The father has a right to see the world as he must see it, but the child will hold it against him unless he or she exercises the same right (which the father rarely grants), namely, to see the world through his or her own eyes and not be deterred by any paternal prohibitions. The potential richness of life bestowed by the father can unfold fully only if the damage caused by the well-intentioned upbringing he has given his child is undone. A growing number of today's young people have a more open relationship with their parents than many analysts of the older generation and than Sigmund Freud himself.

Although Freud courageously uncovered the hypocrisy in sexual matters typical of his time, if he were to hear the open way adolescents or children are permitted to speak about their parents nowadays, he would probably find it hard to accept. He himself reported that every Sunday before his customary visit to his mother, he had stomach pains, but it wouldn't have occurred to him to discontinue these visits, which he obviously rebelled against inwardly. He took it for granted that certain feelings had to be suppressed. In this connection, Freud wrote a great deal about women's penis envy but never a word about his envy of his five younger sisters. We know that he was his mother's first-born child. After him, over the next ten years, she gave birth to a second son—who died at the age of eight months when Sigmund was nineteen months old—and then to five daughters, followed by another son, Alexander. On page 59 of the biography *Sigmund Freud: His Life in Pictures and Words*, there is a reproduction of an oil painting showing the twelve-year-old Sigmund standing to the left of his five sisters and with little two-year-old Alexander in their midst. Alexander later reported that when Sigmund was sixteen he said to him: "Look, Alexander, our family is like a book. You and I are the last and the first of the children, so we are like the strong covers that have to support and protect the weak girls, who were born after me and before you." On p. 55 of the same volume there is another picture, this one a photograph taken in 1864: the mother is sitting with her youngest daughter on her lap, to her right an older one. Sigmund is sitting beside them, not looking at the camera like the others. His intelligent, alert face is turned toward his mother's "pet" on her lap and has an expression somewhere between dislike and scorn.

It is inconceivable that a child in Freud's situation would not have strong feelings of jealousy for the five girls, especially since the family lived in very small quarters at first, and throughout his childhood Sigmund could not escape the fact that his mother often had to devote her time and attention to his sisters. In his remark to Alexander just quoted, there is no sign of this jealousy, with the possible exception of the reaction formation expressed in his role of protector. Yet this analogy to a book is peculiar, for the most important part of a book is its contents, the printed pages, which have value even without a cover, whereas the cover alone would be meaningless without the contents. The sixteen-year-old Sigmund, who had lived with books since childhood, knew this very well. Since an analogy like this occurred to him all the same, it must have reflected an only too understandable but deeply repressed jealousy of his five sisters, who were forever depriving him of the mother he loved, even though they were not so clever and perhaps not so considerate as he. It must have seemed to the little boy that these eternal "mother's pets" were in some mysterious way he could not fathom *superior* to him. But how could such a clever boy, whose young mother took so much pleasure in his fine qualities, be envious or jealous? Ignoble feelings of that nature had to be left to women. How often scorn protects older siblings from bitter feelings of jealousy! Be that as it may, the striking oil painting and Sigmund's words to Alexander shed light on the origin of the theory of penis envy and can perhaps give women who justifiably resent this concept a more human impression of Freud: not of the stern, bearded patriarch, but of the brave little protector—defender of his mother and her five girls—who didn't have a chance to express consciously his anger at the houseful of females, to say nothing of expressing it openly.

In his essay "A Childhood Recollection from *Dichtung und Wahrheit*," Freud analyzes Goethe's sibling situation very compellingly and sympathetically; yet, as a result of his own psychological blindness, the genius who discovered the mechanism of repression could write: "Goethe's next youngest sister, Cornelia Friederica Christiana, was born on December 7, 1750, when he was fifteen months old. *This slight difference in age almost excludes the possibility of her having been an object of jealousy*" (emphasis added). We need only observe young children to see the strong and unmistakable envy and jealousy they are capable of if they are free to show these emotions.

Sigmund Freud showed this indirectly as a little boy too, only no one was there who could understand his behavior and his distress. Ernest Jones writes in his biography of Freud:

> An incident which he could not recollect was of slipping from a stool when he was two years old, and receiving a violent blow on the lower jaw from the edge of the table he was exploring for some delicacy. It

was a severe cut which necessitated sewing up, and it bled profusely;
he retained the scar throughout his life.

A more important occurrence, just before this, was his young
brother's death when Freud was nineteen months old and the little
Julius only eight months. Before the newcomer's birth the infant Freud
had had sole access to his mother's love and milk, and he had to learn
from the experience how strong the jealousy of a young child can be.
In a letter to Fliess (1897) he admits the evil wishes he had against
his rival and adds that their fulfilment in his death had aroused self-
reproaches, a tendency which has remained ever since. [pp. 7–8]

Freud was eleven months old when Julius was born. He reacted to his brother's death by having a serious accident. The early
traumatization may explain in large part why he was willing to con-
cede the jealousy Goethe felt when he was older but not that which
he felt as a small child toward his sister Cornelia, who was just a
little over a year younger than he. The likelihood of experiencing
jealousy of his five sisters and coming to terms with it without reaction formations was greatly reduced because of the wish-fulfillment
represented by his brother's death and the accompanying guilt he
must have felt.

⊸§ 16 §⊛

Facets of the False Self

THE attitude stemming from a conscious identification with the
child as victim, which I contrast to an unconscious identification with the adult (see chapter 1), is not altogether new, nor did
it originate with me; it has already been more or less consciously
adopted by individual therapists. The theoretical inferences to be
drawn from my experiences are nothing new either. The only unusual thing is for someone to think through to its logical conclusion
what everyone knows and doesn't speak about. The fact that the
child has been the victim of the adult for millennia is brought out
not only in Lloyd de Mause's *History of Childhood* (1974) but also
in countless other documents and pedagogical tracts going all the
way back to the time of King Solomon, yet this idea is hardly ever
stated openly. It has always been the case that it is not cruelty itself that arouses public indignation but rather calling attention to
the cruelty. Baudelaire described things everyone knew about, but
as a result his book *Fleurs du mal* was initially banned by the official
censors of the day. The victimization of children is nowhere forbidden; what is forbidden is to write about it.

The more one-sided a society's observance of strict moral principles such as orderliness, cleanliness, and hostility toward instinctual drives, and the more deep-seated its fear of the other side
of human nature—vitality, spontaneity, sensuality, critical judgment, and inner independence—the more strenuous will be its efforts
to isolate this hidden territory, to surround it with silence or in-
stitutionalize it. Prostitution, the pornography trade, and the almost
obligatory obscenity typical of traditionally all-male groups such
as the military are part of the legalized, even requisite reverse side
of this cleanliness and order. Splitting of the human being into two

parts, one that is good, meek, conforming, and obedient and the other that is the diametrical opposite is perhaps as old as the human race, and one could simply say that it is part of "human nature." Yet it has been my experience that when people have had the opportunity to seek and live out their true self in analysis, this split disappears of itself. They perceive both sides, the conforming as well as the so-called obscene, as two extremes of the false self, which they now no longer need. I knew one woman who had been avid about attending wild Fastnacht masquerades because this had been her only chance to be free and creative. Later, however, when she was able to show her other side through her creativity rather than by wearing a mask, her interest in Fastnacht restricted itself to making decorations and costumes. She no longer wanted to disguise herself, because it would remind her of the unhappiness of her former secret life. This case and similar ones make me wonder if it will not one day be possible to let children grow up in such a way that they can later have more respect for all sides of their nature and not be forced to suppress the forbidden sides to the point where they must be lived out in violent and obscene ways.

Obscenity and cruelty are not a true liberation from compulsive behavior but are its by-products. Free sexuality is never obscene, nor does violence ever result if a person is able to deal openly with his or her aggressive impulses, to acknowledge feelings such as anger and rage as responses to real frustration, hurt, and humiliation.

How can it have come about that the split I have just described is attributed to human nature as a matter of course even though there is evidence that it can be overcome without any great effort of will and without legislating morality? The only explanation I can find is that these two sides are perpetuated in the way children are raised and treated at a very early age, and the accompanying split between them is therefore regarded as "human nature." The "good" false self is the result of what is called socialization, of adapting to society's norms, consciously and intentionally passed on by the parents; the "bad," equally false self is rooted in the child's earliest observations of parental behavior, visible only to the child, who is used as an outlet. Perceived sympathetically by the child's devoted, unsuspecting eyes and stored up in his or her unconscious, this behavior is what comes to be regarded automatically, generation after generation, as "human nature."

It is without doubt offensive and disquieting for people to discover that the escape valves they believed they had found in raising their children—so well concealed until now (and so necessary because of their upbringing)—are proving to have a poisonous effect on the next generation. What is one to do without these outlets? Isn't Freud's discovery of the unconscious to blame for everything? But Freud would not have made his discovery if there had not been countless patients in his day whom he found to be suffering from the double standard to such a degree that they could no longer be cared for by their families and thus began to fill the psychiatric wards. The situation is no better today than it was then; indeed, with the increase in population it is even more serious. Therefore, as a psychoanalyst one is faced with the difficult task of calling attention to the poison produced by the early exercise of parental power, a poison we have been storing up inside from the very beginning and then inflicting on our own children. Further, it is our task to recognize that it is not a matter of assigning blame to individual parents, who, after all, are themselves victims of this system, but of identifying a hidden societal structure that determines our lives, like practically no other. Once recognized, it can be found in a wide variety of society's forms. To take this step will necessarily cause us anxiety if we have been raised according to pedagogical principles, which is no doubt the case for most of us. It is understandable, then, if fear of our introjected parents' anger, the child's fear of losing their love, compels us to overlook striking societal patterns for the sake of sparing our parents.

If a psychoanalyst succeeds in experiencing and working through this fear stemming from earliest childhood, then he will perhaps ask himself: "Do I still have to show my parents the same consideration I did as a child, or can I understand their behavior better by seeing them as parts of an overall system whose victims they are as much as I? Won't I be able to get closer to my parents, regardless of whether they are deceased or still living, by recognizing the tragic nature of our mutual victimization instead of trying to gloss it over? Glossing over, denying, concealing—this was what caused me so much trouble in my childhood and probably is the reason why I chose this profession. I know from my own case as well as from my patients' the price children have to pay for doing this and how dangerous it can be if chocolate is secretly laced with poison. Parents who bought the chocolate with the best of intentions and gave it to their children are totally innocent. But what if a pediatrician who has already seen the effects of this poison on several other children were to conceal the truth from the parents to keep them from feeling guilty?"

Those rare analysts who are inwardly prepared to pose questions like these will find the answers as they follow their patients' progress. Then even the most complicated and long-accepted theories will lose their hold over them. They will refuse to abandon their patients or themselves for the sake of these theories.

⊷§ 17 §⊶

Eighty Years of the Drive Theory

I T is not only people who celebrate birthdays; cities, for example, do too, and in congratulatory addresses, speakers cite the attacks the city has survived, extolling its stability and its powers of resistance that enable it to withstand every danger. But what are we to say about the stability of a theory that has been able to withstand all attacks only because it has not perceived them as threats to its validity and survival?

Since the beginnings of psychoanalysis, particularly in the past twenty years, there has been an enormous increase in our knowledge about childhood, which would have led to a major revision in the drive theory had the latter not become a petrified dogma. For dogma is immune to new insights and developments. I shall indicate the areas in which these new findings occur.

1. I regard what adult patients tell us concerning the fantasies they have about their children and the way they act toward them to be fundamental to this new knowledge. In a preanalytic age, they would never have been able to divulge authentic material of this nature. We learn from it to what a powerful and intense degree a child can be the object of narcissistic needs, sexual desires, and pent-up feelings of hatred. Further, we see that these impulses, arising from the patient's own traumatic experiences, need not damage the child—that is, they will no longer be subject to the repetition compulsion once they can be integrated into the patient's total personality and allowed to mature, thanks to his or her opportunity to express them.

2. Numerous works treating the history of childhood by psychohistorians such as Ariès and de Mause corroborate our analytic material. They show with devastating clarity the purposes for which

adults have traditionally used children without, of course, recognizing the unconscious motives involved. To these publications we can
now add more recent ones about child abuse, which bring us face
to face with an inconceivable and yet undeniable *contemporary*
situation (see the works by Louise Armstrong, Sandra Butler, Susan
Griffin, and Florence Rush mentioned in the Afterword to the
American edition).

3. Direct observations reported by René Spitz, John Bowlby,
Margaret S. Mahler, Donald W. Winnicott, and many others, as
well as the practical results of numerous psychoanalysts who work
with children, have opened our eyes even more to the unconscious
conflicts of the children's parents. An analyst who sees both child and
parents will find it harder to be rigid about interpreting children's
symptoms exclusively as a form of defense against their "sexual and
aggressive drives," although such interpretations still can be found.

4. Analysts and psychiatrists such as Theodor Lidz, Harold
Searles, Helm Stierlin, Ronald D. Laing, and Morton Schatzman,
who have worked with schizophrenic adolescents and drug addicts,
have gradually developed the concept of family therapy because
they could no longer countenance interpreting the patient's reaction
to what has been done to him as a form of defense against his aggressive and libidinous drives. They saw the need to take the total
familial context into account, both in trying to understand the patient's pathogenesis and to a certain extent in their therapeutic
methods. Helm Stierlin's "delegation" and Horst Eberhard Richter's
"narcissistic projections" are examples of new directions being taken
that have not, however, been integrated into classical theory.

5. Analytic treatment of the grown children of Holocaust victims
provides additional evidence in this area. Since the parents' fate was
a collective and therefore ascertainable one, it was easy to demonstrate the connections between their fate and very early narcissistic
traumatizations in their children (cf. p. 182). An analyst can
learn something about the origins of narcissistic disturbances, perversions, obsessional neuroses, and other illnesses from studies that
have been made about the offspring of Holocaust victims. The parents' traumas, which they have been unable to come to terms with
because of the excessive horror involved, become their children's
"neurotic misery." Since this can be demonstrated in relation to the
massive traumatizations known about in the parents' adulthood, it

is, in my opinion, all the more valid for those traumas, not caused by war and racial persecution, occurring in their childhood and puberty.

6. Finally, in recent years works by William G. Niederland and Morton Schatzman have acquainted us with the ideas and behavior of the father of Paul Schreber, whose memoirs are the subject of a well-known essay by Freud. The shock effect of their discoveries is missing in the presentation made by Niederland, to whom we actually owe the new findings, whereas Schatzman confronts analysts with questions we can no longer evade: Can we attribute the fears of a patient who was treated cruelly as an infant to his attempts to ward off his instinctual drives, ignoring the true nature of his early childhood? If we attempt to empathize with our patients, must we not consider their parents' psychic reality, of which their own is an inevitable reflection?

In Freud's famous presentation of Schreber's case, he tells the story of this paranoid patient by drawing on Schreber's own *Denkwürdigkeiten eines Nervenkranken* (Memoirs of a Neuropath). Freud traced all Schreber's fears of persecution back to resistance against a homosexual love for his father. Schatzman carries his investigation an important step beyond Niederland's, comparing passages from the son's memoirs with the father's pedagogical writings and discovering some startling connections. It turns out that even the ill son's most absurd ideas, fantasies, and fears of persecution are a retelling, without his realizing it, of the story of the persecution he was subjected to in early childhood. The father's writings reveal the way he raised his sons, a method of child-rearing leading to suicide for one and paranoia for the other. Freud's idea that Paul Schreber had a homosexual fixation on his father is perhaps not wrong, for the father who continually manipulated his sons physically (and only them, not his daughters), even in infancy, sometimes with the help of various mechanical contrivances, no doubt stimulated the boy sexually. Besides, every child loves his father, even if he is persecuted by him, and this combination of love and hate was also present in the young Schreber. But it would be totally misleading to insist on understanding paranoia in general and the genesis of this case in particular as the child's defense against his (and not the father's!) homosexual desires. Perhaps this approach was necessary in Freud's time, but in our day it would mean ignoring the data available to us. The refusal of many analysts to see their patients' "psychic reality" (which they wish to make their sole focus) as a reflection of the psychic reality of the patients' parents reveals vestiges of a rigid, behavioristic attitude.

If we did not take the social factor into account, it would be amazing that the Freudian drive theory has remained virtually untouched by all these scientifically verifiable findings concerning the true nature of early childhood. With striking regularity, the new data presented in most of the investigations referred to above are not followed through to their logical conclusions. Some creative thinkers like Horst Eberhard Richter and Helm Stierlin, who were able to free themselves from the rigid system of the drive theory because they learned from their own practice what parents unconsciously do to their children and who even codified these discoveries in their concepts of "narcissistic projection" and "delegation" respectively, nevertheless failed to apply the implications of their findings to individual therapy. Instead, like many other psychiatrists in the United States, Great Britain, and France who reached the same conclusions, they abandoned individual therapy and concentrated on family or group therapy. In order to justify this change of focus, they present a number of sound and compelling arguments, e.g.:

1. In view of the widespread incidence of mental illness, a therapist should not be available only to a select few. It is his or her duty to help a greater number of people.

2. Individual analysis takes a very long time and only rarely results in substantial success.

3. It is often the case that if the analysand was the bearer of hidden family conflicts, an improvement in his or her symptoms will result in other family members becoming ill.

No one will have any trouble agreeing with these arguments, yet they neglect to take into consideration what I see as the essence of an individual therapy free of all pedagogy—for the following reasons:

Regarding the first point: if an individual begins to discover the truth about his early childhood and to free himself from the internalized taboos and compulsions of his upbringing, including those of his introjects, this is a social factor and not a purely private matter. Even if this person cannot forgive his parents as easily as a "successfully" brought-up child, because he is just beginning to perceive his deep wounds, those around him will still benefit. For now he will not be tempted to "educate" others or to appeal to them to be conciliatory, to have understanding for their parents, to be reasonable; he will know that it was his attempts in this very direction that made him ill as a child, and he will make it his business not to conceal the truth from himself. This will inevitably have political significance, for falsehood will be unmasked automatically whenever there is even one person in the crowd who refuses to go along with the prevailing dishonesty, whenever—as, for instance, in Andersen's tale "The Emperor's New Clothes"—a child's spontaneous exclamation, "But the Emperor is naked!" restores the adults' lost capacity to perceive the truth. If a psychoanalyst can help one individual to discover his true self instead of covertly trying to educate him, he is doing something of benefit for society as well as for his profession.

Regarding the second point: the therapeutic goal of improved interaction between partners or with other members of the family can be a legitimate one but cannot be compared with the individual's liberation from the results of the harm done to him as a child. This liberation usually has a positive effect on the entire family, providing that the early childhood history and the therapist's awareness of the power exercised over the child by the adult are not suppressed. The family therapist observes the interaction between adults or between adolescents and their parents. In these relationships the manifest power structure may be different or even entirely opposite from what it was in the original setting of early childhood. It often looks as though parents are being victimized by their adolescent offspring and not the other way around. Yet the key to understanding the present situation lies in the past, which does not always become visible in a group. Only in the intrapsychic world of the individual does the past go on running its unwavering course and keep on being enacted anew in his or her present surroundings. The psychoanalytic method makes use of free association, transference, and countertransference in its attempt to decode the meaning of these intrapsychic, often tortured reenactments and can thereby free the patient from his tormenting repetition compulsions.

Regarding the third point: if the goal of analysis to lead the patient back to the feelings of his early childhood is achieved, the people around him at present will be less likely to suffer from psychological disturbances unless they were already disturbed and had been making the patient the bearer of their symptoms; this rarely happens in such a clear-cut form, but if it does, it can be an opportunity for the family member now ill to get at the roots of his or her own problems. In general, at the end of analysis the patient no longer needs to reproach his parents as they are today, because he has now been able to experience his tragic past with the parents of his early childhood, which he had until now buried deep inside him. If other members of the family fall ill, it can be a sign that even though the patient's symptoms have disappeared, he is still using the family setting as the stage for the reenactment of his early history or that his recovery has made another family member aware of his or her own plight.

At the present time we can find that one group of psychoanalysts, remaining faithful to the drive theory, is protecting itself from any new insights about early childhood by hiding behind the dogmas of infantile sexuality and the Oedipus complex, and that another group, seeing through the dogmatic nature of these theories, thanks to their experience as practicing therapists, is moving away from individual treatment and as a result is losing sight of the factor of the individual's early childhood. Something similar happened with C. G. Jung when he introduced the concepts of the archetype and the collective unconscious after having been clearly and unmistakably aware of the role of trauma in the development of neurosis.

In 1909 Jung wrote the following words:

> What influences him [the growing child] more strongly than anything else is his particular affective environment, of which his parents and teachers are totally unconscious. Concealed dissension between the parents, secret suffering, repressed and hidden desires all engender in the individual an affective state that slowly but surely, even though unconsciously, finds its way into the child's psyche, where it produces the same state. . . . If adults are as sensitive as they are to the influence of their surroundings, then we must expect this to be true to an even greater extent for the child, whose mind is still as soft and malleable as wax.

I certainly cannot deny the truth of these remarks, for they are based on experiences paralleling my own. Since they are formulated in general terms and do not deal directly with the painful aspects of the subject, they are more easily acceptable to the public than Freud's "seduction" theory, which refers to a specific childhood trauma. Thus, Jung would not have had to contend with the same degree of rejection Freud did had Jung pursued to its logical conclusion the important truth about human existence he stated in 1909. But how little the external world counts for an adult (as opposed to a child) compared to the commandments of the internalized father, who in Jung's case was a theologian and minister. Consequently, the children who are mistreated and abused in their earliest years ultimately disappear in the forest of Jungian archetypes and the collective unconscious, just as they do in Freud's drive theory. The patient of a Jungian analyst, for instance, can allow himself to confront the "savage goddess Kali"—that is socially acceptable, because Kali is abstract and not the concrete mother. Then painful memories, such as being dragged across the floor as a child by his drunken mother, unfortunately will not have to come to the surface, and he will consequently be unable to free himself from the repetition compulsion. When he later reenacts his repressed experiences with his own child, other archetypal explanations can be offered.

What strange fruit can be produced by an intellectual construct that disguises the truth and how easily it can confuse even its highly gifted creator is indicated by Jung's words written in 1934 (already quoted on p. 87), which speak of the depths of the Aryan unconscious and the Germanic psyche, which is "anything but a garbage-bin of unrealizable infantile wishes and unresolved family resentments." This sentence relegates to the garbage bin not only Freud's insights but also those Jung himself advanced in 1909 concerning the crucial significance of childhood traumas.

The concealment of a previously recognized truth in the case of both famous thinkers of our century is tragic, but it is all too understandable in view of the strong influence their upbringing had on them. It is meaningful that these two such different intellectual systems are essentially concealing the same situation: the real traumatizations of the first years and the necessity of denying and repressing them by means of childhood amnesia. Freud, the Jewish son, atones for his forbidden insight with his drive theory, and Jung, the Protestant son, is united with his theological forefathers by locating all evil in an abstract and harmless unconscious that is oblivious to the concrete, individual realities of a specific childhood. The commandment "Thou shalt not be aware" gained a hearing in the later life of both thinkers. It was as though the forbidden fruit of the Tree of Knowledge had never been tasted.

If we analyze the development of Freud and Jung from this perspective, it will hardly seem a coincidence that in the entire body of professional literature after 1897 no one, at least no psychoanalyst, has as far as I know attempted to come to serious grips with Freud's trauma theory, despite the fact that of late there has been a striking increase in arguments in favor of it. This phenomenon would seem to be explained by my hypothesis that beginning with Freud the theory fell victim to the Fourth Commandment and that the force of the commandment also prevented other analysts from making use of these new discoveries in individual analysis.

It is scarcely possible for a psychoanalyst to believe that what happens in early childhood will have no influence on a person's later life. We can no longer assume, as our forebears did, that "the strictness that must prevail will have no after-effects." As a result, waking up to the cruelty inflicted in childhood comes as a shock to anyone who no longer refuses to see the power imbalance between parents and child. Those who do not seek protection from the effect of such a shock by retreating behind the drive theory will be inclined to favor group therapy over individual therapy or to construct the theory of the collective unconscious and thereby escape once again the danger of coming into conflict with the Fourth Commandment.

These considerations help me to understand why so many analysts seem to shrink from their own discoveries. An example of this is offered by Helm Stierlin in *Separating Parents and Adolescents* (1974) when he uses the parable of the Prodigal Son to illustrate his therapeutic goals. The son returns from death to life by obediently coming back to his father, claims Stierlin, who thus, although he knows better, assigns obedience its biblical value. This means that the father designates as death everything that separated his son from him—the son's youthful disobedience occurring at a time when the father was not part of his life—and describes as life his son's return: *"For this my son was dead, and is alive again; he was lost, and is found"* (cf. Stierlin, p. xi). Since Stierlin sees it as his therapeutic task to bring about a reconciliation between children and parents, he doesn't notice that he is identifying with the father's interests, at least in this case, or that the son finds his way back to his father and wins his love *by being obedient*. Stierlin does not realize that a restoration of harmony is being celebrated here only at the price of the son's acquiescence in his father's definition of everything that separated his son from him as "death." In terms of the symbolism of this scene, one could say that in Stierlin's therapeutic endeavors to bring about reconciliation, the relevance of his concept of delegation and its usefulness to the profession must be sacrificed for the sake of reunion with the father.

A similar phenomenon can be found in the case of Horst Eberhard Richter. The same author who in 1963 published a brilliant book, *Eltern, Kind, Neurose* (Parents, Child, Neurosis), which described parental power and the child's victimization within the family with virtually unprecedented accuracy, speaks in 1979 in his book *Der Gotteskomplex* (translated into English in 1983 with the title *All Mighty*) of the child's escape from fantasized, fatal helplessness into narcissistic omnipotence. How did it come about that one of the leading experts on the child's family situation now refers to *fantasized* and no longer *real* helplessness? Furthermore, how can we explain the fact that someone who sees and describes the formative influence of the social milieu on adults as clearly, empathically, and with such dedication as Richter can do so without any concern for the very earliest imprints? This would not be so puzzling in itself, for a great many professional psychologists still do not know how markedly and lastingly the individual is shaped by his or her childhood. But Richter already knew this full well in 1963. What became of his knowledge?

Without a doubt it is a great relief for anyone who finds a supportive person in the figure of an individual or group therapist, someone who does not attribute all the patient's suffering and symptoms to drive conflicts but who regards the severe and very real burdens of living in today's society as serious traumas because he suffers from them himself. If, however, the person seeking help has fallen prey to depression (as a result of the denial of childhood trauma), he is not likely to find any lasting relief as a result of interpretations critical of social conditions. Although it is comforting (and essential) for someone to know that he is not the only one with feelings of indignation, rage, helplessness, anxiety, and worry —over the nuclear arms race, the exploitation of human beings, and

the growing dangers of technology—and that he is being sustained
by the shared (conscious!) feelings within the group, this form of
support cannot reach the early, unconscious roots of the depression.
Depression is not caused by suffering from a present-day situation.
This is why there may be people who suffer from the state of today's
world and devote all their energies to bringing about change without becoming depressed or grandiose (cf. *Drama of the Gifted
Child*, pp. 99–102).

In the preceding pages I have addressed myself to three arguments advanced by family therapists without discussing their techniques. The following case outline presented by Luc Ciompi can
serve as an example of the extent to which the values of "poisonous
pedagogy" can lead a family therapist to assume a judgmental role
in his practice.

> A talented young man, now 30, the only son of the wealthy, authori-
> tarian owner of a large farm, had been told since childhood that he
> must follow in his father's footsteps and take over the family farm,
> even though this was contrary to his own inclinations [cf. here
> Stierlin's concept of "delegation"]. His father keeps him from going
> to an academic secondary school because this might put "other ideas"
> in his head. From that time on (approximately age 11) the boy becomes
> eccentric and "strange."—Outbreak of a severe catatonic-mutistic
> psychosis at age 18 the very day after the agricultural school's entrance
> examination that he had taken (and passed) to please his parents.
> Immediate chronicity, hospitalization for several years until the father
> finally has to sell the farm and become a traveling salesman! Gradual
> improvement since that time; almost uncannily sensitive insight into
> his own illness; in a private session, for example, he immediately
> understands that he was ultimately "the stronger" of the two and had
> forced his father to his knees; the latter in the meantime has joined a
> parents' group and preaches to the other members about parents hav-
> ing to let their children choose for themselves. . . . Until recently their
> strong feelings of guilt toward each other seemed too overpowering
> and explosive to attempt therapy that would uncover the truth.

The patient "immediately understands" that he had forced his
father to his knees, and the accompanying guilt feelings, intensified
by the therapist's attitude, are interpreted as the patient's insight
into his illness. Aside from the fact that a traveling salesman does
not work "on his knees," there are more than a few farmers in

Switzerland who sell their land for development and take up a new
career. The resultant guilt feelings toward these farmers' own parents can be dealt with more successfully if the sale of the family
property is explained by saying that their children are not interested
in becoming farmers. This may sometimes be the real reason but
need not lead to blaming the child. What was the son's guilt in this
particular case? In his therapist's eyes, apparently the fact that he
suffered for many years from a severe catatonic-mutistic psychosis.
Shouldn't this catastrophe be sufficient to indicate to the therapist
the panic it would cause the only son of an authoritarian father if
he were to resist openly his father's determination to make a farmer
out of him? To work with the patient to uncover his anxiety and the
real threat causing it seems like too risky an undertaking to the
therapist; he prefers to speak of "strong feelings of guilt toward each
other" and presumably will appeal to both parties to be forgiving or
will apply other strategies. It is no wonder that this therapist makes
every effort to systematize psychoanalysis and to destroy its last
remaining signs of life. For whatever reasons, he is obviously prevented from appreciating what is vital about psychoanalysis (without systematization!).

After *The Drama of the Gifted Child* appeared, a German analyst wrote to ask me whether my "taking the victim's side" was at
all compatible with psychoanalysis. As far as I am concerned, psychoanalysis is unthinkable without taking sides in this way. I know
such an act must be forbidden under any totalitarian regime since
this question struck me at the time as symptomatic for the second
generation in a country that had experienced a twelve-year dictatorship. Ever since I have given more attention to the attitudes
of psychotherapists and analysts, however, I realize that Germany
is no exception here and that it is very much in vogue all over the
world *not* to take the side of the victim, to deny that victimization
has occurred, and to develop new strategies to "influence the system"
from a pedagogical perspective. Unfortunately, all the new and creative attempts, be they transactional analysis or Gestalt therapy,
insist on making reconciliation with the parents the ultimate goal of
therapy. But efforts in this direction frequently undo the progress
that has been made, not only in the area of theory, but also in
therapeutic practice.

If it should become possible for a patient to gain access to the true feelings of his childhood by means of various techniques (e.g., the empty chair in Gestalt therapy, the group situation in transactional analysis, or a session of family therapy), then he will soon be exhorted to admit that his fears are now groundless, his defiance no longer necessary, his need for acceptance long since met by the group—to be sure, without his noticing it. He will also be told that he doesn't only hate his parents but also loves them and that what they did wrong was done only out of love. The adult patient already knows all this, but he is glad to hear it again because it helps him once more to deny, pacify, and control the child within him who has just begun to cry. In this way, the therapist or the group or he himself will talk the child out of his "silly" feelings because they are no longer appropriate in the present situation (although still intense); a process that could have produced positive results—namely, the awakening and maturation of the child's true self—will be undermined by a method of treatment that refuses to offer support to the angry child.

When I read the transcripts or see the videotapes of sessions of this kind, it seems to me that an attempt is being made to rescue something (not someone) at all costs, i.e., the *good name* of an authority figure. For no one's life would have to be saved, no one would have to die if one of the patients in the group were to direct his or her hate-filled reproaches at the imaginary parents sitting in the chair without having to search for the parents' "positive sides." Perhaps the therapist's unconscious aggression toward his own parents is so strong at times that he indeed needs the group to help assuage it. But no matter how strong the therapist's aggression, it is still only a feeling, and his parents, whom he sees in the empty chair, are not really sitting there. If these rescue operations were abandoned, no one would actually be harmed; only the idealized image, only the *fantasized parents* in the chair would be wounded, offended, angry, and would perhaps become threatening. But what can a therapist hope to achieve if he believes even this risk must be avoided?

In my opinion, Arthur Janov's primal therapy has recognized the liberating significance of grief to an extent that probably no other form of therapy has; moreover, as I understand it, he does not attempt, as many therapists do, to bring about a reconciliation with the parents or make the patient undergo corrective experiences for the sake of sparing the parents and covering up past traumas. But since I have had no practical experience with primal therapy and have not yet been able to see any video presentations, my impressions are based solely on reading Janov's books. As for Casriel's scream therapy, when I watched videotapes I was struck by the way the liberating force of the painful experiences facilitated by the group is canceled out by the illusion of having found the "good" mother in the group or in the group leader. For this only involves a new denial of reality (since as an adult one can no longer find the mother of one's early childhood), and the first steps toward healing already present—including the experience of pain (grief), which is the precondition for coming to terms with the past—will be taken in vain if the patient is allowed to fall victim to this illusion. The positive side of scream therapy as practiced by Janov, Casriel, and others can certainly be useful once it is understood that empathic support is (absolutely!) essential if early traumas are to be reexperienced, whereas there is no room for illusions that supposedly "make up for the past."

Because I repeatedly emphasize that it is not one of my therapeutic goals to bring about the adult patient's reconciliation with his or her still-living parents, as urged by Stierlin and other family therapists, this of course does not mean that the patient's growing familiarity with the internalized parents of his early childhood (his introjects) will not give him a large measure of freedom. But this intrapsychic reconciliation has little in common with the return of the Prodigal Son, and therefore there is no need for any pedagogical pressure in this direction. Rather, it is the result of reliving earlier traumas with intense feelings of anger, rage, impotence, despair, helplessness, and—eventually—grief. From this experience the parents as they once were emerge more and more clearly: they are not so strong as they then appeared, but neither are they so powerless as they are now that they are older; not so clever as they pretended to be, but also not so stupid as the patient experienced them in his emotional reliving of the past; not so bad as many of their actions indicated, but also not so good as the patient wanted to believe; and above all, not so truthful and trustworthy as they wanted their child to believe—and as the patient needed to think they were.

To become reconciled with these parents does not mean to beg their forgiveness on bended knee, like the Prodigal Son; it merely means to find out what one's parents were really like (one's own parents, not one's siblings') and to accept this fact. Such acceptance is a part of the process of mourning and is thus connected with the patient's emotional awakening to the reality of his childhood. Learning to feel, which leads to acknowledging and accepting the past, has the function of uncovering the truth; moral imperatives do not apply to it and it cannot be brought about by pedagogical exhortations, which at the most have the opposite effect —that is, they conceal childhood reality, which then can—and must—express itself only in the form of repeated reenactments. Becoming reconciled with one's introjects thus provides protection from the repetition compulsion, at least in the area of those traumas that have now been consciously experienced. This form of reconciliation simply means that the patient has become familiar with the figures living inside him, whom he no longer blindly permits to direct his actions; he is less at their mercy, because he now knows them well and knows approximately what to expect and what not to expect from them. I have explained on various occasions what I mean by coming to terms with the introjects (cf. *The Drama of the Gifted Child*, pp. 108–9).

Group therapy's attempt to rescue the "good name" of authority figures corresponds to psychoanalysis's attempts to interpret the patient's plight in terms of the drive theory. Even René Spitz, who discovered the phenomenon of hospitalism and did pioneering work in identifying traumatic factors in the infant's environment, tried to adapt his vocabulary to that of the timeworn drive theory.

Initially, Heinz Kohut also used the same terminology, which sounds very out of place alongside his sensitive and empathic case studies. In spite of knowing better, many original and creative thinkers, such as Michael Balint and Masud Khan, tried to maintain connections between their findings and Freud's drive theory. Even Donald W. Winnicott made repeated efforts to adhere to the terminology of Melanie Klein. In his case, the incongruity is particularly striking, for psychoanalysis has him to thank, more than almost anyone else, for some of its most profound and creative impulses. Basically, Winnicott offers proof that psychoanalysis need not observe its dogmas in order to exist. His published findings are an inexhaustible but often still untapped goldmine of information for every analyst, due to the fact that in his practice he was able to free himself from the constraints of dogma. Yet in his writings he often tries to do justice to Kleinian theories, and this may explain why many analysts say they have trouble understanding him. Reading Winnicott's *Piggle* made me particularly aware of the discrepancy between the openness of his approach and the occasional limitations imposed by his use of Klein's concepts.*

At first glance, Margret S. Mahler, on the other hand, does not seem compelled to adapt to the categories of the drive theory. She simply delineates her findings, which—like those of René Spitz—point to a wide variety of traumatizations, but since she tries to derive her patients' material from standard occurrences (such as the stage of separation), she is able to avoid coming into conflict with the Fourth Commandment. Yet conflict can scarcely be circumvented if due consideration is given to the significance of repressed trauma in a patient's individual history. Today, to be sure, a new point of view has emerged, at least regarding Freud's four-year-old "Oedipus" and Klein's "cruel infant," because environmental factors are being given more attention in connection with the pathogenesis of neurosis. This is clearly the case with Kohut, Mahler, Masterson, Winnicott, Khan, Bowlby, and others. However, in their theoretical writings (as opposed to their case presentations), they all attempt to identify in the child's development something resembling objective, universal factors, which might play a role in pathogenesis. They refer to a lack of closeness and empathy (Kohut), difficulties arising in the stage of separation (Mahler), being devoured or deprived of affection in one's attempts at autonomy (Masterson), lack of a holding mother (Winnicott) or of

---

* It unquestionably helped the little girl (Piggle) that at the time of her great crisis she was able to express herself in play and in words to a listening, attentive, sincere, and creative person. But we will never know what might have happened if the therapist had violated Kleinian principles by asking what Piggle's mother was trying to communicate to Winnicott through her daughter's neurosis, at least after she herself wrote that when she was Piggle's age her mother gave birth to a son; Piggle's mother rejected her new brother. Moreover, Winnicott knew that she came from Germany and had probably spent her childhood there during the war. If he had been completely free to pursue his fantasies, he might have asked whether the "black mommy" who upset not only Piggle but, even more, her mother, didn't have something to do with the mother's own childhood experiences.

maternal protection from overwhelming stimuli (Khan), absence of the father, etc. Of course, all these factors have traumatic significance but perhaps would not necessarily lead to neurosis if they could be experienced as painful traumas. Yet this is the very thing that is impossible with parents a child must fear or spare; as a result, the trauma will then be repressed, and it is the repression that produces neurosis. For this reason, I consider it important that psychoanalysis (or psychotherapy) not go along with this compulsion to spare the parents. Only then can it help the patient to relive his or her traumatic experience, thereby nullifying the role repression had in causing neurosis. A theoretical formulation of this insight does not yet exist, although we can see steps being taken in that direction. I detect it in the recent work of John Bowlby, who has remained aware of the reality of early childhood in spite of his psychoanalytic training. Jan Bastiaans is also trying to apply the discoveries he has made about early traumatic experiences (by means of treatment using LSD) to psychoanalytic theory and practice.

I must content myself here with these brief remarks, for it was not my intention to deal in any great detail with the work of these specific analysts. What I have tried to do is merely use them as illustrations to clarify a general situation: namely, the way individual analysts shrink in later life from their own findings and return to earlier ways of thinking they had already left behind.

Psychiatrists who treat young schizophrenics are often witness to the incredible torment and victimization children can be subjected to. If, nonetheless, they routinely close their eyes to the truth or suppress this knowledge, preferring to speak in terms of "inherited," "congenital" psychosis, or of complicated theories that conceal the most obvious facts, there must be important reasons for this. No one who has read the manuals of "poisonous pedagogy" with care and has been open to their import will have difficulty understanding what these reasons are. The parents' right to victimize their children and the child's fear of destroying his parents (thereby losing them) if he perceives his own victimization prevents many gifted therapists from giving full weight to their findings. Sparing the parents is our supreme law; under its sway the Abrahams of this world sacrifice their Isaacs over and over again, unless God, touched by His sons' obedience, should take pity on them. If, however, future Isaacs someday want to understand why they should be expected to wait quietly, with hands bound, for their father's knife to descend, then it might come to pass that even psychoanalysis may be willing to incorporate the ubiquitous social phenomenon of the victimization of children into its theory. Not only would this have far-reaching implications for analytic practice, but with time the victimization might even diminish, since its justification, which has prevailed for millennia, would be seriously challenged by the introduction of psychoanalytic material.

And yet, in spite of widespread societal repression, in spite of our parents' need to be spared, the victimization of children is actually no secret. Their sacrifice is certainly not glossed over in the Bible, and we learned in school that in Sparta babies who were sickly were put to death; these facts have never been disputed. Even today, it is still taken for granted in certain circles that a pregnant woman, instead of seeking an abortion, should subject her unwanted child to a life of being shunted from one foster home to the next (sometimes totaling as many as fifteen). Equally familiar are cases where parents cruelly domineer their already grown children by forcing them into careers or marriages they don't want. Countless novelists have recognized and candidly described these tragedies.

All of this, then, is no secret, nor is it anything new. Perhaps all that is new is the recognition that the individuals involved, and ultimately the whole society, must bear the consequences. Obvious as this assertion appears to some, it appears unacceptable to others, in whom it arouses intense resistance. But wouldn't analysts' therapeutic efforts have to be regarded as hypocritical if they were based on the assumption that victimization of the child—legitimized by society and even including the legal use of the child to satisfy the parents' needs, which is called child-rearing—does *not* have far-reaching consequences for the future "patient" and for society? Such an assumption is apparently possible for analysts today because the drive theory can protect them from any reality, no matter how dreadful. How long can this continue to be the case?

If psychoanalysis is not to lose contact with present-day reality, is not to alienate itself through its technical jargon suited to computer use and comprehensible only to those few experts willing to make the effort, then it must at the very least integrate into its theories the scientific evidence gleaned from modern studies of childhood. It must take into account those phenomena that were less well known or even totally unknown in Freud's day but that have come to light over the past twenty years (thanks in part to his own methods): namely, parents' self-discoveries, adults' projections onto the child, use of the child as outlet and victim, the power game, mistreatment and sexual abuse of the child, and the ideology of "poisonous pedagogy." As long as these factors are disregarded as "unanalytic material," psychoanalytic theory will be of little relevance and will not be equipped to contribute to an understanding of the contemporary human condition.

As far as psychoanalytic practice is concerned, it could be demonstrated that, even within the classical setting, the following goals are attainable:

1. To apply what we know about childhood (as outlined on pp. 196–97, nos. 1–6) to what we hear in the analytic session.

2. To be aware of the socially sanctioned role of the child as an outlet for the adult's pent-up feelings.

3. To be aware of the traces of "poisonous pedagogy" within ourselves and to have more respect for the patient as a result.

4. To relinquish pedagogical goals for the sake of creativity.

As I have repeatedly stressed, the ability to perceive and understand someone else's suffering depends more than anything else on the degree to which one has experienced the suffering of one's own childhood. I see this as the first step in becoming sensitive to what actually happens in childhood. Someone who has reached this emotional level knows it is not sentimentality that comes into play here; rather, the ability to feel sharpens our sensitivity, i.e., our vision, thus enabling us to see the other person's situation and the hidden cruelty in society's institutions. For example, only *one* obstetrician had to gain access to his feelings in order for the cruelty of present-day childbirth methods to be exposed (see Frédéric Leboyer, *Birth Without Violence*). Astonishingly enough, virtually no one had noticed this cruelty before. Therefore, when I speak and write about the desirability of becoming sensitized to the narcissistic needs and wounds of early childhood, I am by no means trying to arouse feelings of pity but to awaken an understanding of those conditions that are concealed from us as a result of our having been forbidden to feel.

Sometimes I have to ask myself how many children's corpses psychoanalysts require as proof before they will stop ignoring their patients' childhood suffering or trying to talk them out of it with the aid of the drive theory. It is unlikely that analysts will be able to alter the incidence of child abuse, but as long as they go on espousing theories that can be used to deny and cover up flagrant mistreatment, they will prevent their patients as well as the general public from becoming conscious of the truth. They will be lending support to the collective repression of a phenomenon whose consequences directly affect each one of us.

We cannot expect parents' child-rearing practices to change in a single generation, for they are deeply rooted in the internalizations of early childhood. One would think, however, that people could give up theories learned during adolescence and even later at college age if these theories run counter to experience and new information. This would no doubt be the case if the content of the theories as well as belief in the infallibility of the great authorities who advanced them were not grounded in the ideology of "poisonous pedagogy."

Many professionals respond to the new information available about child abuse with insensitivity and indifference, which I assume are primarily a reflection of their loyalty to theory and not of their own heartlessness. Their reaction is a particularly clear indication of the dangers of the theory in question. These dangers stem from the simple fact that psychoanalysts are forced back into the framework of "poisonous pedagogy," from which they had hoped to free themselves with the help of their psychoanalytic training, and that they force their patients back with them. For when Freudian theory prescribes that patients' reports about their childhood are to be regarded as fantasies originating in drive conflicts and not in real experiences, the analyst continues to be insensitive to childhood suffering. This has the following consequences:

1. Analysts will have to make light of their own childhood suffering and will be unable to help the patient become sensitive to his or her suffering but will, on the contrary, minimize it the same way they did in their own case and the same way all well-raised

children do. Then the emotional grounds for minimizing it can be legitimized and shrouded in mystery in conjunction with the drive theory.

2. When patients make uncertain and anxious attempts to portray the atmosphere of humiliation, mistreatment, or psychological rape they were once subjected to, their perceptions will be interpreted as drive fantasies or projections of their own desires. This will make patients (a) stop expressing their grievances; (b) feel ashamed for having them; (c) dwell on guilt feelings; and (d) repress their traumatization again, this time more deeply than before. Such a process will add greatly to their self-alienation. Autonomy cannot develop, and as a result, patients will often respond obediently to the analyst's pedagogic efforts without even noticing them. With this method of psychoanalysis, the patients' own truth will be buried, which can, to be sure, temporarily reinforce their resistance to their traumas, usually by means of intellectualization; yet in the long run this approach will increase the likelihood of the incidence of new depression.

3. If patients are not given the opportunity to air their grievances against their parents and educators—which is more often the case than not—then of course they don't have to be talked out of their "negative attitudes" at all; the analyst can simply build directly upon their "good upbringing" and teach them very quickly how they "can learn to understand their parents better and forgive them." The religious notion that a "gesture of forgiveness" will make you a better person has also found its way into psychoanalytic treatment. As if this gesture could do away with something slumbering deep within a person since childhood that can be articulated only in neurosis. Who would know this better than psychoanalysts, had they not reached an agreement that the true nature of childhood should not be the subject of their investigations?

The drive theory, then, entails denial of reality, insensitivity to childhood suffering, refusal to give credence to the patient's grievances—which ultimately means refusal to take him or her seriously —and, above all, misunderstanding and denial of the roots of neurosis. As I have already emphasized more than once, it is my belief that these roots lie in the enforced repression not of the child's so-called instinctual drives but of his or her awareness of having been traumatized and in the prohibition against articulating this, which was internalized at a very early age. Freudian drive theory reinforces this prohibition to the fullest because it is still caught up in the system of assigning blame and thinks parents must be protected from their children's recriminations. Since guilt must be assigned in this system, it is the child's drives and, just as in "poisonous pedagogy," ultimately the child himself who is found guilty. Presumably, his aggressions and the sexual desires he blames his parents for not fulfilling are what often make his parents (by projection) "appear" cruel to him. Thus, cruelty on the part of parents is always interpreted as the product of the child's drive fantasies, generated by the child's own cruelty. For this cruelty is always real and present for the psychoanalyst (as it is for the pedagogue/educator). Significantly, in classical psychoanalytic literature I have never encountered the question of what actually becomes of children's cruelty later when they grow up and have children of their own. As if, when children attain the power accompanying adulthood, such questions would automatically disappear. This interpretation can be observed most clearly in the Kleinian literature. I have selected some of Klein's definitions, taken from Hanna Segal's *Introduction to the Work of Melanie Klein.*

> ANXIETY: is considered to be the ego's response to the operation of the death instinct. When the death instinct is deflected it takes two major forms:
>
> *Paranoid Anxiety* is due to the projection of the death instinct into an object or objects which are then experienced as persecutors. The anxiety is lest these persecutors should annihilate the ego and the ideal object. It originates in the paranoid–schizoid position.
>
> *Depressive Anxiety* is the anxiety lest one's own aggression should annihilate or has annihilated one's good object. It is experienced on behalf of the object and on behalf of the ego, which feels threatened in identification with the object. It originates in the depressive position, when the object is perceived as a whole object and the infant experiences his own ambivalence.
>
> *Castration Anxiety* is mainly of a paranoid type originating in the child's projection of his own aggression, but it may contain depressive elements as well; for instance, the anxiety of losing one's penis as an organ of reparation.
>
> BIZARRE OBJECTS: are the outcome of pathological projective identifications in which the object is perceived as split into minute fragments, each containing a projected part of the self. These

bizarre objects are experienced as being charged with great hostility. . . .

Early Envy is experienced by the infant mainly in relation to the feeding breast. It is possibly the earliest external manifestation of the death instinct as it attacks what is felt to be the source of life. . . .

Persecutors are objects into whom part of the death instinct has been projected. They give rise to paranoid anxiety. . . .

Envy can fuse with greed, making for a wish to exhaust the object entirely, not only in order to possess all its goodness but also to deplete the object purposefully so that it no longer contains anything enviable. It is the admixture of envy which often makes greed so spoiling and so apparently intractable in analytic treatment. But envy does not stop at exhausting the external object. The very nourishment that has been taken in, so long as it is perceived as having been part of the breast, is in itself an object of envious attacks, which are turned upon the internal object as well. Envy operates also by projection and often mainly so. When the infant feels himself to be full of anxiety and badness and the breast to be the source of all goodness, in his envy he wishes to spoil the breast by projecting into it bad and spoiling parts of himself; thus, in phantasy, the breast is attacked by spitting, urinating, defaecating, passing of wind, and by projective, penetrating looking (the evil eye). As development proceeds, these attacks are continued in relation to the mother's body and her babies, and the parental relationship. In cases of pathological development in the Oedipus complex, envy of the parental relationship plays a more important rôle than true feelings of jealousy. [pp. 125–28, 41]

A theory such as Klein's can have been advanced only by someone who herself has found the infant to be wicked, greedy, and threatening. This attitude occurs frequently because many people see their own parents or siblings in the infant. The only way infants can defend themselves against all that is ascribed to them is with violent feelings or, if these are forbidden, with depression ("depressive position"!) and other symptoms. But these are *reactions to parental feelings* and not manifestations of innate drives, for many cases can be observed of infants who do not demonstrate the behavior described by Klein because the mother does not experience them as greedy, demanding monsters who want to destroy her breast out of envy but as hungry little creatures still groping in the dark who are testing things and sometimes lose their patience quickly if everything doesn't work out immediately and if the indispensable object is not available. Parental attitudes have a decisive effect on the child's behavior and development. The same is true in therapy. Our attitude has a crucial influence on our diagnosis of the patient; it determines whether he is a person who is suffering (from anger and hatred) or an evil, envy-filled, incurable case. This is why the therapist is always "right," and a proponent of the Kleinian approach will always be able to produce "proof" for this theory. It cannot be otherwise.

If we grasp the implications of Hanna Segal's definitions, it will not surprise us that psychoanalysts usually do not lose their composure when they hear reports of child abuse and that they fail to make any connection between these facts and their theories. They have already disposed of "evil" by locating it in the young child and his or her drives. We might not begrudge them the peace of mind their theories provide if it were not disquieting to think that they are the ones so many people turn to in their attempt to be rescued from neurosis, people who were narcissistically and often sexually mistreated, violated, and abused as children and who need help in interpreting the information revealed in their symptoms and in regaining their original vitality. Tragically, they cannot receive the help they need from the drive theory; the most they can achieve is to reinforce their defense mechanisms against what they know to be the truth and to make their adaptation to society more rigid, thereby cutting themselves off from access to their own self. This self is like a prisoner in a cell; no one believes in his innocence, and as a result, rather than remain alone and isolated with the truth, he too finally loses all knowledge of it (cf. *The Drama of the Gifted Child*, pp. 10–14). Only by sacrificing his true self does he reestablish ties to other people.

The advice regularly given in the old pedagogical manuals was to "break" the child's will at as early an age as possible, to combat his "obstinacy," and always to impart to him the feeling that he is guilty and bad; they stressed that one should never allow the impression to arise that an adult might be wrong or make a mistake, should never give the child an opportunity to discover adult limitations, but that the adult should, on the contrary, conceal his or her weaknesses from the child and pretend to divine authority. Later, if this child becomes a patient, it might be that during analysis he will realize for the first time that something essential is being "taken away" from him, i.e., his own way of expressing himself, and that his analyst is treating him just as his parents did earlier when he was still too little to be conscious of it. This is a form of psychological castration, which unfortunately may be repeated in analysis if the analyst assumes a didactic attitude. Even if he does not, it is still possible for the patient to experience him as the "castrating father" if he indeed had that kind of father. Only by granting the patient the right to do this and by not regarding his fears as paranoid delusions but as a long-overdue breakthrough of repressed perceptions can the analyst avoid taking on the parents' castrating attitude and instead enable the patient to make "new discoveries."

I can't help it if my attempt to point out the societal (and in my opinion pernicious) function of the drive theory offends or wounds certain Freudians or Kleinians. When I exposed the ideology behind child-rearing with the aid of the manuals of "poisonous pedagogy" (see pp. 8–63 in *For Your Own Good*), many parents felt I was attacking them personally and reacted with guilt feelings, in keeping with their upbringing and without realizing I was only pointing to a system of which they, too, were victims and will continue to be until they see the system for what it really is.

My criticism of the drive theory represents a similar attempt to expose its true nature, and it is not my intention to blame specific individuals for teaching and promulgating this theory, since I am convinced that they themselves are victims of a pedagogical attitude that is difficult to see through. Of course, no one has to share my conviction, but those who do will understand why my attack on the drive theory as well as on "poisonous pedagogy" is not an attack on individual colleagues or parents. I have been obliged to mention names of psychoanalytic authors because I need examples, but I have purposely used the names of those therapists whose work and originality I esteem, and some of them are aware of this.

Sometimes my view that mental illness is the result of repressed traumas is met with the objection that early childhood traumatizations cannot be "unearthed" in analysis. In the first place, this does not correspond to my experience, for I have frequently found the opposite to be true. I do not doubt, however, that certain attitudes on the part of the analyst impede or prevent earlier memories from coming to the surface. In the second place, the question of the etiology of mental illness does not depend on the success of any one analyst in getting through to the traumatizations of early childhood. The basic question is: What method must be developed in order to bring to consciousness material that once had to be repressed for the sake of survival?

Among the reasons Freud gave for rejecting his trauma theory he included the fact that genuine cures gradually became much less frequent and took longer than they had in the beginning. If it is true that the earlier treatments were successful and brief, then the decline in success does not argue against the trauma theory but can be explained by the circumstance that Freud, under pressure of the Fourth Commandment and his own guilt feelings, was beginning to doubt the conclusions he had drawn earlier. That was sufficient to make it impossible for his patients to relive and acknowledge their traumas, for the supportive function of the analyst was missing. We still find this situation to be prevalent today.

The repression of early childhood trauma required in our society by the Fourth Commandment leads to a state of collective repression, which is also at work in the analyst's office. This appears to be no different today than it was in the year 1897, when Freud wrote his famous letter to Fliess giving his reasons for abandoning the trauma theory. An easily understandable note of depression can be detected in this letter.

His conscious reason for backing away from his earlier theory is first and foremost the increasing number of failures in treatment, and it is significant that Freud makes use of arguments he had very convincingly refuted a year earlier in "The Aetiology of Hysteria," a work that met with great resistance at the time. But we must not overlook the fact that in his detailed argumentation of 1897 there is the sentence: "Then there was the astonishing thing that in every case blame was laid on perverse acts by the father, my own not excluded" (see *Origins of Psychoanalysis*, p. 215).*

---

* In the original German edition of 1950 and in the authorized English translation the phrase "my own not excluded" has been replaced with ellipsis. What could have moved the editors to omit such an important phrase if not the desire to spare an internalized "authority figure"? In a footnote they make the following comment on Freud's decision: "It seems reasonable to assume that it was only the self-analysis of this summer that made possible rejection of the

Marianne Krüll's book, *Freud und sein Vater* (Freud and His Father), contains an extremely careful study of Freud's relationship with his father and the role it played in causing him to abandon the trauma theory. Her arguments are very convincing; however, I believe it is not only Freud's personal history that is important here but also a certain aspect of our culture, overshadowed as it is by a particular kind of image of the father and the Deity. God the Father is easily offended, jealous, and basically insecure; He therefore demands obedience and conformity in the expression of ideas, tolerates no graven images and—since "graven images" included works of art for the Hebrew God—no creativity either. He dictates beliefs and imposes punishment on apostates, persecutes the guilty with a vengeance, permits His sons to live only according to His principles and to find happiness only on His terms.

It is fear of this God/father figure that made the drive theory into dogma and causes so many new discoveries to be rejected the way God rejected the graven images of His people.

> For the carved images of the nations are a sham,
>   they are nothing but timber cut from the forest,
>   worked with his chisel by a craftsman;
> he adorns it with silver and gold . . .
> They can no more speak than a scarecrow in a plot of cucumbers;
>   they must be carried, for they cannot walk.

---

seduction theory." Quite aside from the fact that in 1896 Freud was not talking about "hypotheses" but about empirical findings (cf. pp. 110–11 above) and that it was in regard to the drive theory that he first put forward a hypothesis (which later had to be made dogma for the simple reason that it is *not* empirically verifiable), I think it correct to assume that the trauma theory was abandoned of necessity in the course of Freud's self-analysis because it is not possible to relive one's own early traumas without the help of an empathic, supportive, and nonjudgmental person (who was not available to Freud); otherwise the pain and fear of revenge on the part of the offended internalized figure would be intolerable. On the basis of numerous passages from his correspondence with Fliess, it is obvious that the latter was poorly equipped to play this supportive role. Once the unabridged correspondence is released for publication, we will certainly learn more of this subject. Meanwhile, random statements of Freud's can be found even now that shed light on the unconscious motives behind his step, which had such far-reaching repercussions. In this book, however, I do not see it as my task to analyze the early childhood of Sigmund Freud but rather to indicate the overall, societal motives that were decisive not only for Freud but for Jung and many other thinkers in making them relinquish the trauma theory (cf. p. 201 above).

Do not be afraid of them: they can do no harm,
and they have no power to do good. . . .
They are fools and blockheads one and all,
learning their nonsense from a log of wood. . . .
all are the work of craftsmen and goldsmiths . . .
    all the work of skilled men.
But the Lord is God in truth,
    a living god, an eternal king.
The earth quakes under his wrath,
    nations cannot endure his fury. [Jeremiah, Chapter 10]

And elsewhere in Jeremiah we read:

Beware, I am sending snakes against you,
    vipers, such as no man can charm,
        and they shall bite you.
        This is the very word of the Lord. . . .
These are the words of the Lord:
    Let not the wise man boast of his wisdom
        nor the valiant of his valour;
    let not the rich man boast of his riches;
    but if any man would boast, let him boast of this,
    that he understands and knows me.
For I am the Lord, I show unfailing love,
    I do justice and right upon the earth;
        for on these I have set my heart.
        This is the very word of the Lord. [Chapter 8]

This is the tradition from which Freud came. Unable to free himself from the emotional imprisonment it entailed, he was forced to abandon his great discovery concerning traumatization in early childhood.

Although we today are still part of that same religious and cultural tradition, now we know, at least theoretically, that only a very insecure and therefore very easily offended person becomes a tyrant; nevertheless, our intellectual knowledge has little effect on our fear of his tyranny, since this fear is rooted in childhood. However, there will always be those patients in analysis who are confronted with their parents' insecurity in such an intense and crucial way that they can no longer deny what they perceive to be true; they will also be the kind of people who no longer desire a Paradise whose autocratic ruler demands perfect obedience and renunciation of the search for knowledge.

There lived in the Land of Uz a man of blameless and upright life named Job, who feared God and set his face against wrongdoing. . . . The Lord asked Satan, "Have you considered my servant Job? You will find no one like him on earth, a man of blameless and upright life, who fears God and sets his face against wrongdoing." Satan answered the Lord, "Has not Job good reason to be God-fearing? Have you not hedged him round on every side with your protection, him and his family and all his possessions? Whatever he does you have blessed, and his herds have increased beyond measure. But stretch out your hand and touch all that he has, and then he will curse you to your face." Then the Lord said to Satan, "So be it. All that he has is in your hands; only Job himself you must not touch." And Satan left the Lord's presence.

When the day came that Job's sons and daughters were eating and drinking in the eldest brother's house, a messenger came running to Job and said, "The oxen were ploughing and the asses were grazing near them, when the Sabaeans swooped down and carried them off, after putting the herdsmen to the sword; and I am the only one to escape and tell the tale." While he was still speaking, another messenger arrived and said, "God's fire flashed from heaven. It struck the sheep and the shepherds and burnt them up; and I am the only one to escape and tell the tale." While he was still speaking, another arrived and said, "The Chaldaeans, three bands of them, have made a raid on the camels and carried them off, after putting the drivers to the sword; and I am the only one to escape and tell the tale." While this man was speaking, yet another arrived and said, "Your sons and daughters were eating and drinking in the eldest brother's house, when suddenly a whirlwind swept across from the desert and struck the four corners of the house, and it fell on the young people and killed them; and I am the only one to escape and tell the tale." At this Job stood up and rent his cloak; then he shaved his head and fell prostrate on the ground, saying:

> Naked I came from the womb,
> naked I shall return whence I came.
> The Lord gives and the Lord takes away;
> blessed be the name of the Lord.

Throughout all this Job did not sin; he did not charge God with unreason. . . .

Then the Lord asked Satan, "Have you considered my servant Job? You will find no one like him on earth, a man of blameless and upright life, who fears God and sets his face against wrongdoing. You incited me to ruin him without a cause, but his integrity is still unshaken." Satan answered the Lord, "Skin for skin! There is nothing the man will grudge to save himself. But stretch out your hand and touch his bone and his flesh, and see if he will not curse you to your face."

Then the Lord said to Satan, "So be it. He is in your hands; but spare his life." And Satan left the Lord's presence, and he smote Job with running sores from head to foot, so that he took a piece of a broken pot to scratch himself as he sat among the ashes. Then his wife said to him, "Are you still unshaken in your integrity? Curse God and die!" But he answered, "You talk as any wicked fool of a woman might talk. If we accept good from God, shall we not accept evil?" Throughout all this, Job did not utter one sinful word.

When Job's three friends, Eliphaz of Teman, Bildad of Shuah, and Zophar of Naamah, heard of all these calamities which had overtaken him, they left their homes and arranged to come and condole with him and comfort him. But when they first saw him from a distance, they did not recognize him; and they wept aloud, rent their cloaks and tossed dust into the air over their heads. For seven days and seven nights they sat beside him on the ground, and none of them said a word to him; for they saw that his suffering was very great.

After this Job broke silence and cursed the day of his birth:

> Perish the day when I was born
> and the night which said, "A man is conceived"!
> May that day turn to darkness; may God above not look for it,
> nor light of dawn shine on it.
>
> May blackness sully it, and murk and gloom,
> cloud smother that day, swift darkness eclipse its sun.
> Blind darkness swallow up that night;
> count it not among the days of the year,
> reckon it not in the cycle of the months.
> That night, may it be barren forever,
> no cry of joy be heard in it.
> Cursed be it by those whose magic binds even the monster of
>   the deep,
> who are ready to tame Leviathan himself with spells.
> May no star shine out in its twilight;
> may it wait for a dawn that never comes,
> nor ever see the eyelids of the morning,

because it did not shut the doors of the womb that bore me
and keep trouble away from my sight.
Why was I not still-born,
why did I not die when I came out of the womb?
Why was I ever laid on my mother's knees
or put to suck at her breasts?
Why was I not hidden like an untimely birth,
like an infant that has not lived to see the light?
For then I should be lying in the quiet grave,
asleep in death, at rest,
with kings and their ministers
who built themselves palaces,
with princes rich in gold
who filled their houses with silver.
There the wicked man chafes no more,
there the tired labourer rests;
the captive too finds peace there
and hears no taskmaster's voice;
high and low are there,
even the slave, free from his master.

Why should the sufferer be born to see the light?
Why is life given to men who find it so bitter?
They wait for death but it does not come,
they seek it more eagerly than hidden treasure.
They are glad when they reach the tomb,
and when they come to the grave they exult.
Why should a man be born to wander blindly,
hedged in by God on every side?
My sighing is all my food,
and groans pour from me in a torrent.
Every terror that haunted me has caught up with me,
and all that I feared has come upon me.
There is no peace of mind nor quiet for me;
I chafe in torment and have no rest.

Then Eliphaz the Temanite began:

If one ventures to speak with you, will you lose patience?
For who could hold his tongue any longer?
Think how once you encouraged those who faltered,
how you braced feeble arms,
how a word from you upheld the stumblers

and put strength into weak knees.
But now that adversity comes upon you, you lose patience;
it touches you, and you are unmanned.
Is your religion no comfort to you?
Does your blameless life give you no hope?
For consider, what innocent man has ever perished?
Where have you seen the upright destroyed?
This I know, that those who plough mischief and sow trouble
reap as they have sown;
they perish at the blast of God
and are shrivelled by the breath of his nostrils.

The roar of the lion, the whimpering of his cubs, fall silent;
the teeth of the young lions are broken;
the lion perishes for lack of prey
and the whelps of the lioness are abandoned.

A word stole into my ears,
and they caught the whisper of it;
in the anxious visions of the night,
when a man sinks into deepest sleep,
terror seized me and shuddering;
the trembling of my body frightened me.
A wind brushed my face
and made the hairs bristle on my flesh;
and a figure stood there whose shape I could not discern,
an apparition loomed before me,
and I heard the sound of a low voice:
"Can mortal man be more righteous than God,
or the creature purer than his Maker?
If God mistrusts his own servants
and finds his messengers at fault,
how much more those that dwell in houses whose walls are clay,
whose foundations are dust,
which can be crushed like a bird's nest
or torn down between dawn and dark,
how much more shall such men perish outright and unheeded,
die, without ever finding wisdom?"

Call if you will; is there any to answer you?
To which of the holy ones will you turn?
The fool is destroyed by his own angry passions,
and the end of childish resentment is death.

I have seen it for myself: a fool uprooted,
his home in sudden ruin about him,
his children past help,
browbeaten in court with none to save them.
Their rich possessions are snatched from them;
what they have harvested others hungrily devour;
the stronger man seizes it from the panniers,
panting, thirsting for their wealth.
Mischief does not grow out of the soil
nor trouble spring from the earth;
man is born to trouble,
as surely as birds fly upwards.

For my part, I would make my petition to God
and lay my cause before him,
who does great and unsearchable things,
marvels without number.
He gives rain to the earth
and sends water on the fields;
he raises the lowly to the heights,
the mourners are uplifted by victory;
he frustrates the plots of the crafty,
and they win no success,
he traps the cunning in their craftiness,
and the schemers' plans are thrown into confusion. . . .

Then the Lord said to Job:

Is it for a man who disputes with the Almighty to be stubborn?
Should he that argues with God answer back?

And Job answered the Lord:

What reply can I give thee, I who carry no weight?
I put my finger to my lips.
I have spoken once and now will not answer again;
twice have I spoken, and I will do so no more.

Then the Lord answered Job out of the tempest:

Brace yourself and stand up like a man;
I will ask questions, and you shall answer.
Dare you deny that I am just
or put me in the wrong that you may be right?

225

Have you an arm like God's arm,
can you thunder with a voice like his?
Deck yourself out, if you can, in pride and dignity,
array yourself in pomp and splendour;
unleash the fury of your wrath,
look upon the proud man and humble him;
look upon every proud man and bring him low,
throw down the wicked where they stand;
hide them in the dust together,
and shroud them in an unknown grave.
Then I in my turn will acknowledge
that your own right hand can save you. . . .

Can a man blind his eyes and take him
or pierce his nose with the teeth of a trap?
Can you fill his skin with harpoons
or his head with fish-hooks?
If ever you lift your hand against him,
think of the struggle that awaits you, and let be.

No, such a man is in desperate case,
hurled headlong at the very sight of him.
How fierce he is when he is roused!
Who is there to stand up to him?
Who has ever attacked him unscathed?
Not a man under the wide heaven. . . .

Then Job answered the Lord:

I know that thou canst do all things
and that no purpose is beyond thee.
But I have spoken of great things which I have not understood,
things too wonderful for me to know.
I knew of thee then only by report,
but now I see thee with my own eyes.
Therefore I melt away;
I repent in dust and ashes. . . .

Thereafter Job lived another hundred and forty years, he saw his
sons and his grandsons to four generations, and died at a very great
age. [from the Book of Job]

But the Truth Will Out

❀

I T may still be decades or even centuries before humankind stops regarding the knowledge stored up in the unconscious as immaterial, as pathological fantasies of the insane or of eccentric poets, and comes to see it for what it really is: a perception of reality, stemming from the period of early childhood, which had to be relegated to the unconscious, where it becomes an inexhaustible source of artistic creativity, of the imagination per se, of fairy tales and dreams. Once such knowledge is legitimized as pure imagination, all doors are opened to it. It can be admired as art, handed down in fairy tales as "the wisdom of the ages," and interpreted in our dreams as an expression of the never-changing archetypal collective unconscious. We are proud of this cultural heritage, of its wisdom, of "the knowledge of good and evil" we possess, but we do not have to let it affect us deeply unless we happen to be poets or insane ourselves. We can read fairy tales to our children because, after all, "they should also learn something about life's cruelty"; we can write with great detachment and intelligence about the baseness of society, yet not become emotionally aware of cruelty until the stones thrown by rebellious youth break our own windows. Then people whose profession involves the study of society—historians, for example, who have been teaching for years about the persecution of the Christians in ancient Rome, about the Crusades, the Inquisition, the burning of witches, and about history's countless wars—may say that the violence of our times is the result of children being raised permissively. Violence doesn't exist for these people until it is directed against them personally, because everything they learned in school and college has only an abstract and not a living significance for them.

The opposite is true of creative writers. They suffer from cruelty inflicted on others as well as on themselves, and they suffer doubly because usually they are isolated in their suffering, for no one wants to believe them. Often, people try to talk them out of their awareness in order not to have to become aware themselves. If these writers are not renowned they will be dismissed as fools, or, if famous, will be admired and celebrated as great prophets, but always with the proviso that the source of their awareness remain hidden from society. It has not been hard to meet this demand, for the source in question has been hidden from them too, deeply repressed in their unconscious; they have tended to be convinced that they had a higher or divine spirit or their own talent to thank for what they wrote. But if writers begin to describe their childhood, as has been happening more and more frequently in the past decade, then they will soon be confronted with the hostility of society, which sees the customs and rights it has enjoyed for thousands of years threatened.

The term "fairy tale" refers to something that isn't true. On the other hand, it is generally acknowledged that fairy tales convey deep insights into life, that they communicate truth in the form of vivid parables. A similar ambivalence can be observed in our attitude toward dreams. We often reassure ourselves with remarks like "It was only a dream" or even "Dreams don't mean anything"; yet anyone who works with the unconscious knows what an amazing amount of information dreams can provide about a person's life. This ambivalence is a reflection of our attitude toward truth per se: we want to know it and at the same time we don't because it hurts, can frighten us, places excessive demands on us, and robs us of the security of our cherished illusions.

~§ 18 ê~

Fairy Tales

A child asks, "Where do babies come from?" and is given the prompt reply "Out of the mother's tummy." But when this same child wants to know how the baby got into the mother's tummy, the answer is not as prompt and straightforward. I find myself in a situation similar to the child's when I do not content myself with the generally recognized fact that there is truth to dreams and fairy tales but would also like to know how this truth has come to be there. Then I am offered a variety of answers. Just as the questioning child can be told, "The stork brought the baby" or "Mommy and Daddy loved each other very much and that made a baby" or "The egg was fertilized by a seed" (or any number of other clever explanations), my questions are answered with, "Fairy tales and folk wisdom have been handed down from generation to generation" or (somewhat nostalgically), "We used to have time for telling stories" or (on a more learned level), "Wisdom's timeless treasures are stored up in the collective unconscious."

This and similar information awakened in me the image of wise forebears who lived at the beginning of human history. No one could tell me precisely when or where they lived, but it was certain that they had possessed great insight into life, which they then transmitted to following generations. Unfortunately, their precious truths became more and more diluted in subsequent generations. I couldn't understand why this was so. Why were our forebears wiser and better than we are here and now? In early times, God even found the Flood necessary because people had sinned so much and because apparently He couldn't find a single person besides Noah who had pleased Him with his good sense and good deeds. All this contradicts the assumption that there was more wisdom to be found at the beginning of our history than there is now. I have already indicated in these pages that the wise and famous King Solomon wrote things that can now, thanks to the insights of our own century, be proven to be clearly false. Human history begins with the temptation to want to know, with punishment for being curious, with Abel being favored over Cain, Cain's jealousy, and a series of bloody deeds. Even as a child I searched in vain for the wise people who were supposed to be found at the beginning of our history.

And yet there may be a measure of truth in this reference to the past. I believe what it meant is the past of each individual human being, namely, his or her early childhood, when knowledge of the world as it actually is is absorbed. At that time the child experiences evil in its undisguised form and stores this knowledge in the unconscious. These early childhood experiences provide the source for the fantasies of adults, who, however, subject them to censorship. The fantasies then find a home in fairy tales, sagas, and myths, where the whole truth about human cruelty, as only a child can experience it, finds expression. In Greek mythology and its view of human nature, these experiences were still virtually uncensored. In the Christian mind, on the other hand, the commandment to love thy neighbor caused some of this material to be repressed or met with other defense mechanisms. Since the term "fairy tale" by definition implies unreality, censorship can be minimal, especially if in the end good triumphs over evil, justice reigns, the sinner is punished, and the good person is rewarded; that is, if denial undoes the tale's insights into the truth. For the world is not just, goodness is seldom rewarded, and the cruelest deeds are seldom punished. Yet we tell all this to our children, who, like us, would naturally like to believe that the world is the way we are presenting it to them.

The themes of fairy tales are like wild animals during the hunting season (permission is not required to shoot them down). Someone who is himself an artist can use them any way he pleases, expand them or alter them; they can also be interpreted psychologically and distorted in the name of various theories. At the same time, there need be no fear of offending anyone, for the original author is unknown, the story has been recast countless times, and the truth has often been turned upside down, although sometimes it has managed to remain intact because it is so well hidden behind an innocuous mask that no one has been upset by it.

I should also like to take advantage of the same liberty now in presenting my associations to "Rumpelstiltskin." I make no claims to validity but am simply indulging in an intellectual exercise; one could also say that I am making free use of a story to illustrate my ideas.

The beginning of the fairy tale describes the relationship between the king and one of his subjects, the miller. The miller holds his sovereign in esteem but has no hope of being esteemed in return or even respected or taken seriously unless he can perform an extraordinary service for the king. He hits upon the idea of boasting that his daughter knows how to spin gold out of straw. The king orders the miller to bring his daughter to the castle and then takes her to a chamber filled with straw, gives her a spinning wheel and spindle, and before locking her in says, "If you have not spun this straw into gold by tomorrow morning, you must die." The miller's daughter sits down and cries. How is she to make the impossible possible? Yet her life depends on it. She must, like so many children, perform a miracle in order to survive. Suddenly a little man appears before her. He can turn the straw into gold with no trouble at all, and this he does for her. But the king is insatiable and demands even more. The same situation is repeated, and again the little man rescues the miller's daughter. The third time, the king promises to marry the girl, for he "cannot find a richer woman in all the world." This time, however, Rumpelstiltskin demands a high price: she must give him her firstborn child. And when the time comes and the new queen gives birth to a beautiful baby, he arrives to claim the child. The queen is horrified and offers him all the riches of the kingdom if only he will let her keep her child. But what do the world's treasures mean to someone who can make gold himself? They do not outweigh a living creature. Nevertheless, Rumpelstiltskin takes pity on the queen and says, "If you can tell me my name within three days' time, then you may keep your child." The queen would never have been able to guess his name had not her messenger happened to see the little man in the forest. He was dancing and singing a song:

> I've won the game
> For no one knows
> Rumpelstiltskin is my name!

When he returns, only to find that the queen does know his name, he shrieks, "The devil told you!" Angrily he stamps his right foot so hard that his whole leg sinks into the earth; then, in a rage, he seizes his left leg with both hands and tears himself in two.

Strangely enough, this fairy tale does not have a happy ending. The queen, to be sure, is freed of the troublesome little man, but how will she be able to go on spinning gold now? Possibly she can use her child for this purpose; just as her father and the king (grandfather) required her to do the impossible, perhaps she will be able to do the same with her child. But the real tragedy of the fairy tale is the story of Rumpelstiltskin, who tears himself in two. He commits this act of despair upon hearing his name revealed, when he is no longer able to hide and no longer has any hope of being able to alter his fate by means of a living child (the vital part of himself). The little man had been living (we do not know why) all alone in an isolated cottage in the forest, without ties to other human beings. Perhaps he hoped to escape the world's sorrows there if, in his seclusion, he was no longer subjected to human cruelty.

Rumpelstiltskin was lonely, even though he was able to achieve the ultimate according to human standards, namely, to produce gold in great quantities. But little by little he could no longer bear being lonely and separated from others, and he hoped to restore his vitality with the aid of a beautiful woman. An opportunity might have been provided by his encounter with the miller's daughter, but this entailed the loss of his anonymity. The woman removed his mask, exposing his true face, not by searching for and finding his true name, his true self—which had been his hope when he gave her three days in which to solve the riddle—but by means of trickery. She *exposed* him with the aid of the devil but did not *find* or understand him. How can the little man go on living after his expectation of being rescued by love and human contact has been so sorely disappointed? He had known for a long time that gold and the world's treasures meant nothing to him in his loneliness. His anger over the treachery of a woman, perhaps the mother, who used him as long as she needed him and then betrayed him, does not lead to life but to an act of desperation, since his anger is not experienced in connection with the mother but with the miller's daughter.

This is not an interpretation of "Rumpelstiltskin"; it is an attempt to understand the fairy tale as if it were the dream of a patient, a highly successful person suffering from grandiosity who dreams that he is Rumpelstiltskin. There could of course be other readings: the king might be seen as the father and the miller as the mother, who tries to win her husband's favor at the expense of her children. Or the miller's daughter and Rumpelstiltskin might be regarded as parts of the same person or as two siblings, one of whom, highly talented, offers the other his help and skills; the latter, in spite of being very grateful, envies or eventually even hates the former, since feelings are not always as lovely and harmonious as we would like them to be.

I have chosen a fairy tale that does not display obvious reflections of the structure of the family. But if we learn from this example to catch these reflections, we will have no trouble seeing them in "Cinderella," "Rapunzel," "Sleeping Beauty," "Snow White," "Hansel and Gretel," and "Little Red Riding Hood." Despite many misleading interpretations, a great deal has been written about these tales that is valid. There is, for instance, a short play by Robert Walser entitled "Snow White," which expresses with startling clarity the ambivalent feelings a mother has for her daughter. There can be no doubt that someone who writes such a work must himself have gone through what he is presenting. How conscious Walser was of this connection is difficult to judge.

The way parents actually feel toward their children is brought out very clearly in fairy tales, and it has long been known that the stepmother represents one aspect of the real mother. In psychoanalytic literature, on the other hand, parents' feelings toward their children have scarcely been examined and are hardly ever the subject of research. One of the rare exceptions is Donald W. Winnicott's paper "Hate in the Counter-Transference," in which he discusses feelings in the countertransference in relation to the mother's hatred for her child. Without touching on the taboo nature of his subject matter, he investigates the causes of this maternal hatred as if it were something self-evident (which, for him, it is). Significantly, however, in the intervening years since his important essay appeared in 1949, it has awakened little response.

⤚§ 19 §⤙

Dreams

WHEREAS the importance of early childhood for the creation of fairy tales will presumably continue to be debated on all sides, the connection between dreams and early childhood has long been recognized and even thoroughly explored, at least in psychoanalytic circles. But in orthodox psychoanalysis the manifest dream content must be interpreted as a disguised form of a repressed infantile instinctual drive. We know that for Freud every dream was the fulfillment of an infantile wish, which could not always be identified in the manifest content but certainly could be in the latent content inaccessible to the patient. Freud himself as well as his followers always took great pains to demonstrate these wishes to patients by way of their dreams, something that was not always possible without considerable mental acrobatics. At the same time, a patient's first attachment figures, who appeared in all his dreams and who repeatedly displayed there the attitudes they had taken toward him in his childhood, were interpreted merely as projections of his unconscious wishes.

Such interpretations may be valid for a certain percentage of dreams but surely not for all of them. Unfortunately, someone who remains fixated on a certain point cannot learn to see and understand these other dreams, not even if they are obvious and easy to understand. A hunter whose total attention is concentrated on the deer running past him will not hear the birds singing nearby. Similarly, if an analyst is fixated on his patients' "libidinous wishes," this may prevent him from discovering with them their true childhood history, which their dreams often reveal with astonishing clarity. One woman dreamed during her first analysis that she was being raped by her analyst and that he was surprised in the act by his wife. The patient was routinely given the correct Oedipal interpretation: that she would like to seduce her father in her mother's absence. In the course of her second analysis it became clear that at a very early age she had actually been sexually stimulated by her father when her mother was going to work on a regular basis and he was taking care of her. After this hypothesis had been established through her dreams and the transference in her second analysis, the patient was able, not without great difficulty, to confirm it with her mother, who had once happened to come home early and had discovered her husband abusing the child. The patient's amnesia in the first analysis was total, but her recurrent dream was relating a real event, an experience from childhood to which she could not gain access as long as her analyst turned a deaf ear to it. Moreover, her dreams were telling her not only about her past but also about present reality in the transference, for the first analyst's Oedipal interpretations also resembled a very real violation of her vague but nevertheless persistent memory.

I am indebted to William G. Niederland for telling me the following story, which he published in 1965. A patient told him he had dreamed he was lying in bed at the North Pole; he became frozen solid in the bed, and then some people came in. The patient was sitting up as he recounted the dream, and at his last words, he turned toward the door. Niederland was struck by this, and he interpreted the movement as that of a child in bed who notices when adults enter the room. During this session they both were intent on discovering the memory behind the dream. Later the same day Niederland received a telephone call from his patient's mother, who reproached him severely for having revealed her secret to her son. It turned out that at the age of eight months the boy had slept by an open window on a very cold New York night and the next morning had to be taken to the hospital with pneumonia. The parents had forgotten to close the window in the evening, and when the baby screamed without interruption, his mother refrained from going in to him because she didn't want to spoil him. Meanwhile, his excreta and vomit had frozen solid. It is understandable that his parents felt guilty and wanted to forget the incident, which they carefully kept a secret from their son, supposedly to spare him from something that had already happened. From this perspective, we can also understand the reproaches his mother directed at the analyst.

Here again we see the principles of "poisonous pedagogy" at work: First, don't go into the child's room when he is screaming or he will grow up to be a tyrant; second, remain silent about what happened for the child's benefit. Had Niederland not pursued his creative hunch but abided by analytic principles instead, this early trauma would never have been uncovered, and the unintentional early cruelty would have been unintentionally repeated in the form of officially approved interpretations.*

The informative function of dreams is not always as transparent as in the two examples cited here. The degree of distortion in the dream can vary greatly. Some patients often dream they are their own parents, and their children then represent a part of themselves. Or they dream about various persons in the present who resemble certain aspects of their parents. Naturally, the dream content is also related to the particular situation in the transference. What is important, however, is that the analyst take seriously the connection between dreams and early childhood experience in order to see and hear the patient's story, which the parents tried to keep secret and which the patient is therefore keeping secret now.

---

* I am drawing here on Niederland's verbal report. In the written description of the case, the reader will find interesting details concerning the course the patient's treatment took (see "The Ego and the Recovery of Early Memories" in *Psychoanalytic Quarterly* [October 1965]).

❀

"Nobody will read what I say here, no one will come to help me; even if all the people were commanded to help me, every door and window would remain shut, everybody would take to bed and draw the bedclothes over his head, the whole earth would become an inn for the night. And there is sense in that, for nobody knows of me, and if anyone knew he would not know where I could be found, and if he knew where I could be found, he would not know how to deal with me, he would not know how to help me. The thought of helping me is an illness that has to be cured by taking to one's bed.

"I know that, and so I do not shout to summon help, even though at moments—when I lose control over myself, as I have done just now, for instance—I think seriously of it. But to drive out such thoughts I need only look around me and verify where I am."—Franz Kafka, "The Hunter Gracchus"

Literature: Franz Kafka's Suffering

THOMAS Mann wrote of Franz Kafka: "He was a dreamer, and his fiction is often conceived and fashioned altogether along the lines of a dream. His works are a laughably precise imitation of the a-logical and uneasy absurdity of dreams, those strange and shadowy mirrors of life." Alfred Döblin wrote: "What he writes bears the stamp of absolute truth, not at all as if he had made it up. Curiously jumbled, to be sure, but organized around an absolutely true, very real, center. . . . Many have said that Kafka's novels have the nature of dreams—and we can certainly agree with that. But what is 'the nature of dreams'? The spontaneous course they take, entirely plausible and transparent at every moment; our feeling and awareness of the profound rightness of the things taking place and the feeling that these things concern us very much" (quoted in Wagenbach, *Franz Kafka*, p. 144).

I would say that Kafka was not imitating the structure of dreams in his works but that he was dreaming as he wrote. Without his realizing it, experiences from early childhood found their way into his writing, just as they do into other people's dreams. Looking at it this way, we get into difficulty: for either Kafka is a great visionary who sees through the nature of human society and his wisdom somehow "comes from on high" (in which case this can have nothing to do with childhood) or his fiction is rooted in his earliest unconscious experiences and would then, according to popular opinion, lack universal significance. Could it be, however, that we cannot deny the truth of his works for the very reason that they *do* draw upon the child's intense and painful way of experiencing the world, something that has meaning for all of us? Rainer Maria Rilke wrote: "I have never read a line by this author that I did not find relevant or amazing in the most peculiar way." In this chapter, devoted to Kafka's suffering, I cannot hope to do full justice to his work but shall only use some examples from it to show how the writer, without knowing it, tells about his childhood in what he writes. Kafka scholars who are receptive to my approach and do not try to apply ready-made psychoanalytic theories to this author will be able to add an endless number of examples to mine. In any case, having read his letters, I see clear signs of his childhood suffering on every page of his fiction.

In other words, this chapter is not to be understood as the application of psychoanalytic theory to a writer of genius or as a literary interpretation of Kafka's works. It owes its existence both to my oath of professional secrecy, which prevents me from discussing what I know about the backgrounds of writers who are still alive, and to the question that kept occurring to me as I was reading Kafka: What would have happened if Kafka's despair over not being able to bring himself to marry, over his tuberculosis—whose psychological significance he saw with great clarity—and over the torments of insomnia and numerous other symptoms had driven him to seek out an analyst who subscribed to Freudian drive theory? I know that detractors of psychoanalysis who have had no experience with the unconscious would smile at such a question and might say Kafka would have had the good sense, after the first session, not to go back a second time to a situation in which he was so totally misunderstood. I do not share this assumption at all; I am even convinced that a person like Kafka, who from childhood to puberty never had the good fortune to find someone who understood him, would not have sensed this same lack in his psychoanalyst all that quickly. He might have struggled with all his might to find understanding, the way he did with his fiancée Felice nearly every day for five years. He would have had equally little success, however, with a psychoanalyst who was of the opinion that Freud had uncovered all the secrets of childhood and of the unconscious with his Oedipus complex and concept of "infantile sexuality." Thus, it is hard to say how quickly Kafka could have freed himself from such an involvement.

Yet I do not doubt that Kafka's insomnia and his unrelenting anxiety would have abated or even disappeared entirely if it had been possible for him to acknowledge and experience in analysis his feelings from early childhood—especially his anger at not being understood, his feelings of abandonment, and the constant fear of being rejected and manipulated—and to connect these feelings with his original attachment figures. Neither do I doubt that his ability as a writer, rather than being diminished, would even have been enhanced (cf. pp. 305–6).

Psychoanalysis, like pedagogy, can very easily be destructive of the soul if it is used to indoctrinate the patient. But if it is not manipulative, instead allowing the patient full freedom to discover his past, then it cannot help but encourage his creative potential. Furthermore, if we understand art as a creative expression of what a person has experienced and stored in the unconscious and not as "the sublimation of instinctual drives," every kind of therapy that has the goal of paving the way to self-expression will promote, not impede, creativity. The fear that the infinite riches of the unconscious might be exhausted by bringing a small but tormenting portion of it to consciousness will not be shared by anyone who has been moved by the paintings of Picasso, Miró, Paul Klee, or Chagall. Their brushes were guided by the unconscious, not by neurosis.

When we hear that a writer had an unhappy childhood, we frequently attribute his or her artistic achievement to early traumatization. This view seems particularly applicable to Kafka, in whose works an exploitative society takes over the role of the parents, with the philosophy common to both being summed up in the words: "The beating was good for you [us]." Unquestionably, it is scarcely conceivable that someone who is not capable of suffering can produce a great creative work, but the capacity for suffering is not a result of traumatization; rather, both are the result of a very high degree of sensitivity.*

The same event may have a devastating effect on a sensitive child and elicit scarcely any visible response (at least for the moment) in another, who has perhaps already become apathetic. For

---

* I use this term for lack of a better one, for I cannot say what causes one child to react more sensitively at a very early age than another, an undeniable phenomenon we can observe every day. There certainly must be good reasons for this, but I have not pursued the question in enough depth to discover them; possibly the key lies in a study of the prenatal period. It strikes me as quite likely that fear on the pregnant mother's part, for example, could lead to great alertness (sensitivity) in the fetus.

this reason, the view cited above could just as well be turned around to read: There was much suffering in the childhood of all great writers *because* they experienced the wounds, humiliations, fears, and feelings of abandonment that are an inevitable part of that period of life much more strongly and intensely than others. By storing up the pain they suffered, by making it an essential part of themselves and of their later imaginative life and then expressing it in transfigured form, they guarantee the survival of their painful feelings. But the dissociation of these feelings from the first attachment figures, toward whom they were directed, and their association with new, unreal fictitious figures guarantees the "survival" of the neurosis. This can be clarified by the following example:

At the age of fifteen, Gustave Flaubert wrote a story that he entitled "Quidquid volueris." The hero of the tale is sixteen-year-old Djalioh, the offspring of an orangutan and a slave girl, a union that was planned and brought about in Brazil by Monsieur Paul, a young and ambitious scientist "with a cold heart." Monsieur Paul takes the child and raises him, but he is unable to teach him human speech. Fifteen years later, when Paul returns to his native France to marry Adèle, he brings Djalioh with him. The boy loves Adèle, who regards him only as a poor, feeble-minded creature or a good-natured ape. Here are the final scenes of the story in the words of the fifteen-year-old Flaubert:

It was in one of these city mansions that Djalioh lived with Monsieur Paul and his wife, and for almost two years much had been taking place in his soul, and the tears he had held back had hollowed out a deep cavity therein.

One morning—it was that day I'm telling you about—he got up and went into the garden, where a baby about a year old, wrapped in fine silks and linens, embroideries, and colorful ribbons, was asleep in a cradle whose top was gilded by the rays of the sun.

The child's nurse was not there. Djalioh looked all around, approached the cradle, going right up to it, and quickly pulled back the covers; then he stood there a while—looking at this poor, drowsy, sleeping creature, its chubby hands, its rounded contours, its white neck, its little fingernails. Finally he seized it with both hands, swung it round in the air over his head and dashed it with all his might to the ground, which reverberated from the impact. The baby cried out, and its brains spurted out ten paces away next to a gilly-flower.

Djalioh opened his pale lips and gave a forced laugh that was cold and terrible like the laughter of the dead. He immediately went to the house, up the staircase, opened the door to the dining room, closed it again, took the key to that room as well as to the hall door, and— entering the vestibule of the salon—threw them both out the window into the street. Finally, he entered the salon, softly, on tiptoe, and once there he double-locked the door behind him. What little light the carefully closed shutters allowed to penetrate into the room fell dimly upon him.

Djalioh stood still and heard only the sound of the pages Adèle's white hand was turning. . . .

Finally, he approached the young woman and sat down beside her. She trembled suddenly and turned her troubled blue eyes to him. Her flowing dressing-gown of white chiffon was open at the neck, and her legs were crossed in such a way that in spite of her gown one could see the contours of her thighs. Surrounding her was an intoxicating perfume; her white gloves lying on the armchair with her sash, her handkerchief, her scarf—all that had such a delicate and distinctive scent that Djalioh's large nostrils opened wide to take in the aroma. . . .

"What do you want of me?" she asked in fright as soon as she saw him.

And a long silence followed; he didn't answer and fixed his de-vouring gaze on her. Then, drawing closer and closer, he seized her around the waist with both hands and pressed on her neck a burning kiss that seemed to stab Adèle like the bite of a serpent. He saw her flesh redden and quiver.

"Oh! I'm going to call for help," she cried in fright. "Help! Help! Oh! The monster!" she added, looking at him.

Djalioh did not respond, he only stammered and struck his head in rage. What! Not to be able to say a word to her! Not to be able to enumerate his torments and his sorrows and not to have anything to offer her but the tears of an animal and the sighs of a monster! And then to be thrust aside like a reptile! To be hated by what one loves and to be aware of the impossibility of saying anything! To be accursed and not be able to blaspheme!

"Leave me alone, have mercy! Leave me alone! Don't you see that you fill me with horror and disgust! I'm going to call Paul; he will kill you."

Djalioh showed her the key he had in his hand, then paused. The clock was striking eight, and the birds were twittering in the aviary; a cart was heard rolling by, and then it was gone.

"Well, are you leaving? Leave me alone, in the name of heaven!"

And she tried to get up, but Djalioh held fast to the hem of her robe, which his fingernails ripped. "I want to go, I must go . . . I have to see my baby, surely you'll let me see my baby!"

A frightful thought made her whole body tremble, she grew pale and added:

"Yes, my baby! I must see it . . . and at once, this instant!"

She turned and saw the grimaces of a demon's face; he began to laugh so long, so hard, and all in one outburst that Adèle, petrified with horror, fell on her knees at his feet.

Djalioh knelt too; then he took her, forced her to sit on his knees, and with his two hands he tore all of her clothes to shreds and ripped the veils that were covering her; when he saw her trembling like a leaf and crossing her arms over her exposed breasts, crying, her cheeks red and her lips bluish, he felt himself under the weight of a strange oppression; then he took the flowers, strewed them on the floor, closed the curtains of pink silk, and removed his own clothes.

Adèle saw him naked; she trembled with horror and turned her head away. Djalioh went to her and held her pressed against his chest for a long time. She felt the cold and hairy flesh of the monster against her own warm, silky skin. He leapt onto the sofa, threw down the cushions and balanced himself for a long time on its back with a mechanical and regular motion of his flexible spine; from time to time he let out a guttural cry and he smiled, showing his teeth.

What more could he want? A woman before him, flowers at his feet, a rosy light shining on her, the sounds of an aviary for music and a pale ray of sun to cast light on her!

He soon gave up his gymnastics, ran to Adèle, buried his claws in her flesh and pulled her toward him. He removed her chemise.

Seeing herself totally naked in the mirror, in Djalioh's arms, she let out a cry of horror and began praying to God; she tried to call for help but found it impossible to make a sound.

When Djalioh saw her thus, naked and with her hair flowing down to her shoulders, he stood immobilized by stupor, like the first man who ever saw a woman. For a moment he didn't touch her, only pulling out some of her blond hair, putting it in his mouth, biting it, kissing it; then he rolled on the flowers on the floor, among the cushions, on Adèle's clothes, satisfied, crazed, drunk with love. . . .

Finally his wild brutality knew no more bounds; he sprang at her with one leap, pulled apart her two hands, stretched her out on the floor and rolled her frenziedly from side to side. Often he let out wild cries and stretched out both arms, limp and motionless, then he moaned with lust like a man who . . .

Suddenly he felt Adèle's convulsive movements beneath him, her muscles grew rigid as iron, she emitted a plaintive cry and a plaintive sigh that were smothered by his kisses. Then he felt her grow cold, her eyes closed, she rolled to one side, and her mouth opened.

When she had remained motionless and cold as ice for a long time, he got up, turned her from side to side, kissed her feet, her hands, her mouth, and ran leaping into the wall. He repeated this several times; once, however, he ran head first into the marble chimneypiece and fell motionless and bleeding on Adèle's body.

When they found Adèle, she had broad, deep claw marks on her body; as for Djalioh, he had a horribly crushed skull. It was believed that the young woman, in defending herself, had killed him with a knife.

All this was in the newspapers, and you can imagine the "ahs" and "ohs" it caused for a week.

The next day the corpses were buried. The funeral procession was magnificent; there were two coffins, one for the mother and one for her baby, along with black plumes on the horses, candles, chanting priests, the jostling crowd, and men attired in black with white gloves.

Many admirers of Flaubert's style, of his restraint and literary greatness, may well call this passage from "Quidquid volueris" melodramatic and adolescent. The work *was* written during puberty, a time when childhood comes alive again. This explains the uncontrolled intensity of love, hate, pain, loneliness, of the feelings of degradation and powerlessness displayed here. Yet even in this work there are passages depicting in authentic poetic form the tragic loneliness of the sensitive child every writer once was. One example:

> . . . he asked himself why he wasn't a swan and as beautiful as these animals; when he approached people they fled, he was despised among men; why wasn't he beautiful like them? Why hadn't Heaven made him a swan, a bird, something airy that sings and is loved? Or why wasn't he nothing at all? "Why," he said, kicking a stone ahead of him with his foot, "why am I not like that? I kick it, it flies up and doesn't suffer!"

Did Flaubert know that he was telling a great deal of his own story in the scene with Adèle? To the casual observer all indications are that he did. Flaubert's father was a respected physician, whereas Flaubert himself was considered "the family idiot" (the title of Sartre's study) as a child and had trouble learning to speak, read, and write. According to Sartre, there was the same distance between Gustave and his mother as between Djalioh and Adèle; his father was an ambitious scientist like Monsieur Paul; Gustave had to conceal his jealousy of his little sister, who was named after her mother—many other similarities could be mentioned. In spite of this—or rather because of it—I would answer in the negative the question whether Flaubert knew he was writing about his own life. Djalioh could not have torn the baby from the cradle and flung it on the ground if Flaubert had known that a brother's love was not the only feeling he had for his sister. In Djalioh's attack on Adèle, the fifteen-year-old author (and hero of the story) could also give free rein to his pubescent fantasies, since he *didn't* know that he was seeking from Adèle the closeness and affection he had never experienced with his mother.

It is this rift, the dissociation of feelings from those who caused them, along with the preservation of their content in a fantasy world, that shapes an artist's work, although the artistic expression of suffering does not do away with neurosis. Suffering can, however, be blunted in the process of writing, for the writer possesses in his art an imaginary object with ideal qualities: it is available, can always understand him, take him seriously, and be supportive. He can tell his woes to this imaginary object, but always with the understanding that his parents be spared, that is, that no one (not even he) is to find out toward whom his feelings are actually directed. A similar situation can be seen in the case of Samuel Beckett.

Beckett claims to have had a protected and happy childhood because his parents were well-to-do. But the isolation of a Protestant boy who lived in Catholic Ireland on a secluded country estate near the sea and with parklike gardens, along with the daily oppression and intimidation of being forced to examine his conscience because his mother hoped this would bring about a religious awakening, must have had an impact on him, although he was obviously unable to relate these experiences to his childhood on an emotional level. Even though he can experience the accompanying emotions in his writing, he does not associate them with his own past. Unlike people who must completely ward off their feelings by means of the

intellect, poets and writers can experience and express strong dif-
ferentiated feelings as long as the connection with their own tragic
childhood remains unconscious.

Long before writing *Waiting for Godot*, the twenty-three-year-
old Beckett wrote a story entitled "Assumption." The nameless hero,
who often finds himself in noisy crowds of people, develops the
ability literally to "whisper the turmoil down." The real theme of
the story, however, is not this art of whispering down but the hero's
fear of one day breaking out—despite all precautions—into an ele-
mental, unnatural, inhuman scream, for this, he firmly believes,
would destroy him; and a woman who forces herself upon him and
finally spends every night with him actually brings him to this
point. The scream reverberates "with its prolonged, triumphant
vehemence," shaking the house and merging with "the throbbing cry
of the sea." The woman was found "caressing his wild, dead hair."

It is inconceivable to me that someone who had the opportunity
to express his feelings and thoughts relatively freely as a child could
have written this disquieting story with such intensity. But it is
most understandable that in certain severe cases an adult does not
retain any memories—or only idealized ones—from childhood, because the truth was unbearable for the lonely child. The content of
this story reflects very accurately Beckett's denial ("whispering
down") of his childhood suffering and his belief that he is portraying only "society's" suffering and absurdity, which he perceived as
an adult. His tragic position is explained in part by the fact that his
works, which reveal the anguish of his childhood, convey nothing
to him of this anguish; he cannot detect its roots because they are a
part of him and because he has tried all his life to preserve a mask
of indifference regarding that period. This need for a split in the
emotional realm in the case of a sensitive and highly gifted person
clearly demonstrates the severe reprisal the child was once threatened with if he should become aware of how things really were.
Since the prohibition is internalized at such an early age, it can
take its toll undiminished for the rest of his life.

On the basis of the foregoing, the conclusion could be drawn
that neither Flaubert nor Beckett would have written these stories
I have discussed here had they been fully conscious that in them
they were describing their own problems. This line of thinking
brings some to the cruel conclusion that it is a good thing that the

major writers had an unhappy childhood; otherwise we wouldn't have their great works now. I would respond that these writers simply would have written something different that could have been just as powerful as long as it, too, emanated from the unconscious. The unconscious is endless; it resembles an ocean from which we, in analysis, can remove perhaps one glassful of water, that portion which has made the person ill. A great artist will be able to draw all the more freely from the ocean the less he has to protect himself from the suspected poison in the glass. He will be free to try out different approaches and to keep discovering himself anew, as can be observed in the life of Pablo Picasso, for one. In contrast to Picasso, we might mention Salvador Dali, who, although undoubtedly a great painter, has, like Samuel Beckett, been preoccupied all his life with the poison in the glass. What I am saying here is not intended as a value judgment but merely as a comment on the personal tragedy of artists. A glassful is tiny in comparison with the ocean, but if we imagine a person to be the size of an ant, then even a glassful can seem like a great ocean.

The common belief that neurosis is an asset for art may possibly be rooted in an exploitative attitude that is somehow understandable. We could, for instance, argue: What would the works of Kafka, Proust, or Joyce be without their authors' neuroses? Aren't these the very writers who have described our own inner perils and inner prisons, our compulsions and absurdities? Therefore, we would not want them to have been mentally sound, to have written like a Goethe, because then we would have been deprived of a significant experience and unconscious mirroring. In Kafka's *The Trial*, for example, we experience our own incomprehensible guilt feelings, in *The Castle* our powerlessness, and in "The Metamorphosis" our loneliness and isolation; yet the portrayal of these existential situations does not cause us to despair, for they apply only to Kafka's "fictitious" characters. Such writers fulfill an important function for us that we would not like to forgo—that of mirroring—and nothing is required of us in return. We, as these authors' posterity, take on, in a sense, the role of their parents, since we, too, profit from their artistic gifts without having to deal with their actual suffering.

This thought first struck me when I read the letters written to Mozart by his father, quoted in Florian Langegger's fascinating study, *Mozart—Vater und Sohn*. The father wrote: "Above all you must devote yourself with all your soul to your parents' well-being, otherwise your soul will go to the devil. . . . I can expect everything from you out of a sense of filial obligation. . . . I'll live for another few years, God willing, pay my debts—and then as far as I'm concerned you can go knock your head against a stone wall if you're so inclined" (pp. 86 and 92). These and similar passages don't quite fit the image of the loving father that history has handed down to us. But they show very plainly the narcissistic abuse of the child, which in most cases need not exclude great affection and strong encouragement (cf. my review of Langegger's book in *Psyche* 23, pp. 587–88). After reading Leopold Mozart's "loving" letters selected by Langegger, it should come as no surprise to us that the son outlived his father by only a short time, dying at the age of thirty-seven, and that before his death he suffered from a fear of being poisoned. Yet how unimportant the tragic fate of this human being seems to posterity when weighed against his outstanding achievement.

Although the subjective side of an artist's tribulations usually is of no importance to posterity, I should like to devote this chapter to the tragic personal life of the writer Franz Kafka. I do this because I suspect there are numerous patients with a similar background; even though they may turn to psychoanalysis, they are not helped, since traditional analysts, following in Freud's footsteps, generally believe that the work of art is "a substitute for healthy drive fulfillment," that is, a sign of neurosis, or, put differently, that as "a product of culture" it is the result of "drive sublimation."

If there should be someone like Kafka today (and I don't doubt that we encounter many similarly constituted people with a similar childhood history), what would happen if he underwent an analysis based on the drive theory?

We can find possible answers to this question in the extensive literature about Kafka's Oedipal, pre-Oedipal, and (recently) even homosexual drive desires. Gunter Mecke, for instance, writes in "Franz Kafkas Geheimnis" (Franz Kafka's Secret):

> The central subject of *The Trial* is the test of Josef K.'s sexuality, which he does not pass, either heterosexually (with Miss Bürstner) or homosexually (with the "painter" Titorelli). As a consequence, K. is finally punished by being sodomized by two bailiffs. [*Psyche* 35, 214]

From the particulars of this article we can gather what Kafka would have been up against if Mecke had taken on his analysis. Mecke confesses:

> Kafka's writings have always been far more of a stumbling block for me than they have been food for thought. . . . Heaven knows why I of all people was assigned the task of giving several Kafka seminars in succession (beginning in 1970). I led them like a blind man leading the blind, with growing dismay, finally with a feeling of shame. I positively didn't feel up to the subject matter and realized it was driving me to talk nonsense. I was stewing in my own juice and had to admit—and be told by my very outspoken students—that I too had allowed myself to become an intellectual counterfeiter with my "interpretations" of Kafka.
>
> *Initially*, psychoanalysis as a method was of little help to me, sometimes it was a hindrance; that is to say, with its preconceived constructs it tricked me into taking some *leaps* in interpreting individual statements of Kafka's. It doesn't work. You have to have wandered around in Kafka's labyrinthine *system* for a long time before you can get your bearings in any of its individual dead-end passageways. Then, to be sure, the master key can be deduced. . . . I took to heart the advice of Gardena (in *The Castle*), who hates the land surveyor K. You have only to listen to him carefully and then you are on to him. . . . That becomes the heart of my method. Not infrequently this heart beat so wildly that I felt a kind of fury in me. [p. 215]

This fury can occur when a person is trying to understand something or someone and all the available tools for understanding fail. That was also the situation Kafka must have found himself in, and had he undergone analysis, he certainly would have transmitted this feeling to his analyst, the same way his works sometimes do to his readers, who, after thinking they have already understood something, are suddenly confronted with an absurd situation. Therefore, we shouldn't be surprised at Mecke's "fury"; it could be reflecting—in the form of the countertransference, so to speak—the feelings of little Franz. But—and here is the big difference—analysts need not put up with the desperate feeling of powerlessness the way a child or patient must, for they can rid themselves of this unbearable feeling by offering the patient explanations that ignore his or her plight. In this way they take revenge for their inability to understand and are happy finally to have a patient under their control. Mecke, too, is triumphant after he is on to the tricks of the cunning fellow Franz Kafka and describes him as a "poisoner," who conceals his "homosexuality" with "schizophrenic cunning" in a language "analogous to the slang used by criminals." In his long article, Mecke points out exactly those passages in the story where he believes he has caught "Kafka the boy chaser" (p. 227) red-handed in his homosexual fantasies and activities. Mecke is not lacking in thoroughness, but the information about the homosexual abuse Kafka himself supposedly underwent is presented, without documentation or support, in a footnote, which merely says: "Abundant evidence, which must be passed over here, indicates that at the age of fifteen Kafka was homosexually seduced or—what is more likely—raped." Without any substantiation! In my supervisory work and in listening to case presentations in analytic circles, I noticed countless times that no importance was attributed to information of this nature, because all the emphasis was placed on describing the patient's "drive desires" (the child's guilt).

One has every right to see in a work of literature what one must see in it, for however contemptuous a reader's attitude may be, it can have no deleterious effect on the finished work. But the patient in an analyst's office can easily become the victim of this type of attitude. Just as Professor Mecke did not read Kafka voluntarily but was, as he says, obliged to teach a series of Kafka seminars, so too an analyst may take on a patient whose nature is totally foreign to him, perhaps because at that moment he happens to need a case for economic reasons. If the patient then unconsciously confronts him with certain absurdities from his, the patient's, childhood, this can easily lead the therapist to adopt an attitude not unlike Mecke's toward Kafka and will thus cause him to rely on complicated theories. Should the patient become aware of the therapist's powerlessness or complain that he is not being understood, he will be told that he is now becoming aggressive because the analyst is not responding to his homosexual advances. In my own training I often heard explanations like this, and it took me a long time to see through their nature as a defense mechanism on the part of supervisors and other analysts. A well-trained candidate will inevitably think, "Perhaps there is some truth to it." And the patient, who sees the godlike qualities of his or her first attachment figures in the analyst, cannot resist the powerful grip of the interpretation given, especially if it is presented in a self-assured tone of voice allowing no room for alternatives. If analysts could acknowledge and experience their occasional despair over their lack of understanding, then they might gain important access to their patients' childhood. At least this has been my personal experience.

Mecke's article is also characteristic of the psychoanalytic approach based on the drive theory, described on pp. 11ff. One might assume that this approach is definitely a thing of the past and rarely encountered today; similarly, we would like to believe that "poisonous pedagogy" has no place in our day and age. Unfortunately, the opposite is true, and there are still frequent attempts to label the patient (here Franz Kafka) a sly deceiver, whose underhandedness can fortunately be exposed by using the right keys. Such attempts are a logical consequence of psychoanalytic training that emphasizes the drive theory.

Of course, not all analysts proceed along these lines: Donald W. Winnicott, Marion Milner, John Bowlby, Jan Bastiaans, Heinz Kohut, Massud Khan, William G. Niederland, Christel Schöttler, and many others have been able to help creative people substantially because they were not compelled to trace their patients' creativity back to drive conflicts and systematically point out their "dirty fantasies" (cf. *For Your Own Good*, pp. 18–21). Yet Mecke's contemptuous, deprecatory, even abusive attitude, reminiscent of the methods of "poisonous pedagogy," is by no means an exception; indeed, it is representative of the (unconscious and unintentional) prevailing tendency in psychoanalysis today. The editorial comment introducing Mecke's article is an indication that the official advocates of this attitude regard it as perfectly normal and even as something new:

> Drawing on Kafka's letters, Mecke reads Kafka's stories and novels as cryptograms, as encoded artistic messages about the experiences of someone who is on the borderline between homosexuality and heterosexuality. This new way of interpreting Kafka is presented here by using his story "The Hunter Gracchus" as an example.

This "new way" of looking at Kafka is not new insofar as someone else had already treated him the same way Mecke does now. As Kafka's *Letter to His Father* makes clear, the father also rejected, scorned, and at times must have hated the little boy, whose questions he didn't understand and simply ignored. Most children whose parents feel threatened by their child's very nature suffer a similar fate. If this trauma is repeated at the beginning of analysis, before an empathic inner object has been established, it can lead to an outbreak of psychosis. Then we say the patient has encountered his "psychotic core," failing to take into account that in his analysis—that is, in the present—he has *once again* been subjected to a real trauma. Because he is unable to endure this without a supportive companion, he succumbs to a psychotic episode.

In the following pages I shall not apply any pat theories to Kafka but shall attempt to set down what I learned about his childhood when I read his fiction and, above all, his letters. By so doing I am also describing indirectly my analytic methodology, which I sum up as the search for my patients' early childhood reality without any attempt to spare their parents. The difference between the psychoanalysis of a literary work and the psychoanalysis of a person is that in the latter case the articulation of suffering occurs not in the work of art but in the patient's associations and reenactments within the transference and countertransference. However, my attitude toward the child within the adult is the same in both cases.

The twenty-nine-year-old Kafka notes in his diary that tears came to his eyes when he read aloud the conclusion of his story "The Judgment." During the night following this reading (between December 4 and 5, 1912), he wrote to Felice Bauer:

> Frankly, dearest, I simply adore reading aloud; bellowing into the audience's expectant and attentive ear warms the cockles of the poor heart. . . . As a child—which I was until a few years ago—I used to enjoy dreaming of reading aloud to a large, crowded hall . . . the whole of *Education sentimentale* at one sitting, for as many days and nights as it required . . . and making the walls reverberate. Whenever I have given a talk, and talking is even better than reading aloud (it's happened rarely enough), I have felt this elation, and this evening was no exception. [*Letters to Felice*, p. 86]

These words do not go particularly well with the popular image of the modest and reserved Franz Kafka. Yet how understandable they are, coming from the pen of someone who had no one throughout his entire childhood in whom he could confide his real and deepest concerns.

Max Brod writes in his biography that Kafka's mother was a kindhearted and wise woman. (The cliché "a kindhearted woman" still seems to fit biographers' mother image.) When we read this, knowing that no one was closer to Kafka than Brod, we realize even more clearly how lonely Kafka's life was. His mother, Julie Kafka, whose own mother and then grandmother died when she was three years old, was essentially a good and submissive child all her life, first for her father and then for her husband. She was constantly at the latter's disposal, during the day to help him in his business and in the evening to play cards with him ("for thirty years, which is my entire life," her son writes Felice). Franz was her first child; then in quick succession she had two more sons, one of whom lived two years and the other only six months. Later, she gave birth to three daughters when Franz was between the ages of six and nine.

All of Kafka's writing, including his letters, gives us only an approximate idea of how much a child of his intensity and depth of awareness is affected by these births and deaths as well as by feelings of abandonment, envy, and jealousy if he has no one to help him experience and express his true feelings. (There are parallels in the childhoods of Hölderlin, Novalis, and Munch, among others.) This alert, curious, highly sensitive—but by no means disturbed—child was hopelessly alone with all his questions, completely at the mercy of the power-hungry household staff. We often say with a shrug that it was normal in those days for wealthy people to entrust their children to governesses. (As if what is "normal" were ever the criterion of what is beneficial.) Certainly there have been many cases of a nurse or governess rescuing a child from cold and unloving parents, but we must also keep in mind what satisfaction it must have given oppressed household servants to pass the humiliation meted out to them from "above" on to the little children in their charge. Since it is difficult for children to tell anyone about what is being done to them, all the psychological cruelty they experience remains a well-kept secret.

How great, how irrepressible must have been Kafka's *hunger* for a sympathetic ear in his childhood, for someone who would respond genuinely to his questions, fears, and doubts without using threats or showing anxiety, who would share his interests, sense his

feelings, and not mock them. How great must have been his longing
for a mother who showed interest in and respect for his inner world.
Such respect, however, can be given a child only if one has learned
to take oneself seriously as a person as well. How could Kafka's
mother have learned to do this? She lost her own mother at an age
when a child can neither grasp nor mourn the loss. Without an
empathic surrogate it was impossible under the circumstances for
her own personality—that is, her genuine capacity to love—to develop. Inability to love is tragic, but it is not a culpable state.

There are signs of a growing awareness in our society that only
a mother's own growth and vitality, not a depressing sense of duty,
enable her to have warm and respectful affection for her child. Men
who take this awareness to be an invention of the women's movement need only look back a bit into the past. Goethe's mother, for
one, wrote her son letters that show clearly how natural and spontaneous love and respect for one's child can be. Not a single un-
authentic word is to be found here, no mention of sacrifice or
fulfilling one's duty. Julie Kafka, in contrast, writes Brod that she
would be ready to sacrifice her life's blood for the happiness of *each*
of her children. Hölderlin's mother writes in a similar hypocritical
vein. But after all, how much blood does a mother have? And what
is the child supposed to do with this blood, when all he needs is a
sympathetic ear?

Her son's unstilled and desperate hunger for authenticity and
understanding, a theme which, by the way, pervades the six
hundred pages of *Letters to Felice*, is expressed in the dream referred to earlier: in place of his mother a crowd of people "with
expectant and attentive ear" have gathered for the express purpose of listening to *him*. And he is permitted to go on reading, whole
nights on end, until they have understood him. But since his doubts
and the tormenting force of his early experiences are just as strong
as his hopes, it is Flaubert he chooses to read aloud. In case his
audience, despite his tremendous effort, should not understand
what he is attempting to communicate to them, then it is Flaubert
whom they do not understand—Flaubert, to whom he feels very
close but who, after all, is not he. To expose *himself* to the risk of
meeting with indifference and incomprehension would be even
more painful and would leave him with the tormenting feeling of
nakedness and shame. For a child is ashamed if he has sought in

vain for understanding; then he feels like a beggar who, after long hesitation and a great inner struggle, finally brings himself to stretch out his hand, only to be unnoticed by the passers-by.

That, too, is part of the human condition—for children to be ashamed of their needs while adults are not even conscious of turning a deaf ear and often haven't the vaguest idea of what is going on right beside them in their child's soul, at least not if their own childhood is emotionally inaccessible to them.

Kafka was described by his nursemaid as an "obedient" and "good" child who "had a quiet disposition."

> The child grew up under the supervision of the cook and the house-keeper, Marie Werner, a Czech who had lived with the Kafka family for decades. . . . The cook was strict, the housekeeper amiable but timid toward the father, to whom she always responded in an argument with, "I won't say anything, I'll just think it." A nursemaid was soon added to these two "authority figures" and later a French governess, obligatory in the "better" families of Prague. Kafka rarely saw his parents: his father had set up noisy living quarters on the premises of his steadily growing business, and the mother always had to be on hand to help him and smooth things over with the employees, whom the father referred to as "beasts," "dogs," and "paid enemies." Kafka's formal training was restricted to being taught table manners and given orders, for even in the evening his mother had to keep his father company and play "the usual game of cards . . . accompanied by exclamations, laughter, and squabbling, not to mention whistling." The boy grew up in this "dull, poisonous atmosphere of the beautifully furnished living room, so devastating for a child"; he found his father's brusque commands incomprehensible and mysterious, and he finally became "so unsure of everything that, in fact, I possessed only what I actually had in my hands or in my mouth or what was at least on the way there." The direction taken by the upbringing his father gave him added greatly to the boy's uncertainty. Kafka describes this upbringing in *Letter to His Father*: "You can only treat a child in the way you yourself are constituted, with vigor, noise, and a hot temper, and in my case this seemed to you, into the bargain, extremely suitable, because you wanted to bring me up to be a strong, brave boy." [Wagenbach, *Franz Kafka*, p. 20]

Seen superficially, this is a description of a "sheltered" home life, a childhood no worse than many others that have produced more or less prominent and undaunted adults. But Kafka's works

reveal how a sensitive child can experience situations we still des-
ignate today as quite normal and unremarkable, situations with
which our children must live without ever being able to articulate
them like Kafka. If we can be empathic, refrain from trying to spare
the parents, and learn to understand that what Kafka wrote was a
description of conditions in his early childhood and of his reactions
to them instead of the expression of his "neurasthenia," his head-
aches, his "constitution," or his delusions, then we will also become
more sensitive to the burdens we are placing on our children here
and now, often simply because we don't know how intensely a
child receives impressions or what later becomes of them inside him.
It may merely be a matter of a harmless joke at the child's expense,
a trick one plays on him, or a threat one never seriously intends to
carry out but makes only in order to encourage better behavior. The
child, however, cannot know this; he waits, perhaps for days, for the
threatened punishment that never comes but that hangs over his
head like the sword of Damocles. Such "harmless" scenes were often
enacted on Kafka's way to school. In a letter to Milena he writes:

> Our cook, a small dry thin person with a pointed nose and hollow
> cheeks, yellowish but firm, energetic and superior, led me every
> morning to school. We lived in the house which separates the Kleine
> Ring from the Grosse Ring. Thus we walked first across the Ring,
> then into the Teingasse, then through a kind of archway in the
> Fleischmarktgasse down to the Fleischmarkt. And now every morning
> for about a year the same thing was repeated. At the moment of
> leaving the house the cook said she would tell the teacher how naughty
> I'd been at home. As a matter of fact I probably wasn't very naughty,
> but rather stubborn, useless, sad, bad-tempered, and out of all this
> probably something quite nice could have been fabricated for the
> teacher. I knew this, so didn't take the cook's threat too lightly. All the
> same, since the road to school was enormously long I believed at first
> that anything might happen on the way (it's from such apparent
> childish light-heartedness that there gradually develops, just because
> the roads are not so enormously long, this anxiousness and dead-eyed
> seriousness). I was also very much in doubt, at least while still on the
> Alstädter Ring, as to whether the cook, though a person commanding
> respect if only in domestic quarters, would dare to talk to the world-
> respect-commanding person of the teacher. . . . Somewhere near the
> entrance to the Fleischmarktgasse . . . the fear of the threat got the

upper hand. School in itself was already enough of a nightmare, and now the cook was trying to make it even worse. I began to plead, she shook her head, the more I pleaded the more precious appeared to me that for which I was pleading, the greater the danger; I stood still and begged for forgiveness, she dragged me along, I threatened her with retaliation from my parents, she laughed, *here* she was all-powerful, I held on to the shop doors, to the corner stones, I refused to go any further until she had forgiven me, I pulled her back by the skirt (she didn't have it easy, either), but she kept dragging me along with the assurance that she would tell the teacher this, too; it grew late, the clock on the Jakobskirche struck 8, the school bells could be heard, other children began to run, I always had the greatest terror of being late, now we too had to run and all the time the thought: She'll tell, she won't tell—well, she didn't tell, ever, but she always had the opportunity and even an apparently increasing opportunity (I didn't tell yesterday, but I'll certainly tell today) and of this she never let go. [*Letters to Milena*, pp. 65–66]

There have been countless interpretations of Kafka's *The Trial*, for this work reflects the situation in which many people find themselves. Kafka's profound awareness of this situation, which made it possible for him to describe it as he did, is probably rooted in the child's early experiences, scenes similar to those just described on his way to school. Joseph K. is still in bed one morning when he is notified that a lawsuit is being brought against him, the rationale for which is as obscure to him, as illogical, as the attitudes of parents and care givers. He cannot simply deny the justification of the suit out of hand, however, since there is always something a child thinks he must conceal, something he feels guilty for and which he always has to face all alone.

Like *The Trial*'s Joseph K., who tries in vain to find out what his crime is, K., the land surveyor in *The Castle*, worries night and day over the question of when he will finally be accepted as a legitimate member of the community.

A child's desperate attempts to adjust to his parents' inconsistencies, to find meaning and logic in them, can scarcely be better stated than in Kafka's story of the surveyor K., who struggles to gain entry to the castle. How can a child be expected to understand that the same mother who continually professes her love for him is totally unaware of his *true* needs and that he can never gain complete access to her, even though he is physically as close to her as K. is to the castle.

Kafka is depicting here in essence a child's unending efforts to gain understanding, which will help him to escape loneliness and his isolation among the household servants (the villagers); this is mirrored in K.'s attempt to see signs of the castle's favor or rejection in insignificant chance words and gestures of the village inhabitants as well as in his hope of one day finally being able to discover a meaning in that absurd world—a meaning that will sustain him and allow him to become integrated into the community of those living in the castle (the parents).

A child thinks: "The fact that I was born means that someone wanted me, but now no one is paying any attention to me. Have they forgotten they had me? That can't be. Sooner or later they are sure to remember. What must I do to make it happen sooner? How should I behave, how should I interpret the signals?" He will magnify infinitely the slightest sign of favor, reinforcing it with many fantasies and wishes, until his hopes are again shattered under the impact of the undeniable indifference of his environment. But not for long—a child cannot live without hopes and fantasies, which help him to disguise his unbearable reality. Once again the surveyor K. builds his castles in the air; again he tries to establish contact, if not with the count himself, then at least with the count's underlings.

We can only suppose that as a child Kafka, like the land surveyor in *The Castle*, was all alone with his thoughts and speculations concerning the relationships of adults among themselves and with him; paradoxically, this intelligent child, again like the surveyor K., was not taken seriously by his family. He, too, was discredited, misled, not paid attention to, shunted off with promises, humiliated, and ignored—without a single person who was sympathetic and explained things to him. Only his youngest sister, Ottla, gave him love and understanding, but since she was nine years younger than he, he had to spend his first years, the most crucial and formative of his life, in the atmosphere he described in such minute detail in *The Castle*. The surveyor K. (like the child Franz) feels that he is the victim of incomprehensible and inscrutable underhanded treatment; he is continually being subjected to inconsistent behavior; he has been summoned (is wanted), yet is useless; he is under someone's total control or is completely neglected and ignored; he is being humiliated and made fun of, or his hopes are being falsely raised; vague demands are being made on him that he can only guess at; and he is constantly unsure of whether he has done the right thing.

He tries to understand his surroundings, to ask questions, to find meaning in all this chaos and disorder, but he never succeeds. When he thinks he is being made fun of, the others are apparently in dead earnest; yet when he counts on their being serious, he is made a fool of. This is what often happens to a child: the parents call it "playing" and are amused when the child tries in vain to learn the rules of this "game," which, like the pillars of their power, they will not relinquish. Thus, the surveyor in *The Castle* suffers from his inscrutable surroundings, just like a child without a supportive attachment figure; he suffers from the meaningless bureaucracy (child-rearing principles), the undependable nature of the women, the self-importance of the employees, and above all from the fact that there seem to be no answers in this environment to his most urgent existential questions.

Among this great array of people there is not one—with the exception of Olga, who is also a victim of the system—who might explain to K. what is going on or might be able to understand him. Yet he never speaks confusedly but always with clarity, simplicity, friendliness, and conviction. The tragedy of never making any headway with even the simplest, most logical ideas and always running into stone walls permeates all of Kafka's works and is also perceptible in the letters as a constant, suppressed lament. Although Kafka repeatedly gives poetic form to this lament, and makes it a manifest theme of his fiction, for this very reason it remains unconnected with its roots in his biography. The suffering caused the little boy by his mother, who did not understand or even notice the child, is emotionally inaccessible for Kafka as an adult, whereas the difficulties he had with his father, which fall in a later period, were something he could grasp and could articulate much better (cf. *Letter to His Father*).

Kafka's friendship with Max Brod as well as his engagement to Felice Bauer left him ultimately alone, just as he always was with his mother. He once wrote about his relationship with Brod:

For example, during the long years we have known each other I have, after all, been alone with Max on many occasions, for days on end, when traveling even for weeks on end and almost continuously, yet I do not remember—and had it happened, I would certainly remember —ever having had a long coherent conversation involving my entire being, as should inevitably follow when two people with a great fund of independent and lively ideas and experiences are thrown together. And monologues from Max (and many others) I have heard in plenty, but what they lacked was the vociferous, and as a rule even the silent, conversational partner. [*Letters to Felice*, p. 271]

A person who was as lonely as Franz Kafka as a child is unable, as an adult, to find a friend or a woman to understand him, since he often seeks unconsciously to repeat his childhood. From the kind of attachment Kafka had to Felice and she to him we can deduce how he suffered in his relationship with his mother. Julie Kafka not only had no time for her son, she also was insensitive to him, and when she concerned herself with his welfare she did it with such tactlessness that she wounded him deeply (cf. pp. 280–81) without meaning to and without his being able to put his feelings into words, for the child of an insecure mother is so concerned about her well-being that he cannot be aware of his own wounds. The same pattern emerges with Felice. Kafka's levelheaded fiancée can understand a great many things but *not* the world of a Franz Kafka. That he sought understanding from someone like her in vain and didn't become aware of his disappointment for a long time is not surprising when we consider that this man had (and loved) a mother who had absolutely no access to his world.

He wrote to Felice:

My mother? For the last 3 evenings, ever since she began to suspect my troubles, she has begged me to get married whatever happens; she wants to write to you; she wants to come to Berlin with me, she wants goodness knows what! And hasn't the remotest idea what my needs are. [p. 312]

And to Felice's father:

I live within my family, among the kindest, most affectionate people —and am more strange than a stranger. In recent years I have spoken hardly more than twenty words a day to my mother, and I exchange little more than a daily greeting with my father. To my married sisters and brothers-in-law I do not speak at all, although I have nothing against them. [p. 313]

Language and the ability to speak meant everything to Kafka, but because it was not permissible to say what he felt, he had to remain silent and suffered as a result.

In my reading of Kafka, his *Letters to Felice* and the novel *The Castle* provided the keys to understanding both the man and his works. On the one hand, the letters helped me to grasp better what was happening in the novel; on the other, the episodes in the novel and the hopelessness of the hero's situation shed light upon why Kafka tried for five long years to explain himself to a woman who was ill equipped to respond to him. The effort he made to communicate with a partner who, for reasons having to do with her own history, was neither able nor willing to communicate on his terms would not be tragic if his efforts had not been accompanied by the compulsion to keep repeating them and to refuse to give up hope at any price. This absurd compulsion loses its absurdity when we picture a little boy who has no choice but to attempt to communicate with his mother, since he cannot pick out another. I often had to think of his predicament while I was reading *Letters to Felice*, in which, as in *The Castle*, Kafka's earliest relationship with his mother clearly emerges. Her presence was as necessary to him as "air to breathe," he wanted to cling to her, have her to himself, but the very thought made him fearful, since he thought he was asking too much, for she couldn't give him what he needed. And so he feared more than anything else that his longing and his hunger for contact were wrong or inappropriate, simply because his mother couldn't still *that* hunger and perhaps for this reason had difficulty tolerating it as well.

Kafka would have been able to break off with Felice after receiving her first letters had this not been his first experience. This he cannot do; he is too familiar with the disappointment he suffers even to recognize it as such. He therefore becomes engaged to her, ends the engagement at a decisive moment, then later becomes engaged to her again. As the truth about their relationship becomes increasingly clear and oppressive, he is saved from the engagement by illness (tuberculosis).

Kafka recalls their first meeting in one of his letters to Felice:

That night you looked so fresh, even pink-cheeked, and indestructible. Did I fall in love with you at once, that night? Haven't I told you already? At the very first you were quite obviously and incomprehensibly indifferent toward me and probably for this reason seemed familiar. I accepted it as a matter of course. Not until we rose from the table in the dining room did I notice to my horror how quickly the time had passed, how sad that was, and how one would have to hurry. But I didn't know how, or what for. [Translation amended.] [p. 81]

Although Felice Bauer lived in Berlin, Kafka met her for the first time in Prague at the home of friends, where she was also a guest. This marks the beginning of a correspondence almost ideally suited to the projection of long-pent-up feelings accumulating since early childhood, for Kafka actually knows just as little about this woman as a very young child knows about his mother. For the little child, the mother is not an autonomous person but the extension of his own self. Her availability is therefore of crucial importance to him (see *The Drama of the Gifted Child*).

It did not take very long for Kafka to notice unconsciously the similarity between the cool, levelheaded, and capable Felice Bauer and his mother ("you were quite obviously and incomprehensibly indifferent toward me and probably for this reason seemed familiar"). Sometimes such similarities can be sensed in the very first minutes after meeting someone. But in the ensuing happiness of falling in love, all the long-buried hopes of finding a person who will listen and understand and care can blossom forth. The return of suppressed hope can restore vitality and bring a feeling of bliss never experienced before. It is comprehensible if the lover is at first willing to overlook the initial signs of lack of understanding, of alienation, of uncertainty in the beloved, or, when this is no longer possible, to blame himself for having too high expectations, for being "complicated" and different. Of course, he will inevitably feel disappointed in the partner, but the reasons he gives to explain this can enable him to postpone admitting the truth for some time. Thus, Kafka begins by complaining about how infrequently Felice writes (which is not the case at all) in order not to have to complain about the content of her letters, for we can see from his answers that Felice, like his mother, often urges him to take care of his health, has virtually nothing to say about his stories, recommends authors he doesn't like, is upset about the feelings he expresses, and probably is also afraid of their intensity. In essence, she seems to be standing unsuspectingly at the edge of a volcano.

When we read the following passages we can easily imagine how upset and confused Felice must have been by them:

> It is now 10:30 on Monday morning. I have been waiting for a letter since 10:30 on Saturday morning, but again nothing has come. I have written every day (this isn't in the least a reproach, for it has made me happy) but don't I deserve even a word? One single word? Even if it were only to say "I never want to hear from you again." Besides, I thought today's letter would contain some kind of decision, but the nonarrival of a letter is also a little decision. Had a letter arrived, I would have answered it at once, and the answer would be bound to have begun with a complaint about the length of those two endless days. But you leave me sitting wretchedly at my wretched desk!
> [*Letters to Felice*, p. 27]

> Dear Fräulein Felice,
>   Yesterday I pretended to be worried about you, and tried hard to give you advice. But instead what am I doing? Tormenting you? I don't mean intentionally, that would be inconceivable, yet even if I were it would have evaporated, faced by your last letter, like evil faced by good, but I am tormenting you by my existence, my very existence. Fundamentally I am unchanged, keep turning in circles, have acquired but one more unfulfilled longing to add to my other unfulfilled ones; and a new kind of self-confidence, perhaps the strongest I ever had, has been given to me within my general sense of lostness. [p. 30]

> Dearest, don't let me disturb you, I'm only saying good night, and to do so I broke off in the middle of a page of my writing. I'm afraid that soon I shall no longer be able to write to you, for to be able to write to someone (I must give you all kinds of names, so for once you must be called "someone") one has to have an idea of the face one is addressing. I do have a clear idea of your face, that wouldn't be the trouble. But far clearer than that is an image that now comes to me more and more often: of my face resting on your shoulder, of my talking, partly smothered and indistinctly, to your shoulder, your dress, to myself, while you can have no notion of what is being said. . . .
>   And don't fly away! This suddenly comes to my mind somehow, perhaps through the word "adieu," which has a certain soaring quality.

I think one could derive extraordinary pleasure from soaring to great heights, if this could rid one of a heavy burden which clings to one as I cling to you. Don't be tempted by the beckoning of such relief. Hold on to the delusion that you need me; think yourself more deeply into it. It won't do you any harm, you know, and if one day you want to get rid of me you will always have the strength to do so; but meanwhile you have given me a gift such as I never even dreamt of finding in this life. That's how it is, even if in your sleep you shake your head. [pp. 40–41]

Dearest, please don't torment me! Please! No letter even today, Saturday—today when I felt sure it would come, as sure as day follows night. But who insisted on a whole letter? Just two lines, a greeting, an envelope, a card! After four letters (this is the fifth) I haven't had a single word from you. Shame, this isn't right. How am I to get through these endless days—work, talk, and do whatever else is expected of me? Perhaps nothing has happened, you just haven't had the time, rehearsals or conferences about the play may have prevented you, but please tell me, who in the world could prevent you from going over to a small table, picking up a pencil, writing "Felice" on a scrap of paper, and sending it to me? It would mean so much to me. A sign of you being alive, a reassurance for me in my attempt at clinging to a living being. A letter will and must come tomorrow, or I won't know what to do; then all will be well and I'll stop plaguing you with endless requests for more letters. . . . [p. 44]

The night before last I dreamt about you for the second time. A mailman brought two registered letters from you, that is, he delivered them to me, one in each hand, his arms moving in perfect precision, like the jerking of piston rods in a steam engine. God, they were magic letters! I kept pulling out page after page, but the envelopes never emptied. I was standing halfway up a flight of stairs and (don't hold it against me) had to throw the pages I had read all over the stairs, in order to take more letters out of the envelopes. The whole staircase was littered from top to bottom with the loosely heaped pages I had read, the resilient paper creating a great rustling sound. That was a real wish-dream! [p. 47]

His clinging to her, his hopes, his pleas for her devotion alternate with his fear of being abandoned and his self-reproaches. Only after some time does he dare to allow a reproachful tone to creep into his letters, which is then followed by great fear of having now placed everything in jeopardy.

Dearest, what have I done that makes you torment me so? No letter again today, neither by the first mail nor the second. You do make me suffer! While one written word from you could make me happy! You've had enough of me; there is no other explanation, it's not surprising after all; what is incomprehensible, though, is that you don't write and tell me so. If I am to go on living at all, I cannot go on vainly waiting for news of you, as I have done these last few interminable days. But I no longer have any hope of hearing from you. I shall have to repeat specifically the farewell you bid me in silence. I should like to throw myself bodily on this letter, so that it cannot be mailed, but it must be mailed. I shall expect no further letters. [pp. 50–51]

Dearest, my dearest, it is 1:30 at night. Have I offended you with this morning's letter? How am I to know about the responsibilities you have toward your relatives and friends! You take all that trouble and I trouble you with my reproaches about your troubles. Please, dearest, forgive me! Send me a rose to show that you have forgiven. I am not actually tired, but numb and heavy, and can't find the right words. All I can say is: Stay with me, don't leave me. And should one of my enemies from within write to you as he did this morning, don't believe him, just ignore him and look straight into my heart. Life indeed is so hard and sad, how can one hope to hold anyone with nothing but written words? To hold is what hands are for. But this hand of mine has held your hand, which has become indispensable to my life, for only three moments; when I entered the room, when you promised me the trip to Palestine, and when I, fool that I am, allowed you to get into the elevator.

May I kiss you then? On this miserable paper? I might as well open the window and kiss the night air.

Dearest, don't be angry with me! That's all I ask of you. [p. 51]

I cannot cry. To me other people's tears are a strange, incomprehensible phenomenon. In the course of many years I have cried only once, that was two or three months ago; but then I was literally shaking in my armchair, twice in quick succession; I was afraid my uncontrollable sobs would wake my parents next door; it happened at night and was brought about by a particular passage in my novel. [p. 72]

And again his fear of becoming a burden to her:

Tired, you are sure to be tired, my Felice, when you pick up this letter, and I must make an effort to write clearly to spare your sleepy eyes. Wouldn't you rather leave the letter unread for the moment, lie back, and go on sleeping for a few more hours after this week of noise and rush? The letter won't fly away, but will be quite happy to wait on your bedcover until you wake up. . . .

But now not another word, only kisses, and many of them for a thousand reasons—because it's Sunday, because the festivities are over, because the weather is fine, or maybe because the weather is bad, because I write badly, and because I hope my writing will improve, and because I know so little about you and kisses are the only means of discovering something that counts, and because after all you are very sleepy and can't offer any resistance. [pp. 76–77]

I am in your way, I hamper you, there will come a time when I shall have to step aside, whether sooner or later will be determined only by the extent of my selfishness. And it seems I shall never be able to do it in a frank and manly fashion; I shall always be thinking of myself, and should never, as would be my duty, succeed in withholding the truth: if I were to lose you, I should be lost. Dearest, my happiness seems so close at hand, only 8 railway-hours away, yet impossible and unthinkable.

Don't be alarmed, dearest, by these constantly recurring complaints, they won't be followed by another letter like the one I burst out with not long ago . . . but there are evenings when I have to complain away, for to suffer in silence is too hard. [p. 80]

If someone learns at a very early age that he is burdensome to his mother, it is hard for him to imagine that he is not burdensome to other people he loves. He may therefore unconsciously provoke the other person into finding him difficult to tolerate by calling that person "indispensable," as essential to him as "the air he breathes." This will certainly make the other person uncomfortable and will be trying, because it places too many demands and can produce in the partner a reserved attitude not originally intended.

Probably Felice also reacted with growing reserve to lines like these:

Dearest, you cannot imagine the way I squeeze life out of your letters, but the careful consideration, the fully conscious Yes is not in them as yet, not even in your last letter. If only it is in tomorrow's letter, or more particularly in your reply to the one I shall send tomorrow. [pp. 274–75]

The more strongly the other person is idealized, the more painful encounters with reality will be.

You believe everything I say; only what I say about myself you call "too harsh." In that case you don't believe any part of my letter, for it is all about me. What am I to do? How make the incredible credible to you? You have already seen, heard, and put up with me in the flesh. Not only you but your family. And still you do not believe me. And it's a question, too, of your losing more than just "Berlin and all that goes with it"; but of this you say nothing, yet it is the most important. "A good, kind husband"? I attached quite different adjectives to myself in my last letter, but you simply refuse to believe them. Do believe me; consider everything carefully and tell me *how* you have considered it. If only you had a little time today, Sunday, and could write and tell me in a little more detail how you visualize everyday life with a man such as the one described by me? Do that, Felice, I ask you, as one who has been pledged to you ever since the first quarter of an hour! [p. 274]

Dearest, this too, and perhaps this above all, you do not take into account sufficiently in your considerations, though we have written a great deal about it: namely, that writing is actually the good part of my nature. If there is anything good about me, it is that. Without this world in my head, this world straining to be released, I would never have dared to think of wanting to win you. It is not so much a question of what you think of my writing now, but, should we live together, you would soon realize that if willingly or unwillingly you do not come to love my writing, there would be absolutely nothing for you to hold on to. In which case you would be terribly lonely, Felice; you would not realize how much I love you, and I should hardly be able to prove my love, even though then I might feel myself especially yours, then as now. [p. 275]

I know, Felice, there is a simple way of settling these questions quickly and favorably—by not believing me, or at least not believing me as concerns the future, or at least not believing me entirely. I fear you are on the point of it. As a matter of fact nothing could be worse. In that case you would be committing the gravest of sins against yourself, Felice, hence also against me. It would mean ruin for us both. You have to believe what I say about myself; which is the self-knowledge of a man of 30 who for deep-seated reasons has several times been close to madness, thus reaching the limits of his existence, and so can see all of himself and what can become of him within these limits. [p. 276]

Poor dearest Felice! That I suffer more with you than with anyone else, and torment you more than anyone else, is both terrible and just. I

break in half, so to speak. I duck to avoid my own blows, while taking
the greatest pains to deliver them. If this isn't the worst possible omen
for us!

Not a bent for writing, my dearest Felice, not a bent, but my entire
self. A bent can be uprooted and crushed. But this is what I am; no
doubt I myself can be uprooted and crushed, but what will happen to
you? You are abandoned, yet live at my side. You will feel abandoned
if I live the way I have to, and you will be truly abandoned if I don't
live that way. Not a bent, not a bent! The very smallest detail of my
life is determined by and hinges on it. You say you will get used to
me, dearest; but amid how much perhaps unbearable suffering! Are
you capable of actually visualizing a life in which, during autumn and
winter at least, as I have told you before, we shall have but *one* hour
a day together? A life in which, as a married woman, you will find
loneliness harder to bear than you can possibly imagine now from afar,
as a single girl in familiar and fitting surroundings? You would shrink
back in derision from the idea of a convent, yet you contemplate living
with a man whose natural ambition (and incidentally his circumstances, too) obliges him to lead a monastic life? [p. 309]

Needless to say, the living man in me is hopeful, which is not surprising. The thinking man, however, is not. [p. 460]

One just has to keep on trying. Roughly—hence with rather more
ruthlessness than the truth would warrant—I can describe my position
as follows. Having as a rule depended on others, I have an infinite
longing for independence, self-reliance, freedom in all directions; I
would rather wear blinkers and go my own way to the bitter end, than
have my vision distorted by being in the midst of frenzied family life.
That's why every word I say to my parents, or they to me, so easily
turns into a stumbling block under my feet. Any relationship not
created by myself, even though it be opposed to parts of my own
nature, is worthless; it hinders my movements, I hate it, or come near
to hating it. The road is long, one's resources few, there is reason in
plenty for this hatred. Yet, I am my parents' progeny, am bound to
them and to my sisters by blood; in my daily life, and because of the
necessary obsession with my particular objectives, I am not conscious
of this, yet fundamentally I respect it more than I know. Sometimes
this too becomes the object of my hatred; at home the sight of the
double bed, of sheets that have been slept in, of nightshirts carefully
laid out, can bring me to the point of retching, can turn my stomach
inside out; it is as though my birth had not been final, as though from
this fusty life I keep being born again and again in this fusty room; as

though I had to return there for confirmation, being—if not quite, at
least in part—indissolubly connected with these distasteful things;
something still clings to the feet as they try to break free, held fast as
they are in the primeval slime. That is sometimes. At other times I
know that after all they are my parents, are essential, strength-giving
elements of my own self, belonging to me, not merely as obstacles but
as human beings. At such times I want them as one wants perfection;
since from way back and despite all my nastiness, rudeness, selfishness,
and unkindness I have always trembled before them—and do so to this
day, for in fact one never stops; and since they, Father on the one hand
and Mother on the other, have—again quite naturally—almost broken
my will, I want them to be worthy of their actions. (Now and again I
think that Ottla would be the kind of mother I should like in the background: pure, truthful, honest, consistent—with humility and pride,
receptiveness and reticence, devotion and self-reliance, timidity and
courage, in unerring equilibrium. I mention Ottla because my mother
after all is also part of her, though altogether unrecognizable.) So I
want them to be worthy of their actions. In consequence, for me, they
are a hundred times more unclean than they may be in reality, which
doesn't really worry me; their foolishness is a hundred times greater,
their absurdity a hundred times greater, their coarseness a hundred
times greater. On the other hand their good qualities seem a hundred
thousand times smaller than they are in reality. Thus they deceive me,
and yet I cannot rebel against the laws of nature without going mad.
So again there is hatred, and almost nothing but hatred. But you belong to me, I have made you mine; I do not believe that the battle for
any woman in any fairy tale has been fought harder and more
desperately than the battle for you within myself—from the beginning,
over and over again, and perhaps forever. So you belong to me. . . .
Yet if this is so, why did I not like what you said? Because, literally, I
stand facing my family, perpetually brandishing knives simultaneously
to wound and to defend them. [pp. 524–26]

As you know, there are two combatants at war within me. During the
past few days I have had fewer doubts than ever that the better of the
two belongs to you. By word and silence, and a combination of both,
you have been kept informed about the progress of the war for 5 years,
and most of that time it has caused you suffering. Were you to ask if I
have always been truthful, I could only say that with no one else have
I suppressed deliberate lies as strenuously, or—to be more precise—
more strenuously than I have with you. Subterfuges there have been,
lies very few, assuming that it's possible to tell "very few" lies. I am a
mendacious creature. . . . [pp. 544–45]

The next lines show how untrue this last sentence is. Kafka's truthfulness goes so far that he does not even succumb to the temptation to hide behind his illness.

> For secretly I don't believe this illness to be tuberculosis, at least not primarily tuberculosis, but rather a sign of my general bankruptcy. I had thought the war could last longer, but it can't. The blood issues not from the lung, but from a decisive stab delivered by one of the combatants.
>
> From my tuberculosis this one now derives the kind of immense support a child gets from clinging to its mother's skirts. What more can the other one hope for? Has not the war been most splendidly concluded? It is tuberculosis, and that is the end. [p. 545]

And even more plainly:

> I will never be well again. Simply because it is not the kind of tuberculosis that can be laid in a deckchair and nursed back to health, but a weapon that continues to be of supreme necessity as long as I remain alive. And both cannot remain alive. [p. 546]

A letter to Max Brod written in mid-September 1917 reveals Kafka's insight into the deeper significance of his illness.

> In any case I stand today in the same relationship to tuberculosis as a child does to his mother's skirts to which he clings. If the disease comes from my mother, this is even more appropriate, and my mother with her infinite concern, far beneath the surface of her understanding of the matter, would have done me even this service as well. I am constantly searching for an explanation for my illness, for I certainly didn't catch it by myself. Sometimes it seems to me as if my brain and my lungs came to an understanding without my knowledge. "It can't go on like this," said my brain, and after five years my lungs agreed to help out. [*Briefe: 1902–1924*, p. 161]

In his biography Brod tells what happened after Kafka bid farewell to Felice:

> The next morning Franz came to my office to see me. To rest for one moment, he said. He had just been to the station to see F. off. His face was pale, hard, and severe. But suddenly he began to cry. It was the only time I saw him cry. I shall never forget the scene, it is one of the most terrible I have ever experienced. I was not sitting alone in my office; right close up to my desk was the desk of a colleague. . . . But Kafka had come straight into the room I worked in, to see me, in the middle of all the office work, sat near my desk on a small chair

which stood there ready for bearers of petitions, pensioners, and debtors. And in this place he was crying, in this place he said between his sobs: "Is it not terrible that such a thing must happen?" The tears were streaming down his cheeks. I have never except this once seen him upset quite without control of himself. [*Franz Kafka*, pp. 166–67]

On the basis of his letters, we have the choice with Kafka, as we do with patients, of speaking and writing about his "narcissistic character," his "intolerance of frustration," his "weak ego," anxiety, hypochondria, phobias, psychosomatic disturbances, and the like, or of looking for and finding in his life and works information about the kind of childhood he had; in other words, of looking at his symptoms not as undesirable or wrong forms of behavior but as visible links in an invisible chain.

If we do not take our patients' suffering seriously, especially that of early childhood, our diagnoses will remain in the realm of normative, moralizing value judgments. As long as psychoanalysis is unable to free itself from these judgments, it is no wonder—and, apart from unconscious resistance and fear, there is probably good reason—that creative people are highly suspicious of it.

Kafka, like Flaubert and Beckett, could not possibly know he was portraying what he experienced in childhood in his novels and stories. His readers, too, regard his works as products of his imagination, emanating from his brain, his talent, his artistic genius, or whatever one chooses to call it. There is no doubt that Kafka was a writer of genius, and it is his ability to see the universal in the concrete and yet portray it concretely that gives us the very special experience that comes from reading his works. The form he gave to his writing seems to show him to be a very conscious artist with words, but since its content stems from the depths of his experience, it has the power to affect our unconscious deeply and directly. This is why his words provide so many young people with their first confirmation that what they find in their interior world is not necessarily madness.

The usually absurd situations portrayed by Kafka can easily be read as symbols of "general conditions," and the extensive Kafka scholarship is full of such interpretations, which may indeed all be correct. We surely will not go wrong if we see in "A Hunger Artist" the problem of the individual's isolation in mass society, of spiritual

hunger, of exploitation, of so-called exhibitionism and the like; or
if we speak of racial discrimination, the deceptiveness of appear-
ances, and hypocrisy in connection with "The Metamorphosis"; or
understand "In the Penal Colony" as an anticipation of the concentration camps or emphasize the primacy of the religious problem in
The Castle and the ethical one in *The Trial*. All this is legitimate,
but it ignores the fact that Kafka gained his knowledge about these
deeply human and essentially everyday situations by means of the
stored-up memories and feelings the world of his childhood produced in him. Like everyone else, he had to dissociate these feelings
from his initial experiences with his first attachment figures, but
they were preserved within, and like every great writer, he was
able to transfer them in his imagination to fictitious characters. Let
us look at some concrete examples of this.

The hunger artist on display at a circus is starving himself out
of an inner need, finally shrivels away to nothing, and explains before dying that the reason he hasn't wanted to eat is that he couldn't
find the food he liked. At first, this sounds totally absurd, even if we
don't think in terms of actual food but of spiritual nourishment. We
can, to be sure, imagine someone saying, "Rather than read bad
books, I won't read any at all," but a grown man needn't "starve to
death" on that account; he could try to find other books or talk with
people, or—if this weren't possible—even talk to himself. What is
a newborn to do, however, whose mother experiences him as threatening (perhaps because she sees one of her parents in him) and
passes along to him with her milk rejection, fear, and not infrequently a need for revenge? There are babies who are so highly
sensitive that they sense their mother's distress and rejection in the
first days of life, in their first contact with her breast, and express
their anxiety in various physical symptoms. Often these symptoms
require the baby to be taken away from the mother and to be cared
for in the hospital, where the nonhostile arms of a nurse can on
occasion save the baby's life. When, after weeks or months, the baby
is returned to the mother, their relationship has been impaired, it
is true, but the child has survived. It may be that the high degree of
infant mortality in past centuries also had something to do with the
emotional situation in which the infant found himself at birth.
Similar to the hunger artist in Kafka's story, infants actually died
because of food they didn't "like," for they had no one who under-

stood their body language and were as isolated in body and soul in their cradles as the hunger artist in his cage.

I have juxtaposed several passages from "A Hunger Artist" in a way that reproduces what I think must have been little Franz's situation.

> Besides casual onlookers there were also relays of permanent watchers selected by the public, usually butchers[!], strangely enough, and it was their task to watch the hunger artist day and night, three of them at a time, in case he should have some secret recourse to nourishment. . . .
>
> There were often groups of night watchers who were very lax in carrying out their duties and deliberately huddled together in a retired corner to play cards with great absorption, obviously intending to give the hunger artist the chance of a little refreshment, which they supposed he could draw from some private hoard. Nothing annoyed the artist more than such watchers; they made him miserable; they made his fast seem unendurable; sometimes he mastered his feebleness sufficiently to sing during their watch for as long as he could keep going, to show them how unjust their suspicions were. But that was of little use; they only wondered at his cleverness in being able to fill his mouth even while singing. Much more to his taste were the watchers who sat close up to the bars, who were not content with the dim night lighting of the hall but focused him in the full glare of the electric pocket torch given them by the impresario. The harsh light did not trouble him at all, in any case he could never sleep properly, and he could always drowse a little, whatever the light, at any hour, even when the hall was thronged with noisy onlookers. He was quite happy at the prospect of spending a sleepless night with such watchers; he was ready to exchange jokes with them, to tell them stories out of his nomadic life, anything at all to keep them awake and demonstrate to them again that he had no eatables in his cage and that he was fasting as not one of them could fast. . . .
>
> So he lived for many years, with small regular intervals of recuperation, in visible glory, honored by the world, yet in spite of that troubled in spirit, and all the more troubled because no one would take his trouble seriously. What comfort could he possibly need? What more could he possibly wish for? And if some good-natured person, feeling sorry for him, tried to console him by pointing out that his melancholy was probably caused by fasting, it could happen, especially when he had been fasting for some time, that he reacted with an outburst of fury and to the general alarm began to shake the bars of his

cage like a wild animal. Yet the impresario had a way of punishing these outbreaks which he rather enjoyed putting into operation. He would apologize publicly for the artist's behavior, which was only to be excused, he admitted, because of the irritability caused by fasting; a condition hardly to be understood by well-fed people. . . .

This perversion of the truth, familiar to the artist though it was, always unnerved him afresh and proved too much for him. What was a consequence of the premature ending of his fast was here presented as the cause of it! To fight against this lack of understanding, against a whole world of non-understanding, was impossible. . . .

A few years later when the witnesses of such scenes called them to mind, they often failed to understand themselves at all. For meanwhile the aforementioned change in public interest had set in; it seemed to happen almost overnight; there may have been profound causes for it, but who was going to bother about that; at any rate the pampered hunger artist suddenly found himself deserted one fine day by the amusement-seekers, who went streaming past him to other more-favored attractions. . . .

Perhaps, said the hunger artist to himself many a time, things would be a little better if his cage were set not quite so near the menagerie. That made it too easy for people to make their choice, to say nothing of what he suffered from the stench of the menagerie, the animals' restlessness by night, the carrying past of raw lumps of flesh for the beasts of prey, the roaring at feeding times, which depressed him continually. But he did not dare to lodge a complaint with the management; after all, he had the animals to thank for the troops of people who passed his cage, among whom there might always be one here and there to take an interest in him, and who could tell where they might seclude him if he called attention to his existence and thereby to the fact that, strictly speaking, he was only an impediment on the way to the menagerie.

A small impediment, to be sure, one that grew steadily less. People grew familiar with the strange idea that they could be expected, in times like these, to take an interest in a hunger artist, and with this familiarity the verdict went out against him. He might fast as much as he could, and he did so; but nothing could save him now, people passed him by. Just try to explain to anyone the art of fasting! Anyone who has no feeling for it cannot be made to understand it. The fine placards grew dirty and illegible, they were torn down; the little notice board telling the number of fast days achieved, which at first was changed carefully every day, had long stayed at the same figure, for after the first few weeks even this small task seemed pointless to the staff; and so the artist simply fasted on and on, as he had once dreamed of doing, and it was no trouble to him, just as he had always foretold, but no one counted the days, no one, not even the artist himself, knew what records he was already breaking, and his heart grew heavy. And when once in a while some leisurely passer-by stopped, made merry over the old figure on the board, and spoke of swindling, that was in its way the stupidest lie ever invented by indifference and inborn malice, since it was not the hunger artist who was cheating, he was working honestly, but the world was cheating him of his reward.

Many more days went by, however, and that too came to an end. An overseer's eye fell on the cage one day and he asked the attendants why this perfectly good cage should be left standing there unused with dirty straw inside it; nobody knew, until one man, helped out by the notice board, remembered about the hunger artist. They poked into the straw with sticks and found him in it. "Are you still fasting?" asked the overseer; "when on earth do you mean to stop?" "Forgive me, everybody," whispered the hunger artist; only the overseer, who had his ear to the bars, understood him. "Of course," said the overseer, and tapped his forehead with a finger to let the attendants know what state the man was in, "we forgive you." "I always wanted you to admire my fasting," said the hunger artist. "We do admire it," said the overseer, affably. "But you shouldn't admire it," said the hunger artist. "Well then we don't admire it," said the overseer, "but why shouldn't we admire it?" "Because I have to fast, I can't help it," said the hunger artist. "What a fellow you are," said the overseer, "and why can't you help it?" "Because," said the hunger artist, lifting his head a little and speaking, with his lips pursed, as if for a kiss, right into the overseer's ear, so that no syllable might be lost, "because I couldn't find the food I liked. If I had found it, believe me, I should have made no fuss and stuffed myself like you or anyone else." These were his last words, but in his dimming eyes remained the firm though no longer proud persuasion that he was still continuing to fast.

The calm, placid hunger artist would fly into an occasional rage if someone tried to tell him "that his melancholy was probably caused by fasting," if, in other words, effect was mistaken for cause, but it was impossible to fight against this unnerving perversion of the truth, "a whole world of non-understanding."

We can surmise the concrete formative experiences behind Kafka's despair over not being understood when we read the letter, dated November 16, 1912, that his mother wrote to Felice Bauer. (Kafka was twenty-nine at the time.)

My dear Fräulein Bauer,

By chance I caught sight of a letter dated Nov. 12, addressed to my son and signed by you. I liked your manner of writing so much that I read the letter to the end before realizing that I was not entitled to do so.

But when I assure you that it was only my son's well-being that impelled me, I feel certain you will forgive me.

Although I have not had the pleasure of meeting you personally, I have enough confidence in you, dear Fräulein Bauer, to confide in you a mother's worries.

What contributes considerably to this confidence is the suggestion in your letter that he should talk to his mother, who surely loves him. Your opinion of me is correct, dear Fräulein Bauer, which is only natural, since any normal mother must love her children, but I have no words to describe the love I feel for my son, and I would gladly give several years of my life if this could ensure his happiness.

Anyone else in his place would be the happiest of mortals, for his parents have never denied him any wish. He studied whatever he felt like, and since he did not want to be a lawyer he chose the career of an official, which seemed to suit him quite well, as the working hours are short and he has the afternoons to himself.

I have known for many years that he spends his leisure hours writing. But I assumed this to be a mere pastime. Actually, this occupation would not harm his health if only he would sleep and eat like other young people of his age. But he sleeps and eats so little that he is undermining his health, and I am afraid he may not listen to reason until, God forbid, it is too late. I would therefore very much like to ask you if you could somehow draw his attention to this fact, question him about the way he lives, what he eats, how many meals he has, and about his daily routine in general. On the other hand, he must not suspect that I have written to you, nor must he learn that I am aware of his correspondence with you. Should it be within your power to change his mode of life, I would be greatly in your debt and you would be making me very happy.

With the expression of my great esteem, Julie Kafka
[*Letters to Felice*, pp. 45–46]

How much easier it would be to protect oneself against this kind of concern if it were not honest and well-intentioned, which it no doubt was, at least consciously. For what child wouldn't like to believe in a parent's protestations of love and willingness to make sacrifices? It is much easier for the son to defend himself against his blustering father and inwardly distance himself from him. But when his devoted mother insists he ought to be "the happiest of mortals, for his parents have never denied him any wish," how can one bring oneself to tell her that she is obviously overlooking her beloved child's most important needs? If she attributes his unhappiness to not sleeping and eating enough, how can one make clear to her that she is mistaking the effect for the cause? She still won't understand and will have to twist everything in such a way that it fits into her own view of life. "Just try to explain to anyone the art of fasting! Anyone who has no feeling for it cannot be made to understand it." Kafka was not able to tell about his childhood relationship with his mother, but he was able to portray situations that express so clearly his early childhood despair, impotence, and rage, his quiet, passive struggle, that many readers see their own experiences reflected in them—perhaps also without quite realizing it.

"The Metamorphosis" is probably Kafka's best-known story. Although it describes an altogether impossible and unheard-of situation—for of course a person cannot be changed overnight into an insect—even the most indifferent and unfeeling reader cannot help being deeply touched and moved by it. Why is this so? Gregor Samsa, the story's hero, a conscientious salesman whose work enables him to provide devotedly for his parents and sister, awakens one morning to find he has turned into a repulsive insect, and in the coming days he feels revulsion, horror, fear, dread, and infinite helplessness. He is aware of his mother's and sister's touching attempts to overcome their disgust, of the unremitting isolation separating him from the world around him, the disgrace he is bringing to his loved ones, who know no other way of responding to the situation than with fear, horror, guilt feelings, murderous desires, shame in front of others, and hypocrisy arising from their anguish. He himself feels the way an unconsciously rejected infant would feel: unable to speak, tiny in comparison to the size of the furniture, weak, with no possibility of articulation or of being understood and taken seriously by the others, left completely to his own devices, and condemned to death unless someone takes pity on him and establishes communication with him, something that is not easy to do (see pp. 47–50).

Probably Franz Kafka often felt this way as a little child and later too, when he could walk and talk, had to bury his true self just as deeply because he would have risked arousing reactions in those around him similar to those experienced by Gregor Samsa after his metamorphosis. Fortunately, however, it was possible for Kafka, at least in puberty, to find deep rapport and understanding with his sister, who was nine years younger than he, to know that he could rely on her sensitivity and mirroring; this helped him through the critical period of adolescence, enabling him to rescue his spiritual riches despite a long period of starvation and preserve them into adulthood. This was not sufficient to cure his severe neurosis, but his capacity for artistic expression was saved. If Kafka himself had not experienced Gregor Samsa's situation intensely at a very early age, he would not have been able to write this story in such a way that many readers, without giving the matter much thought, at once unconsciously recognize in it an underlying aspect of the human condition. They recognize this by the pain they feel while reading it, because they are compelled to identify with Gregor Samsa and because they vaguely sense a part of their past in this act of identification. I am not saying that everyone is the victim of extreme narcissistic frustration like Franz Kafka but that the need for mirroring, attention, and understanding is especially strong and intense in people like Kafka, and it is consequently they who, tragically enough, suffer the most when their need is not met.

This explains why great artists become neurotic almost of necessity; yet the neurosis is a secondary symptom of their situation, an adjunct to their sensitivity and their fate but never the cause of their creativity, which survives *despite* their neurosis and virtually saves their lives, although it never has the power to cure their illness. "The Metamorphosis" describes, among other things, the sensibility of a neurotic person who feels isolated, does not speak the same language as other people, is dependent on their full understanding, which he never finds, can never formulate his tragedy and must remain silent, is hated and scorned by others as soon as they recognize his true self. Indeed, just a short time before, it is true, when he was still his false, accommodating self, living the part of the good, well-behaved son, the others treated him as one of their own, without ever asking themselves who he really was. It is no surprise, of course, that people prefer to remain the good son Gregor Samsa and, in their fear of the isolation Kafka describes, never overstep the boundaries of what is expected of them. Since, however, it *was* possible for Kafka to overstep these boundaries in his imagination and descend into the depths of his own past as well as the common human past— to identify not with the persecutor but with the suffering victim in his extreme powerlessness—a work of rare universality came into being. In it, the defenselessness, impotence, muteness, and isolation of a little child, which each of us once was, is portrayed in such a way that the reader can acknowledge these feelings yet regard the situation involved as absurd and impossible. Despite this absurdity, however, the authenticity of the story can scarcely be questioned.

What could possibly inspire the writer's imagination to describe scenes like the following?

And so Gregor did not leave the floor, for he feared that his father might take as a piece of peculiar wickedness any excursion of his over the walls or the ceiling. All the same, he could not stay this course much longer, for while his father took one step he had to carry out a whole series of movements. He was already beginning to feel breathless, just as in his former life his lungs had not been very dependable. As he was staggering along, trying to concentrate his energy on running, hardly keeping his eyes open; in his dazed state never even thinking of any other escape than simply going forward; and having almost forgotten that the walls were free to him, which in this room were well provided with finely carved pieces of furniture full of knobs and crevices—suddenly something lightly flung landed close behind him and rolled before him. It was an apple; a second apple followed immediately; Gregor came to a stop in alarm; there was no point in running on, for his father was determined to bombard him. He had filled his pockets with fruit from the dish on the sideboard and was now shying apple after apple, without taking particularly good aim for the moment. The small red apples rolled about the floor as if magnetized and cannoned into each other. An apple thrown without much force grazed Gregor's back and glanced off harmlessly. But another following immediately landed right on his back and sank in; Gregor wanted to drag himself forward, as if this startling, incredible pain could be left behind him; but he felt as if nailed to the spot and flattened himself out in a complete derangement of all his senses. With his last conscious look he saw the door of his room being torn open and his mother rushing out ahead of his screaming sister, in her underbodice, for her daughter had loosened her clothing to let her breathe more freely and recover from her swoon, he saw his mother rushing toward his father, leaving one after another behind her on the floor her loosened petticoats, stumbling over her petticoats straight to his father and embracing him, in complete union with him—but here Gregor's sight began to fail—with her hands clasped around his father's neck as she begged for her son's life. . . .

The serious injury done to Gregor, which disabled him for more than a month—the apple went on sticking in his body as a visible reminder, since no one ventured to remove it—seemed to have made even his father recollect that Gregor was a member of the family, despite his present unfortunate and repulsive shape, and ought not be treated as an enemy, that, on the contrary, family duty required the suppression of disgust and the exercise of patience, nothing but patience.

And although his injury had impaired, probably forever, his powers of movement, and for the time being it took him long, long minutes to creep across his room like an old invalid—there was no question now of crawling up the wall—yet in his own opinion he was sufficiently compensated for this worsening of his condition by the fact that toward evening the living-room door, which he used to watch intently for an hour or two beforehand, was always thrown open, so that lying in the darkness of his room, invisible to the family, he could see them all at the lamp-lit table and listen to their talk, by general consent as it were, very different from his earlier eavesdropping.

In his *Letter to His Father* Kafka wrote:

At that time, and at that time in every way, I would have needed encouragement. I was, after all, weighed down by your mere physical presence. I remember, for instance, how we often undressed in the same bathing hut. There was I, skinny, weakly, slight; you strong, tall, broad. Even inside the hut I felt a miserable specimen, and what's more, not only in your eyes but in the eyes of the whole world, for you were for me the measure of all things. But then when we stepped out of the bathing hut before the people, you holding me by my hand, a little skeleton, unsteady, barefoot on the boards, frightened of the water, incapable of copying your swimming strokes, which you, with the best of intentions, but actually to my profound humiliation, always kept on showing me, then I was frantic with desperation and at such moments all my bad experiences in all spheres fitted magnificently together. I felt best when you sometimes undressed first and I was able to stay behind in the hut alone and put off the disgrace of showing myself in public until at last you came to see what I was doing and drove me out of the hut. I was grateful to you for not seeming to notice my anguish, and besides, I was proud of my father's body. By the way, this difference between us remains much the same to this very day.

Kafka sees himself here as "a little skeleton," unsteady, barefoot on the boards, afraid of the water. He speaks of "profound humiliation," "desperation," and "the disgrace of showing myself in public." Every child, after all, is so much smaller than his father; is it always necessary for this to be felt as humiliating? We know from experience that it need not be the case, that the difference in size does not necessarily cause feelings of shame. We know that children often greatly enjoy being taught to swim by their father and can learn to take pleasure in their own body. But the father's attitude toward the little fellow beside him, his visible and invisible *inner gaze*, determines how the child's attitude toward his own body will develop.

Kafka's father was the son of a very robust butcher, an image that appears in "A Hunger Artist," and by age eleven he was getting up early in the morning, often going barefoot even in winter to deliver meat to the surrounding villages in a pushcart. We can assume that Hermann Kafka, in spite of his great physical strength, never had the feeling of being strong enough, because he was overburdened by the tasks assigned him and time and again reached the limits of his endurance. His father, bursting with strength, made his children, who worked for him, painfully aware of their weakness. He had to be respected and obeyed, that was taken for granted. What became of Kafka's father's feeling of being despised, which he was forced to repress as a child? It survived for thirty years and finally found an outlet when he had a son of his own. Since his physical strength had at one time helped him to survive, any weakness was a sign of being unfit for life and posed a threat for him. It would be possible to help a child grow stronger by respecting him for the weak little creature he is, but a father who was himself despised as a child for being weak can accept only the strong part in himself and rejects the despised weak part in his child from the very beginning. This attitude cannot escape the notice of a child like Franz Kafka.

There is no denying the visionary power of "In the Penal Colony," which was written more than twenty years before the Nazi

concentration camps came into being. The situations depicted in
the story apply to our own day as well—for instance, to our enslavement by technology and the absurdities to which this leads. What
Kafka writes can be seen as relevant to so many situations because
it is true, and it is true because it reflects in a symbolic way something that has actually been experienced. In the work in question
an explorer visits a penal colony and is invited to witness an execution. Kafka describes the bizarre method of carrying out the sentence
in such a way that I could not help seeing the child in the condemned prisoner and was repeatedly reminded of methods of child-
rearing and of treating small children still practiced until very
recently. I quote here a lengthy passage from the story:

All the more did [the explorer] admire the officer, who in spite of his
tight-fitting full-dress uniform coat, amply befrogged and weighed
down by epaulettes, was pursuing his subject with such enthusiasm
and, besides talking, was still tightening a screw here and there with a
spanner. As for the soldier, he seemed to be in much the same condition as the explorer. He had wound the prisoner's chain around both
his wrists, propped himself on his rifle, let his head hang, and was
paying no attention to anything. That did not surprise the explorer,
for the officer was speaking French, and certainly neither the soldier
nor the prisoner understood a word of French. It was all the more
remarkable, therefore, that the prisoner was nonetheless making an
effort to follow the officer's explanations. With a kind of drowsy per-
sistence he directed his gaze wherever the officer pointed a finger, and
at the interruption of the explorer's question he, too, as well as the
officer, looked around.

"Yes, the Harrow," said the officer, "a good name for it. The
needles are set in like the teeth of a harrow and the whole thing works
something like a harrow, although its action is limited to one place
and contrived with much more artistic skill. Anyhow, you'll soon
understand it. On the Bed here the condemned man is laid—I'm going
to describe the apparatus first before I set it in motion. Then you'll be
able to follow the proceedings better. Besides, one of the cogwheels in
the Designer is badly worn; it creaks a lot when it's working; you can
hardly hear yourself speak; spare parts, unfortunately, are difficult to
get here.— Well, here is the Bed, as I told you. It is completely
covered with a layer of cotton wool; you'll find out why later. On this
cotton wool the condemned man is laid, face down, quite naked, of
course; here are straps for the hands, here for the feet, and here for

the neck, to bind him fast. Here at the head of the Bed, where the man, as I said, first lays down his face, is this little gag of felt, which can be easily regulated to go straight into his mouth. It is meant to keep him from screaming and biting his tongue. Of course the man is forced to take the felt into his mouth, for otherwise his neck would be broken by the strap." "Is that cotton wool?" asked the explorer, bending forward. "Yes, certainly," said the officer, with a smile, "feel it for yourself." He took the explorer's hand and guided it over the Bed. "It's specially prepared cotton wool, that's why it looks so different; I'll tell you presently what it's for." The explorer already felt a dawning interest in the apparatus; he sheltered his eyes from the sun with one hand and gazed up at the structure. It was a huge affair. The Bed and the Designer were of the same size and looked like two dark wooden chests. The Designer hung about two meters above the Bed; each of them was bound at the corners with four rods of brass that almost flashed out rays in the sunlight. Between the chests shuttled the Harrow on a ribbon of steel.

The officer had scarcely noticed the explorer's previous indifference, but he was now well aware of his dawning interest; so he stopped explaining in order to leave a space of time for quiet observation. The condemned man imitated the explorer; since he could not use a hand to shelter his eyes he gazed upwards without shade.

"Well, the man lies down," said the explorer, leaning back in his chair and crossing his legs.

"Yes," said the officer, pushing his cap back a little and passing one hand over his heated face, "now listen! Both the Bed and the Designer have an electric battery each; the Bed needs one for itself, the Designer for the Harrow. As soon as the man is strapped down, the Bed is set in motion. It quivers in minute, very rapid vibrations, both from side to side and up and down. You will have seen similar apparatus in hospitals; but in our Bed the movements are all precisely calculated; you see, they have to correspond very exactly to the movements of the Harrow. And the Harrow is the instrument for the actual execution of the sentence."

"And how does the sentence run?" asked the explorer.

"You don't know that either?" said the officer in amazement, and bit his lips. "Forgive me if my explanations seem rather incoherent. I do beg your pardon. You see, the Commandant always used to do the explaining; but the new Commandant shirks this duty; yet that such an important visitor"—the explorer tried to deprecate the honor with both hands, the officer, however, insisted—"that such an important visitor should not even be told about the kind of sentence we pass is a new development, which——" He was just on the point of using strong language but checked himself and said only: "I was not informed, it is not my fault. In any case, I am certainly the best person to explain our procedure, since I have here"—he patted his breast pocket—"the relevant drawings made by our former Commandant."

"The Commandant's own drawings?" asked the explorer. "Did he combine everything in himself, then? Was he soldier, judge, mechanic, chemist, and draughtsman?"

"Indeed he was," said the officer, nodding assent, with a remote, glassy look. Then he inspected his hands critically; they did not seem clean enough to him for touching the drawings; so he went over to the bucket and washed them again. Then he drew out a small leather wallet and said: "Our sentence does not sound severe. Whatever commandment the prisoner has disobeyed is written upon his body by the Harrow. This prisoner, for instance"—the officer indicated the man—"will have written on his body: HONOR THY SUPERIORS!"

The explorer glanced at the man; he stood, as the officer pointed him out, with bent head, apparently listening with all his ears in an effort to catch what was being said. Yet the movement of his blubber lips, closely pressed together, showed clearly that he could not understand a word. Many questions were troubling the explorer, but at the sight of the prisoner he asked only: "Does he know his sentence?" "No," said the officer, eager to go on with his exposition, but the explorer interrupted him: "He doesn't know the sentence that has been passed on him?" "No," said the officer again, pausing a moment as if to let the explorer elaborate his question, and then said: "There would be no point in telling him. He'll learn it on his body." The explorer intended to make no answer, but he felt the prisoner's gaze turned on him; it seemed to ask if he approved such goings-on. So he bent forward again, having already leaned back in his chair, and put another question: "But surely he knows that he has been sentenced?" "Nor that either," said the officer, smiling at the explorer as if expecting him to make further surprising remarks. "No," said the explorer, wiping his forehead, "then he can't know either whether his defense was effective?" "He has had no chance of putting up a defense," said the officer, turning his eyes away as if speaking to himself and so sparing the explorer the shame of hearing self-evident matters explained.

The credulity, naïveté, and trust of a child who is the victim of an insane system of child-rearing can scarcely be presented more vividly than in this scene. Perhaps the explorer is the person the child dreams up to witness the injustice; it is characteristic of Kafka's plight, however, that this person does not help or intervene but leaves other people to their fate.

Since Hermann Kafka does not seem to have been a compulsive person, he presumably did not beat his son regularly. Yet this does not mean Franz was never mistreated. He tells about wanting a glass of water once in the night. His father lifted him out of bed (he slept in the same bedroom with his parents), carried him to the balcony, and left him standing there outside the closed door (cf. *Letter to His Father*, p. 17). On the basis of Kafka's works we can also imagine similar scenes quite clearly if we do not feel compelled to protect his father from our own reproaches. Like the condemned prisoner in "In the Penal Colony," Kafka undoubtedly didn't know what he was guilty of when he was beaten or otherwise punished. Hermann Kafka was an impulsive man, often overworked, impatient, and shaped by his difficult childhood; why shouldn't he seek relief from his pent-up affect by means of his only son, since he had the right to? Even today we live with laws that give adults the right to punish children but deny the right to self-defense. If a man suddenly were to fly into a rage right on the street (perhaps because he just remembered something important he had neglected to do or because his boss had irritated him that day) and in his rage attacked someone going by, the police would immediately arrest him, even if the person he attacked was strong enough to defend himself. However, if the man does this to his little child, whose love and physical weakness make him totally defenseless, then this is called child-rearing and is expressly countenanced and even encouraged by the authorities. Why should it have been any different when Kafka was a child? Regardless of the specific form the torture takes in "In the Penal Colony," the author is also describing, although probably unconsciously, a beating given by a person one loves for crimes one didn't commit and for reasons one cannot grasp.

The short story "The Judgment" deals with a later period in Kafka's life. The hero, Georg, has just written a letter to his friend announcing his engagement. An altercation develops between him and his ailing father, as a result of which Georg takes his own life by jumping off a bridge, thus carrying out the sentence his father imposed on him.

In the figure of the father in "The Judgment," I see not only an introject but also Kafka's real father from earliest childhood, who, like many other fathers with a similar background, requires the sacrifice of his little son. Thus, instead of continuing his engagement, Georg goes to his death, just as Kafka contracted a lung disease, which, as he wrote more than once, "rescued him from his engagement."

The role Kafka's mother played in this tragedy can be seen in her reaction to her son's *Letter to His Father*. He sent the letter to her, asking her to pass it on to his father, since apparently he didn't dare to send it directly. His mother refused to be the intermediary and returned the letter to her son with the request that he spare his father and not send it; so the robust, not particularly sensitive Hermann Kafka was spared, and his son became ill with tuberculosis. But just the fact of writing the letter, of articulating his reproaches, enabled Kafka to take a very important step in his life: to give up the tormenting search to find an accessible mother in Felice and instead enter into a new, more mature relationship with Milena Jesenská in which—in contrast to the monologue with Felice—he experienced true dialogue. "The Judgment" also shows Kafka's insight into the function sons have as their father's sacrificial victim, something that can be observed at many points in human history. Georg's father exclaims:

> "Just take your bride on your arm and try getting in my way! I'll sweep her from your very side, you don't know how! . . . So now you know what else there was in the world besides yourself, till now you've known only about yourself! An innocent child, yes, that you were, truly, but still more truly have you been a devilish human being! —And therefore take note: I sentence you now to death by drowning!"

Georg felt himself urged from the room, the crash with which his father fell on the bed behind him was still in his ears as he fled. On the staircase, which he rushed down as if its steps were an inclined plane, he ran into his charwoman on her way up to do the morning cleaning of the room. "Jesus!" she cried, and covered her face with her apron, but he was already gone. Out of the front door he rushed, across the roadway, driven toward the water. Already he was grasping at the railings as a starving man clutches food. He swung himself over, like the distinguished gymnast he had once been in his youth, to his parents' pride. With weakening grip he was still holding on when he spied between the railings a motor-bus coming which would easily cover the noise of his fall, called in a low voice: "Dear parents, I have always loved you, all the same," and let himself drop.

At this moment an unending stream of traffic was just going over the bridge.

Amid all the street sounds (in the noisy Kafka household) the sacrifice of the son goes unnoticed.

If it may be said that Kafka's stories read like dreams, this is particularly true of *The Stoker*, a work (later to become the first chapter of the novel *Amerika*) that portrays in various images and garbs the specific kind of powerlessness characteristic of Kafka's childhood. It must have been the underlying experience of his life that whatever he expressed was never understood or echoed or responded to. The responses he did receive had nothing to do with what he intended but struck him as strange and absurd.

The Stoker begins with sixteen-year-old Karl Rossmann's arrival in America. He is just about to get off the ship with his suitcase when he remembers he has left his umbrella behind. He asks a fellow passenger to watch his suitcase for a moment (the same suitcase he guarded with his life throughout the two-week voyage because he was afraid someone might steal it) and returns to look for his umbrella. Who hasn't encountered similar situations in dreams? Sometimes we wonder, even before the dream is over, how we could have left the most precious thing we possess standing somewhere without giving it a thought and how our cautiousness, even distrust, could suddenly turn into a childlike trust, into naïve unconcern and affability. This can be explained by the fact that dreams express aspects of our personality dating from various times in our life and that the way we behave in a dream can be alternately like a child or like an adult, or even both at the same time. Although such is undoubtedly the case, it may also be that something is being reflected in our behavior in the dream that is indicative of our situation at an earlier time, namely, that the concern shown us as a child was not dependable and ongoing but vascillated between the extremes of constant supervision and total indifference. It was in precisely this way that Karl Rossmann at first constantly guarded his suitcase and then suddenly abandoned it without a thought.

Karl Rossmann goes back onto the ship to look for his umbrella, and like a little child, he thinks: It really should be quite easy to

find since the ship is empty. But now begins the confusion typical
of dreams, for even an empty ship is thoroughly bewildering for
someone who does not know it well, and Karl is relieved when he
at last finds the stoker, someone he can talk to. It soon becomes
clear, however, that the man will be of no help; on the contrary,
Karl tries to console and help *him*. The stoker complains about how
unjustly he is being treated on the ship and how his superior, Schubal, is harassing him. He says he is in the process of packing his
things and is going to leave the ship. Suitcase and umbrella are now
long forgotten, and Karl devotes all his energy, skill, and emotions—
risking his future, virtually his life—to convincing the captain and
the most important members of the crew of how the stoker is suffering under Schubal. Unlike the explorer in "In the Penal Colony,"
who was merely an observer, Karl assumes the role of advocate.
The child Franz would undoubtedly have liked to present his
mother's suffering under the domination of his father (Schubal)
before a court of justice with equal fervor. Essentially, however,
here the stoker stands for different aspects of Kafka's own self.

Then a situation ensues that is often to be found in Kafka: Karl
speaks clearly, argues logically, is friendly, and attempts to reach
the others, but to no avail. He cannot make himself understood, and
to add to the difficulty, the stoker, symbolizing the childish side of
Kafka's personality, behaves inappropriately, tactlessly, and clum-
sily, thereby damaging his own cause; he attacks everyone, including
Karl, who wants to help him. Karl attempts to calm the stoker and
bring him to his senses—a difficult task—until the whole episode
comes to an unexpected end. It turns out that an uncle of Karl's
is present, a senator and a respected man, who suddenly embraces
his nephew and wants to take him home with him.

Kafka's attempts to express himself to his family undoubtedly
met with the same results: whatever the child tried to say was not
taken seriously and was drowned in the indifference of the family's
good will and the kind of good advice that fills his mother's letters.
Karl tries to mediate between the awkward, childish stoker and the
world of the adults by identifying with both sides. He wants to do
all he can on the stoker's behalf, yet he also senses that the stoker's
uncouth ways are getting on the others' nerves:

> Everything demanded haste, clarity, exact statement; and what was
> the stoker doing? Certainly he was talking himself into a sweat; his

hands were trembling so much that he could no longer hold the papers he had laid on the window-ledge; from all points of the compass complaints about Schubal streamed into his head, each of which, it seemed to him, should have been sufficient to dispose of Schubal for good; but all he could produce for the Captain was a wretched farrago in which everything was lumped together. . . .

Accordingly Karl said to the stoker: "You must put things more simply, more clearly; the Captain can't do justice to what you are telling him. How can he know all the mechanics and ship's boys by name, far less by their first names, so that when you mention so-and-so he can tell at once who is meant? Take your grievances in order, tell the most important ones first and the lesser ones afterwards; perhaps you'll find that it won't be necessary even to mention most of them. You always explained them clearly enough to me!"

Now Kafka shifts his perspective from that of the well-meaning intermediary to the little child and his hopeless situation.

The stoker certainly stopped speaking at once when he heard the familiar voice, but his eyes were so blinded with tears of wounded dignity, of dreadful memory, of extreme present grief, that he could hardly even recognize Karl. How could he at this stage—Karl silently realised this, facing the now silent stoker—how could he at this stage suddenly change his style of argument, when it seemed plain to him that he had already said all there was to say without evoking the slightest sympathy, and at the same time that he had said nothing at all, and could not expect these gentlemen to listen to the whole rigmarole over again? And at such a moment Karl, his sole supporter, had to break in with so-called good advice which merely made it clear that everything was lost, everything.

Karl tries to help the little child like an older brother or a well-meaning older sister.

In his fear of being struck by the stoker's gesticulating hands he would have liked to catch hold of them, and still better to force the man into a corner so as to whisper a few soothing, reassuring words to him which no one else could hear. But the stoker was past all bounds. Karl now began actually to take a sort of comfort in the thought that in case of need the stoker could overwhelm the seven men in the room with the very strength of his desperation.

But the opposite occurs. And now the individual aspects of the personality of the dreamer/narrator are all brought together in one scene that reveals, at the same time, a glimpse into Kafka's biography.

Karl himself felt more strong and clear-headed than perhaps he had ever been at home. If only his father and mother could see him now, fighting for justice in a strange land before men of authority, and, though not yet triumphant, dauntlessly, resolved to win the final victory! Would they revise their opinion of him? Set him between them and praise him? Look into his eyes at last, at last, these eyes so filled with devotion to them? Ambiguous questions, and this the most unsuitable moment to ask them!

In the scene in which Karl takes leave of the stoker, his tenderness and his profuse tears show that he is leaving behind his true self in the guise of the stoker and is mourning the fact, for the uncle is taking only the capable, accommodating, and clever Karl with him. When the boy bids the stoker farewell he says:

"Now you must get ready to defend yourself, answer yes and no, or else these people won't have any idea of the truth. You must promise me to do what I tell you, for I'm afraid, and I've good reason for it, that I won't be able to help you any more." And then Karl burst out crying and kissed the stoker's hand, taking that seamed, almost nerveless hand and pressing it to his cheek like a treasure which he would soon have to give up. But now his uncle the Senator was at his side and very gently yet firmly led him away.

Kafka's despair over not being able to express himself with his parents permeates everything he wrote. Numerous keys to his works can be found in his letters—for example, in these to Max Brod:

When the breakfast noises cease to my left, the noonday noises begin to my right. Doors are then opened everywhere, as though the walls were falling down. But above all, the center of my misfortune remains: I cannot write . . . my whole body warns me against each word; each word, before allowing me to write it, first looks around in all directions. The sentences literally go to pieces on me. I see their insides and then have to stop quickly. [December 15 and 17, 1910]

Or in another letter to Brod:

I have a feeling of pressure in my stomach, as if my stomach were a person and were about to cry. [July 19, 1909]

At age twenty Kafka writes to Oskar Pollak:

. . . We are as forlorn as children lost in the woods. When you stand before me and look at me, what do you know of the pain inside me and what do I know of yours. And if I were to throw myself at your feet and cry and tell you things, what more would you know of me than of hell, when someone tells you it is hot and terrible. That is reason enough for us mortals to be as reverent, thoughtful, and loving with one another as though we were standing before the entrance to hell. [September 9, 1903]

And in the same letter we read:

God doesn't want me to write, but I simply must. . . . So many energies within me are bound to a stake. . . . But we don't shake off any millstones from around our necks by complaining, especially not if we love them.

Kafka tried to live with the millstones he loved. Every child loves his parents, no matter what else is superimposed upon this love later on. But it need not hang like a millstone around his neck, at least not if the parents can tolerate other feelings along with it. Then "so many energies" wouldn't be "bound to a stake."

Why have I devoted so much attention to Kafka here? Why have I quoted so many passages from his works and letters in a book in which he appears only as an example of a possible patient? I could just as well have chosen Heinrich von Kleist, Friedrich Hölderlin, James Joyce, Marcel Proust, Robert Walser, or others instead of Kafka. Perhaps it is only by chance that I immersed myself in him first and must now struggle against the temptation to write a whole book about him. This is what happens to us with our patients as well: in the beginning it is a matter of chance who comes to us, whom we take on as a patient, but then that person assumes unique import-ance for us and stops being merely a case. Why, then, not a book about Kafka instead of a chapter in this book? There are several reasons:

1. Narcissism and the "narcissistic character" in particular now seem to be central topics of discussion for analysts as well as soci-ologists and even theologians. As I have already explained in *The Drama of the Gifted Child*, the word "narcissism" can have many connotations, but a disparaging attitude toward the so-called narcis-sistic character is contained in all of them. In this more or less moralizing attitude I see an unconscious identification with the adult, who tries to combat in the child whatever troubles him in

himself. Critics of the "narcissistic character" are often narcissistically disturbed people who seek protection in grandiose behavior
and in the way they raise their children. For this reason I have let
Kafka speak through his letters and his fiction to enable the reader
to identify with the child in the writer and to enable the beginning,
still inexperienced analyst to identify with the child in "the patient"
Kafka. We can unquestionably describe Kafka's relationship with
Felice as narcissistic, but only if, in reading his letters to his fiancée,
we also keep an ear open to the voice of the child abandoned by
his mother will his words become fully comprehensible and will
the uselessness of merely descriptive or even judgmental concepts
(such as "pathological narcissism") become obvious.

2. In the same way that I immersed myself in the life of Adolf
Hitler in my earlier book *For Your Own Good*, in order to comprehend his destructive career from the perspective of his early life, I
have also searched in Franz Kafka's life for the biographical roots
of a narcissistic personality disturbance in someone who is already
well known—or could become so through his works—to many with
similar problems. In the case of both men I am interested not only
in the universal but in the particular; this stems from my method,
which places *subjectivity* in the foreground. For me the individual
is not a case to be used to illustrate a theory (such as the Oedipus
complex, castration fear, narcissism) but a wellspring of awareness,
a source of understanding that enables others to understand themselves in turn. Like the contemporary English painter Francis Bacon
with some of his oil portraits behind glass, I attempt to present a
picture in which the viewer can see his own reflection (but need
not if he doesn't so choose).

3. There are many people who have gone hungry all their lives
even though their mothers were conscientious, saw that they got
enough food and enough sleep, and were concerned about their
health in general. That these people were in many cases deprived
nevertheless of what was most crucial for them does not yet seem
to be understood, even among professionals. It has by no means
become common knowledge in our society that a child's *psycho-*
logical nourishment derives from the understanding and respect
provided by his or her first attachment figures and that child-rearing
and manipulation cannot take the place of this nourishment.

On the contrary, recent developments in psychology, psychotherapy, and psychiatry reveal a tendency to favor "strategic techniques" and to deny collectively the significance of childhood traumas, with psychopharmaceutical treatment replacing corporal punishment. If someone attempts to talk to his doctor about his childhood, he is given pills to keep him from becoming "overly agitated." On the surface, everything possible is being done to spare the patient, but in reality it is the therapist's feared, internalized parents who are being spared at the cost of the patient's failure to discover his own truth.

4. Kafka's letters to Felice describe the development of a relationship that can without a doubt be called narcissistic. In a relationship of this kind the other person is not seen as an autonomously acting human being but as a function of one's own needs (cf. *The Drama of the Gifted Child*). This attitude toward others is a common one and often remains unchanged throughout a person's life. What particularly struck me about Kafka's letters was their demonstration of the author's ability to grow and to change—from the childish and fearful clinging typical of the early ones to the pain of separation and the grief displayed in later ones. These letters, it seems to me, offer proof of Kafka's long inner struggle between fear of losing the person he loves most if he remains true to himself and panic at the prospect of losing his self if he has to deny who he is. A child cannot resolve a conflict of this nature and is forced to conform because he cannot survive by himself. In his early letters to Felice it appears as though Kafka's childhood plight was going to repeat itself. But as the correspondence progresses, it becomes obvious that now, unlike earlier with his mother, he can perceive and articulate his needs more and more clearly, that although he is in constant danger of subordinating his need to be a writer and to be alone to bourgeois ideals of familial happiness, he never succumbs to this danger. In the end, he knows he can never give up his writing without giving up himself, and he accepts the consequences. Since it is not possible for him to go on writing in the world from which he comes without suffering from guilt feelings, he pays for his decision by becoming ill.

5. Kafka's insight into the origins of his tuberculosis can help us in our attempts to understand psychosomatic illnesses and their societal context. Don't we as therapists make it difficult for patients to live their own lives if we have preconceived ideas about what

constitutes happiness, psychic health, social commitment, altruism, and goodness in a person? According to these conventional standards, still very prevalent today, Franz Kafka was a neurotic or an eccentric, whom a psychotherapist would be tempted to "socialize" in order to enable him to marry Felice. One of my goals in this chapter is to make clear how absurd such an attempt would be. A visionary of rare greatness and depth came into being, and it is obvious that his attempts to adhere to bourgeois norms were bound to fail. Whether humankind cares to pay heed or not, the prophetic power of "In the Penal Colony" endures, not because some god or other whispered inspiration in his ear (only in Brod's fantasy was Kafka a religious man), but because he took his own experiences seriously and thought them through to their bitter end.

Advocates of manipulative strategies in psychotherapy could counter my views by saying that not everyone has the talent of a Franz Kafka and that most people seek help because they would like to get along better with others, because they suffer from their symptoms, want to improve their relationships, cannot bring themselves to marry, and the like. I would reply that these were precisely the complaints Kafka had. It would be disastrous, however, not to perceive the longing to find one's true self inherent in these complaints (cf. *The Drama of the Gifted Child*). What can we discover about a person's gifts if we use our strategic measures in psychotherapy to put the finishing touches to the murder of his or her soul begun in the process of child-rearing? Who can tell later how much talent was nipped in the bud as a result? It is not given to everyone to have a sister like Ottla during puberty. And there are countless people who have never in their life met anyone who could truly relate to them without trying to "educate" them, that is, to change them. How can such people be expected to discover their talents?

As for Kafka, in his last years he was finally able, without benefit of analysis, to live with a woman who was not a replica of his mother and with whom he could share his thoughts and feelings the way he did with Ottla. This opportunity would have been denied him if several years earlier he had submitted to therapy that enabled him to marry Felice.

It is very possible that people who are accustomed to interpreting everything on the conscious level will be unable to find anything convincing in my discussion of Kafka, but my remarks are not intended to try to persuade anyone of the existence of the unconscious. I could imagine, however, that there may even be some analysts who respond to my description of Kafka's suffering, typical for a certain group of people, with the usual arguments—namely, that "no mother is perfect and always able to understand her child," that, in addition, too many demands are placed on mothers and I am downplaying women's predicament and making them feel more guilty than ever by dwelling so much on children's suffering, etc. I have encountered these arguments so often in analytic circles that I think it worth examining them more closely.

What good does it do to criticize "society" if we as analysts keep to ourselves our knowledge of how cruelty in a society develops and is handed on, or even refuse to admit these facts at all so that no one need feel guilty?

In my analytic work I have frequently observed that paradoxical guilt feelings instilled at an early age reduce people's ability to make crucial connections and block their way to feeling and thus to grief as well. What I mean by this is expressed with particular clarity by Lea Fleischmann in *Das ist nicht mein Land* (This Is Not My Country).

> To inform against Jews was one's duty—no need for a guilty conscience; provisions were made to cram them into trains and take them away—no guilty conscience about that; it was legal to shoot children in droves—no guilty conscience. Getting to work five minutes late ran counter to regulations—a guilty conscience; to be lax on the job at the train platform went against one's sense of duty—a guilty conscience; turning on the gas in the gas chambers was an order—no guilty conscience; it's not permissible to get back late from lunch—again a guilty conscience.

Without depth psychology but simply on the basis of her everyday experiences as a teacher, the author of this passage seems to have discovered through pure intuition the close connection between extreme indifference to someone's suffering on the one hand and submissiveness to rules and regulations instilled at an early age on the other. My experience of the unconscious can only confirm this discovery. Since I have come to understand how people with the makeup of an Adolf Eichmann became possible (cf. *For Your*

Own Good, pp. 67–75) and what torments they would suffer if they
were to fail to follow orders even once, I refrain from passing hasty
judgment. At the same time, I see with the utmost clarity the potential danger, so inimical to the truth and so destructive of life, that
comes from being trained from earliest childhood to be unfeelingly
docile. There is no doubt that analysts are often also among those
taught to obey at an early age and thus share in this tragic fate,
but they attempt to work it through. We cannot change our past,
it is true, but the present and future will change once increased consciousness makes our past accessible to us, once we recognize the
extent to which our ability to feel and our awareness have been
hampered by paradoxical guilt feelings implanted in us at an early
age.

It is possible that my efforts to bring these mechanisms to
light will fail because of the power of the Fourth Commandment;
the hold it has over us cannot be broken with a single blow. We
internalized this obstacle to awareness at such an early age that anything which threatens it frightens us. We may therefore have to
give up searching for the truth if our discoveries are going to cause
us more anxiety than we can tolerate. No one can be blamed for this,
and unquestionably we are dealing here with a collective fate.

Thus, as analysts we may say that narcissistic and sexual abuse
of children as well as physical and emotional mistreatment, humiliation, and hurt are facts we must accept because we cannot change
them. But we may not say that the necessity of repressing this
knowledge in childhood simply because it is a necessity is not the
cause of neurosis and then trace the neurosis back to drive conflicts
instead. Let us imagine that a film director making a film exposes in
it some very real forms of cruelty, hitherto unknown, that the audience finds disturbing. Should we be allowed to ban his film on the
grounds that nothing can be done to eliminate this cruelty? How is
anything ever to be changed in a society if cruelty is not seen for
what it is? And who can say that something may not be done to
change it someday, after all? But for this change to occur, the truth,
no matter how unpleasant, must not be concealed any longer. If
we would just stop worrying about guilt and turn to the facts instead, without having to spare anyone in our attempts to understand
the origins of neurosis, our new knowledge might then create one

of the necessary preconditions for bringing about change for future generations.

I admit that history gives us little cause to be optimistic or to hope for change. Four hundred years ago Montaigne's views on child-rearing displayed a respect for the dignity of the child that has not been approached by the methods of present-day pedagogues; and more than two thousand years ago Socrates embodied an attitude toward matters of the soul that puts our scientific psychology to shame. The prevalence of evil in the world and our willingness to succumb to superstition seem to remain constant and to be immune to the influence of new findings. Thus, there is little reason to deny the justification for these pessimistic views; complicated systems theories in the fields of psychotherapy and psychoanalysis, no matter how clever and complicated, will not alter the situation either.

What would we say if we brought someone who had been run over by a car to the hospital and the doctors in attendance allowed the driver of the car to interrupt their examination of the victim because the driver was so eager to prove his innocence? Sometimes I feel that I am in a situation similar to that of these doctors when analysts say that the way I view neurosis in my books might make parents feel guilty. I have myself written that the mother who can give her child everything he or she needs doesn't exist, and I have tried to explain in *The Drama of the Gifted Child* why she cannot exist. This does not absolve us as analysts, however, from asking what conditions a child must have in order not to become neurotic or psychotic in later life. We must raise the question if only for the sake of understanding why our patients have become ill. To react to such questions by defending mothers is an indication of guilt feelings rooted in our own (usually religious) upbringing; they are therefore understandable but are of no help to anyone because they stand in the way of experiencing grief (cf. *For Your Own Good*, pp. 247–76). We cannot undo the harm done to children, neither by blaming nor by defending the parents, but perhaps we can help to prevent future damage if we do not have to deny the truth out of our need to defend ourselves or our parents. The truth is that the neuroses of today were not brought about by drive deprivation or drive conflicts but by severe narcissistic traumatizations (such as humili-

ation, hurt feelings, sexual abuse, and also by making light of childhood suffering), coupled with the necessity to repress them. *The
less the public knows of the significance, the pathogenic effect, and
the impact on society of these traumatizations, the more frequently
they occur.* Only knowledge and not merely more spare time can
help mothers to broaden their understanding of their child and to
give him or her as much sympathetic support as possible. Psychoanalysts could impart this knowledge to mothers if they did not have
false pity for them. I say false, because by holding back and concealing the truth, they lead their patients into new entanglements,
new unintentional cruelty, in other words, into a trap. Doesn't it
make more sense, then, to open patients' eyes to the actual situation
instead?

As desirable as this function of the analyst may be for society,
we cannot take it for granted, let alone require it of him or her. We
all grew up in a pedagogical system in which the child's narcissistic
needs for respect, mirroring, understanding, and self-expression
were neither recognized nor tolerated; on the contrary, they were
stifled. Nevertheless, we can still attempt to gain a new outlook. We
know how long it can take a patient to realize how important it is
to articulate and be aware of his or her needs. Even if there should
no longer be any prospect of these needs being satisfied by the environment, it is still important to acknowledge them because only
then can the patient establish an empathic inner object. Thus we
encourage our patients to feel and express even those desires that
cannot be satisfied, usually with the result that a broadening of the
personality takes place. The analyst's function as midwife consists in
assisting the patient to give birth—or rebirth—to these desires and
needs as well as to bring traumas to the level of consciousness. We
can provide this assistance only if we do not perpetuate the ideology
of our parents, who attempted to talk us as children out of our
unfulfillable desires (for example, for understanding)—that is, if
we do not adopt a pedagogical attitude toward the suffering of
people with natures similar to Kafka's by saying, "There are no
ideal mothers, and children like Kafka make it particularly difficult
for their mothers to understand them." The truth of both assertions
is irreversible, yet we must not allow this to have the effect of
minimizing children's suffering; if we do, we will fail to understand
both our patients and many great literary artists, and at the same

time we will unconsciously bequeath to the next generation of analysts the tragic implications of our not having been understood ourselves, either as children or in our training analysis.

I have frequently pointed out in a variety of contexts that it is
far from my intention to cast blame on parents, for I see them, too,
as victims of their childhood and of the child-rearing ideology that
shaped it; I have also carefully explained that *I do not regard external circumstances as the cause of neurosis but rather the child's
psychological situation*—that is, *the impossibility of articulating his
or her strong feelings caused by traumatic experiences*. Nevertheless, these points are often overlooked and my ideas are misunderstood as a result. It is also overlooked that I am primarily trying
to call attention to social factors that—in spite of far-reaching intellectual emancipation—have remained hidden until now, thanks
to very early emotional internalization.*

Often people also overlook the fact that my criticism of permissive child-rearing practices of course does not include the authentic endeavors of many parents and pedagogues (such as A. S. Neill
of Summerhill fame) but is directed solely against those who abuse
a child under the cover of ideological aims. I have described what
I mean by this in appropriate contexts (cf. *For Your Own Good*,
pp. 99–100 *passim*). Neither is my criticism of traditional child-
rearing ideology directed at individual outstanding personalities
(like Janusz Korczak) who regard themselves as pedagogues but
actually are children's advocates, protectors, and psychological
companions. It was this attitude that gave Korczak the strength in
1942 to accompany into the gas chambers of Treblinka the children
from his Children's Home in Warsaw who had been condemned to
death (cf. Korczak, *Das Recht des Kindes auf Achtung* [The Child's
Right to Be Respected] and *Verteidigt die Kinder* [Defend the Chil-
dren]). In the world he lived in, he couldn't save the children in his
charge, but he didn't want them to feel abandoned as they went
to their death. We are not able to alter our children's world either,

---

* The fact that children are sacrificed to their parents' needs is an uncomfortable truth that no adult likes to hear. Even adolescents find it difficult to
bear, because they are bound to their parents by ambivalent feelings and would
much rather direct their split-off hatred toward institutions and "society" in the
abstract. This provides them with objects they can unequivocally reject, and
they hope in this way finally to rid themselves of their ambivalence.

but it makes a great difference whether we are aware enough to give them our sympathetic support or whether we rear them in a way that leaves them with a burden of guilt. For child-rearing methods reinforce a world in which even the most rudimentary support of the child requires sacrifice.

In this book I have taken a stand against such reinforcement, and I willingly take the risk of being accused of one-sidedness for not taking into account other equally valid points of view that have already been advanced by others. When someone casts a spotlight on a certain area, the surroundings are temporarily thrown into darkness, which does not mean that they cease to exist or that the opportunity for them to be similarly illuminated is lost. I do not doubt that there were many wonderful trees in the Garden of Eden, but I was unable to escape the forcefulness and the substance of discoveries based on my experience as analyst and was compelled to devote myself exclusively to the one forbidden tree. If I succeed in making even a few people aware of how the victimization of children is concealed by placing the blame on them, then all the misunderstandings and reproaches for being one-sided that I anticipate would be a very small price to pay, compared to the importance to me of what I shall have achieved.

Those who have read the first chapter of my book *For Your Own Good* will understand why Freud's first theory, his trauma theory, and my own findings that support it inevitably encounter much greater resistance than the theory of the Oedipus complex. I see this resistance as a social phenomenon and am prepared for the misinterpretations and reproaches it engenders. If there were none, it would have been superfluous for me to write this book. The heritage of millennia cannot suddenly be cast aside. As analysts we must be understanding of this, but we cannot be expected, on the other hand, to shut our eyes tighter than ever after analyzing patients all these many years and making some discoveries no one wants to know about. People don't want to listen because they are not yet ready to bear what they will hear. That is justifiable, for to achieve genuine insight is a slow process in which intellectual knowledge plays only a small role. What is decisive is no doubt the willingness to remain open, open to what "the patients" and the poets tell us, to what our children have to reveal to us, and, finally, to the discoveries we can make about our own selves once we are able to take our feelings and our fantasies seriously and see them as messages about earlier situations in our lives.

As soon as opposition to the truth about the damage done to young children under a cloak of silence becomes less widespread and unyielding than it is now, these messages will not need much coding. Mariella Mehr's moving book, *Steinzeit* (Stone Age), is an indication of this. At age thirty-two this woman succeeded in uncovering the almost inconceivable martyrdom of her childhood and youth as well as a whole long and hidden chain of persecution and assault; she did this by experiencing her pain and other accompanying feelings in their full intensity, and in the process found her true self. The change from a petrified, dehumanized creature to a vital, feeling, and suffering human being took place within the context of primal therapy, apparently in its best possible form. In any case, we sense here the presence of a trustworthy, nonpedagogical, empathic support figure, who never is placating, never conceals the truth with theories, ideologies, or mystification. The only concession Mehr makes to the reader's resistance is her designation of the book as a "novel," thereby giving the reader the opportunity to take a psychiatric approach and call the whole thing the product of a "diseased imagination." But even the most horrible imaginings seldom approach the horror of reality. Mehr's book is an exceptional work, both for its conviction as well as for the significance of its findings. This work illustrates and indirectly confirms several of my premises:

1. It is the depth, intensity, and authenticity of experience that gives a literary work its force and not the psychological naïveté (or lack of awareness of the unconscious) of the author; therefore, a writer's familiarity with his or her unconscious does not diminish literary power.

2. The source of creativity lies in the creative person's capacity for suffering, not in his or her neurosis.

3. Liberation and the ability to love are attained by experiencing traumatic childhood situations and articulating the resulting hatred and despair, not by acting them out. Only if these emotions are dissociated from their cause will they lead to destructive and self-destructive behavior.

4. Change in society is brought about by uncovering and recognizing the truth in its entirety, not by manipulative methods based on acceptance of social taboos.

5. Old wounds will heal over if feelings find full acceptance and if emotional access to childhood traumas is provided, not if drive conflicts are intellectually resolved or if improved control and mastery over drive desires are achieved.

6. Access to these traumas will be facilitated by a trustworthy, sincere support figure, not by complicated theories.

Once this access has been won, then the numbness that was needed to survive gives way, even in the case of a woman whose schizophrenic mother twice attempted to murder her as a little girl, a woman who was raped repeatedly and who was forced to undergo electric shock treatments and disciplinary measures of unbelievable brutality. No "mere" imagination could have invented all this, could ever have described it in such a consistent way. There are simply some horrendous things in this world that the philosophers (the fortunate ones) have not yet dreamed of. But at the same time there are an increasing number of people who are able to see these things because at some point along the way they have found an aware and sensitive support figure. To be sure, the truth that individuals discover through their pain can be crushed over and over again by the tomes of pedagogical, psychiatric, and theological wisdom, but it cannot be destroyed, for every newborn child has the capacity to discover the truth anew.

Afterword to the Original Edition

BEFORE sending the manuscript of this book to the publisher, I gave it to four colleagues to read who had shared in the development of my ideas through numerous discussions. The first one said that after our many conversations the material was no longer new to him and he was able to confirm my hypothesis on the basis of his practice. This reaction pleased me very much, since it indicated there was little likelihood that mine would be a lone voice among psychoanalysts. Another analyst said the scales had fallen from her eyes when she read my case presentations. She was relieved to be able to cast aside the ballast from her training that she had never fully accepted and give more credence than before to her own findings and perceptions. The third colleague reacted the same way many parents did to my previous books, i.e., with guilt feelings. She said if my arguments were correct, that would mean she had made grave errors: she recalled patients who, as she now thought, had been desperately attempting to articulate their traumas, whereas she had always felt obligated to regard what they said as an expression of their childhood fantasies and desires. I could only tell my colleague that I had felt this way for a long time, too, and without that experience I would not have been able to write this book. Whether someone reacts to my views with sorrow or guilt feelings, or even with total denial, depends on his or her own history.

My fourth colleague said she felt as though blinders had been removed from her eyes, but at the same time, now that she was seeing new connections, she was also feeling disloyal to her teachers, to whom she was grateful for a great deal and who had insisted that the drive theory was the central factor in analysis. Her observation gave me food for thought.

Both sorrow and a conflict of loyalties will undoubtedly be required of us if we are to recognize and come to terms with "poisonous pedagogy's" influence on our childhood and specifically on our training as analysts. But if we succeed in working through our sorrow, we shall gain the freedom to judge for ourselves and with this the possibility and the right to make use of our own eyes and ears and to take our own perceptions seriously.

The direction in which I have moved in writing this book as well as the countless unfortunate childhoods I have read about in letters from my readers caused me to question how the truth could have remained hidden from me, too, for such a long time and what role the drive theory played in concealing it. It troubled me that so few of my colleagues were able to accompany me on my journey, and in trying to find the societal reasons for this, I came upon the drive theory, the Fourth Commandment, and the traditional methods of child-rearing, a combination of factors that explained the collective denial of childhood trauma. But this was my personal journey. My colleagues' reactions showed me that the ways in which one responds to new experiences can vary greatly; what led to a radical change of direction in my attempt to understand neurosis may elicit different responses in others. How we integrate new insights into our existing fund of knowledge depends on our character, our age, and our previous experience. The discoveries I have made bear my own personal stamp and therefore cannot be prescribed for others. But the hypotheses I have adopted can be examined, again from a personal perspective, and can serve as a basis for new findings.* The purpose of this book is not to win support for my conclusions, for that would only encourage the uncritical stance I object to; rather, it is my hope that the findings I have presented here will challenge readers to go on to make their own discoveries.

---

* My hypotheses have been confirmed much more quickly than I expected; significantly, verification was provided not by my psychoanalytic colleagues but by life itself (see my Afterword to the American edition).

Afterword to the American Edition

W HEN this book appeared in Germany in 1981, I was virtually alone in my thinking, for the sexual abuse of children was still a forbidden subject in Europe. I didn't know then that the situation had already changed in the United States, that the topic was being discussed openly there and had become a matter of public concern.

As a result of my first visit to America in 1982 and of meeting the women authors Florence Rush, Louise Armstrong, Sandra Butler, and Susan Griffin,* I read several books and papers on the facts concerning the sexual abuse of children. Meanwhile, the silence had been broken in Europe as well: increased media coverage is now being supplemented by authentic reports given us by the victims themselves. A German translation of Florence Rush's important book, *The Best Kept Secret*, appeared in 1982, and Louise Armstrong's *Kiss Daddy Goodnight* will soon appear. In response to an article about sexual abuse of children I had written in 1982 for the women's magazine *Brigitte*, over 160 letters were received from victims who reported—for the first time in their lives—what had once happened to them. These letters appeared in book form in 1983 and encouraged many women to form self-help groups to overcome their fear and speak out.

We are observing a new situation, unprecedented in history, not because the sexual abuse of children is a new problem (as Florence Rush has indicated in her book, it is as old as our culture itself), but

---

* Florence Rush, *The Best Kept Secret: Sexual Abuse of Children* (Englewood Cliffs, 1980); Louise Armstrong, *Kiss Daddy Goodnight: A Speak-Out on Incest* (New York, 1978); Sandra Butler, *Conspiracy of Silence: The Trauma of Incest* (San Francisco, 1978); Susan Griffin, *Pornography and Silence: Culture's Revolt Against Nature* (New York, 1982).

because it *is* new for the phenomenon to be *discussed in public.*
This development gives rise to the hope that the victims will now
have more opportunity than before to work through their confusion,
isolation, and disturbed perception of reality. I shall treat this last
point in greater detail below.

Even if certain therapeutic schools are unable to draw the logical
conclusions from the new information being made available because
they are still rooted in the nineteenth century, the truth will prevail
in spite of them. Two books with similar titles (*The Best Kept Secret*
and the German edition of *Thou Shalt Not Be Aware*) appeared
within a year of each other (1980 and 1981). They were written by
women who did not know of each other's existence, who had different professions, lived on different continents, and nevertheless discovered the same shocking truth. What I as a psychoanalyst found
in the unconscious of my patients, Florence Rush was able to confirm
in her historical research. This information will be of importance in
future forms of therapy, for an effective method can be developed
only if it is based on the truth and not on the techniques of traditional
pedagogy.

At the turn of the century the occurrence of sexual abuse of
children was still considered "inconceivable" (although demonstrably taking place), at least in bourgeois circles, where the subject
was embarrassing and considered indecent. Since practitioners in
those fields dealing with psychology (physicians, psychiatrists, psychologists) felt obligated to observe the rules established by these
circles, they reacted with indignation to Freud's discovery that all
his hysterical patients had been sexually abused as children, and
they were unable to reconcile it with their own findings. Although
intimate matters of this nature were more apparent among the less
privileged classes, there was obviously no one who could formulate
the question of what behavioral patterns a person sexually abused
in childhood brings to society. Questions of this sort could scarcely
have been posed earlier, even by professionals, because so little was
known about the child's true situation. The victims involved actually think they must blame themselves for what happened. Also,
the psychoanalytic theory of infantile sexuality denies the cruelty
inflicted on children. Thus, the question of what children do with
their unresolved traumas, of how they later, as adults, turn the

cruelty to which they were subjected against themselves or others, never really arose in psychology or the other social sciences.

General information that has been made public about the sexual abuse of children occurring every day of course addresses only a small part of the problem, for the effects of this abuse on the victims' interaction with others and on the next generation are not altered, nor is the question of the best therapeutic treatment for the damage that has been caused resolved simply by providing more information. Nevertheless, growing public awareness is gradually making it easier for psychologists and psychotherapists to become better informed about the subject and to pay more attention to its significance. Sooner or later they will feel compelled to ask: What becomes of the feelings arising from such traumas, feelings that must be repressed or split off? How do these children develop as adults and what happens when they become parents themselves? Or put differently: What is the significance of the fact that eighty percent of all female drug addicts and seventy percent of all prostitutes were sexually abused as children?

It was not reports about real and verifiable cases of sexual abuse of children such as are now fortunately being disclosed that made me aware of the problem but rather the unconscious messages of people severely wounded in childhood who initially denied these wounds. The form their symptoms took, their way of idealizing their childhood and their parents, of blaming themselves for all their suffering, of keeping the secret from others as well as themselves—but also their strong desire, on the other hand, to escape the confusion they felt and learn to live with the truth—led me to make some assumptions that unfortunately proved to be true. On the basis of my experience I concluded that the extent of sexual abuse of children throughout all levels of society must be greater than is generally believed, and the statistics I have since seen have already far exceeded my own estimates.

In my books I had formulated the hypothesis that as children we are used and misused for adults' needs, including sexual needs, to a much greater extent than we realize. It also became increasingly clear to me that the blocked feelings resulting from this abuse inevitably lead to psychic and physical disturbances. Initially, I attempted to integrate my insights into the body of psychoanalytic

theory, but gradually I became painfully aware that this would be
impossible. It took time for me to accept the fact that psychoanalysis,
too, of necessity shares the taboos of the society to which it belongs;
realizing this, I tried to understand from what source these taboos
received their extraordinary power. I began my search within the
framework of psychoanalysis because this was the field I knew best,
but the answers I found fell outside its boundaries and cast new
light on the foundations of society as a whole. In almost every area
of life I found the tendency to ignore the prevalence of child abuse
and to deny its lasting effects. This attitude is found not only in
psychoanalysis, where it has been given additional reinforcement by
the drive theory, but also in the new therapeutic schools, for it
conforms to the unwritten laws of our society and remains unconscious as long as it is not directly confronted.

That is why I found it crucial to describe this tendency in as
much detail as possible so that it would be more easily identifiable
for therapists of varying persuasions as well as for their patients;
only if therapists no longer have the need to protect adults from
the reproaches of the injured child, because they have experienced
and accepted their own unconscious reproaches dating from childhood, will they be able to support the victims and to help them
work through a painful past. I shall try to explain here why I think
the presence of a supportive person is of particular importance for
victims of sexual abuse.

For millennia it has been permissible and customary for children to be used to satisfy a wide variety of adult needs. They have
provided a cheap source of labor, an ideal outlet for the discharge
of stored-up affect, a receptacle for unwanted feelings, an object
for the projection of conflicts and fears, compensation for feelings
of inferiority, and an opportunity for exercising power and obtain-
ing pleasure. Among all the different ways of misusing a child, sexual abuse is of particular significance, stemming as it does from the
major role sexuality plays in our body and from the hypocrisy still
surrounding it in our society.

Since beatings and the tormenting, demeaning, and humiliating
treatment of children have always been regarded as forms of discipline "for their own good," these methods have been applied quite
openly. There are still many people today who are fully in favor of
child-rearing principles of this nature, and therefore child-beating

can be widely observed, for it need not take place behind closed doors. This can lead to the fortunate circumstance that children find an adult witness who has the courage to come to their aid and defend them, for the adult knows how wounding this humiliating treatment is. Such support can help children perceive that a wrong has been done them and thus make it possible for them to integrate this unhappy segment of reality into their lives. Then they will not have to spend the rest of their lives blaming themselves for what happened to them. But in the case of sexual abuse, which, unlike beatings, usually takes place surreptitiously and under cover of darkness, the likelihood of finding the help of a courageous witness who can facilitate the integration of what has happened is much slimmer. Children cannot achieve integration by themselves. They have no choice but to repress the experience, because the pain caused by their fear, isolation, betrayed expectation of receiving love, helplessness, and feelings of shame and guilt is unbearable. Further, the puzzling silence on the part of the adult and the contradiction between his deeds and the moral principles and prohibitions he proclaims by light of day create an intolerable confusion in the child that must be done away with by means of repression.

If older children who earlier had the good fortune to be able to trust their perceptions with their first attachment figure are sexually molested, they may be able to acknowledge the trauma and take it seriously, retain the memory of it, and with time work the experience through. If, however, this essential feature is missing, as it often is, and if children are talked out of what they perceive, then the experience they undergo will later be seen in a diffuse, hazy light; its reality will remain uncertain and indistinct, laden with feelings of guilt and shame, and as adults these children either will know nothing of what happened or will question their memory of it. This will be even more the case if the abuse occurred in early childhood. Since very young children do not find support within their own self or a mirror in the eyes of a witness, they must deny the truth. Later, the patient will repeatedly and unconsciously reenact this reality, will tell the story by way of symptoms, including physical ones, and will hope that the whole thing is only a matter of fantasy. In the preceding pages I have used the example of Freud's famous patient known as the Wolf-Man to describe this process.

The Wolf-Man, who was sexually abused, probably by his nurse in his second year of life and thereafter repeatedly by his sister, struggled all his life to avoid being abused by others but kept falling into situations in which this indeed happened. Unconsciously, he had to bring about these situations in order to keep repeating his childhood traumas, which he could not remember and therefore could not talk about. The traumas occurred at a tender age and without witnesses; in spite of endless analysis, there was never anyone all his life who was able to empathize with the situation of the little boy, although this was what he needed, for his repression made it impossible for him to empathize with himself. Even Freud misused the Wolf-Man for the sake of proving his theories and was unable to give his patient this desperately needed empathy because he himself had had similar experiences as a child and had not been allowed to be aware of the feelings aroused as a result. At first Freud approached these experiences by way of his dreams but was unable to deal with them and work them through without the presence of a supportive person; therefore, he repressed them again, devising a theory to help him ward off what he had experienced. With this theory he created a whole army of analysts, skilled in warding off, who help their patients talk themselves out of their trauma instead of experiencing it, with the result that the victims of abuse continue to feel responsible for what happened to them.

The Freudian ideology ensures that the patient need not face up to the unendurable pain of confusion and helplessness felt by a sexually abused young child but can gain a feeling of power through the illusion of "Oedipal" guilt. If this illusion of power can be achieved without having to pay the price of severe symptoms, that is perhaps better than the reawakening of early childhood feelings if they must be faced alone. It is understandably difficult to find a supportive therapist to talk to about these experiences as long as society ignores or minimizes the fact of sexual abuse of children.

The psychoanalytic drive theory has done a great deal to encourage this societal attitude. More than eighty years ago Freud claimed he had "established" that his patients' memories of being sexually molested as children by adults were not memories of real events after all but merely fantasies. How was he able to establish this? Only since I have become more familiar with the circumstances surrounding sexual abuse (thanks to Armstrong, Butler, Herman, and

Rush) has it struck me that Freud's conclusion, which provides an important premise for his drive theory and has been repeated in good faith countless times since by students in examinations, "establishes" something that he can only have conjectured, for it can be established with the aid of witnesses that a certain act took place, but we can never be certain that something did *not* take place if both parties to the act have an interest in keeping it secret. This is usually the case with sexual abuse, for even the victim cannot bear the truth because of the accompanying feelings of fear, shame, and guilt.

I cannot emphasize enough the importance of this point, for whether it is understood or not will determine whether the patient in society, like the child in the family, is left alone with his or her trauma or finds the necessary understanding in the therapist, i.e., understanding for the fact that reality is more tragic than all fantasies, which do indeed contain certain aspects of the trauma experienced but essentially serve to conceal the unbearable truth. A particular difficulty—indeed, an actual hindrance—on the path to remembering in therapy comes about as a result of the mechanism of warding off, once required for survival, which can manifest itself in fantasies and imagery from fairy tales or in chronic perversions. Perversion, addiction, and self-destructive enactments—like fantasies—take on the function of concealment. They organize present suffering in exact accordance with the pattern of the past and in this way guarantee that the earlier, unbearable suffering remains repressed.

Only liberation from pedagogical tendencies will bring about crucial insights into the child's actual situation. These insights can be summarized in the following points:

1. The newborn is always innocent.
2. Each child needs among other things: care, protection, security, warmth, skin contact, touching, caressing, and tenderness.
3. These needs are seldom sufficiently fulfilled; in fact, they are often exploited by adults for their own ends (trauma of child abuse).
4. Child abuse has lifelong effects.
5. Society takes the side of the adult and blames the child for what has been done to him or her.

6.   The victimization of the child has historically been denied and is still being denied, even today.

7.   This denial has made it possible for society to ignore the devastating effects of the victimization of the child for such a long time.

8.   The child, when betrayed by society, has no choice but to repress the trauma and to idealize the abuser.

9.   Repression leads to neuroses, psychoses, psychosomatic disorders, and delinquency.

10. In neuroses, the child's needs are repressed and/or denied; instead, feelings of guilt are experienced.

11. In psychoses, the mistreatment is transformed into a disguised illusory version (madness).

12. In psychosomatic disorders, the pain of mistreatment is felt but the actual origins are concealed.

13. In delinquency, the confusion, seduction, and mistreatment of childhood are acted out again and again.

14. The therapeutic process can be successful only if it is based on uncovering the truth about the patient's childhood instead of denying that reality.

15. The psychoanalytic theory of "infantile sexuality" actually protects the parent and reinforces society's blindness.

16. Fantasies always serve to conceal or minimize unbearable childhood reality for the sake of the child's survival; therefore, the so-called invented trauma is a less harmful version of the real, repressed one.

17. The fantasies expressed in literature, art, fairy tales, and dreams often unconsciously convey early childhood experiences in a symbolic way.

18. This symbolic testimony is tolerated in our culture thanks to society's chronic ignorance of the truth concerning childhood; if the import of these fantasies were understood, they would be rejected.

19. A past crime cannot be undone by our understanding of the perpetrator's blindness and unfulfilled needs.

20. New crimes, however, can be prevented, if the victims begin to see and be aware of what has been done to them.

21. Therefore, the reports of victims will be able to bring about more awareness, consciousness, and sense of responsibility in society at large.

Thanks to these honest reports of childhood experiences, other men and women will be encouraged to confront their own childhood, take it seriously, and talk about it. In so doing, they in turn will provide information to others about what so many human beings have had to undergo at the beginning of life without even knowing about it in later years and without anyone else knowing about it either. Earlier, it simply was not possible to be aware of these matters and there were virtually no published reports by the victims that did not idealize the perpetrators. But now such reports are available and will continue to appear, presumably in growing numbers. I do not believe this process can be reversed.

I have not founded a psychoanalytic school or an institute nor have I established any groups, and I am not in a position to provide names and addresses of therapists. My intention has been to describe the unstated commandment that forbids us to see the true situation of children in our society. Once their plight has become visible, it will be easier to offer therapeutic help through existing channels, and the danger that therapeutic practices will be used to subjugate people (in sects, for instance) will be reduced. Research in the field will also be of more use to therapists than before, once researchers have accepted the truth, which is no less true because it is painful and which for that very reason has healing and transforming powers.

The truth about our childhood is stored up in our body, and although we can repress it, we can never alter it. Our intellect can be deceived, our feelings manipulated, our perceptions confused, and our body tricked with medication. But someday the body will present its bill, for it is as incorruptible as a child who, still whole in spirit, will accept no compromises or excuses, and it will not stop tormenting us until we stop evading the truth.

Daughters Are Breaking Their Silence*

R OD McKuen, the fifty-one-year-old poet and singer, recently
addressed a meeting of the National Committee for the Pre-
vention of Child Abuse, held in Washington, D.C., and revealed for
the first time that when he was seven years old he was sexually
abused by both his step-aunt and his step-uncle. Only when he said
he would tell his mother and everyone on his block did they leave
him alone. He described this period of his life as a time of terrible
humiliation. In this case, a child managed to rescue himself from
the torment of a frightening and degrading situation by threatening
to tell other people about it. But to make a threat like this, to say
nothing of carrying it out, requires a psychological strength that a
sexually abused child is seldom able to summon up. And above all,
it requires the confidence that "everyone on the block" will take a
child seriously, will listen to him and believe what he says. If this
were indeed the case, the lot of our children would be greatly
improved. But where are we to find such enlightened listeners? I
know a woman who was sexually abused by a priest when she was
seven and after going to her mother about it was beaten for telling
"such wicked lies." We have been taught to respect those in authority
and to protect them from any criticism and at the same time to
"educate" those who are weak and helpless and dependent. This is
what we have come to expect. One of the Ten Commandments says,
"Honor your father and your mother . . . that it may go well with
you . . ."; nowhere does it say, "Honor your children so that they will

---

* This is a somewhat shortened version of an article that originally appeared
as "Die Töchter schweigen nicht mehr" in a special issue of the German magazine *Brigitte* (October 1982).

be able to honor others as well as themselves." As a result, victimized children in our society must contend with the knowledge that they will not be protected but will be blamed and humiliated while those who abuse them will be defended. This attitude on the part of society is reflected in the way rape cases are handled by the courts, and the ramifications are particularly ominous when child rape is involved, because this is where the roots of new violence are nurtured. It is nonsense to think that there will be no lasting consequences when harm is done to a child, since he or she is "still so little." The opposite is true, although not yet widely recognized. Children only *seem* to forget what has been done to them, for they have a photographic memory in the unconscious, and it has been demonstrated that under certain conditions this memory can be reactivated. If these conditions are not present, however, if the crucial traumas are forgotten and childhood remains highly idealized, then there is often the danger that as adults these people will torment others or themselves the same way they were once tormented —without their even remembering the past. In order to protect the culprits, the "authority figures," from the accusations of their victims, our society, including professional experts, stubbornly denies or glosses over and minimizes the *connection* between what was endured in childhood and later symptoms of illness. Quentin Bell's biography of Virginia Woolf serves as an example of this.

Woolf, known to many women not only as a writer but as a proponent of women's rights, was subject to schizophrenic episodes beginning at the age of twelve and took her own life in 1941 at the age of fifty-nine, although she had no apparent grounds for doing so. From the time she was four until she reached puberty she was sexually molested by her much older half-brother, virtually on a daily basis, without being able to tell anyone about it. The appearance of her later delusions of persecution is without a doubt a logical consequence of this situation, and yet the connection is carefully ignored. Bell, for example, writes that he doesn't know whether this trauma had any permanent effect on Virginia or not!

How can an author who describes with great empathy Woolf's trauma and the entire dishonest atmosphere surrounding it at the same time question its importance? One would think that by now such an obvious compartmentalization of knowledge would be a thing of the past. Yet Bell's book is a recent one, and it faithfully reflects our society as it is today.

At the moment, however, there are hopeful signs of an impending change: thanks to the American women's movement, conditions that have been kept carefully hidden by society until now are becoming more visible and are beginning to be discussed in public.

In this connection, a number of books that have appeared in the United States over the past five years ought to be extremely enlightening for the younger generation. In these works, women writers—some of them quite successful—have tried to come to terms with the traumatic sexual abuse their fathers inflicted on them in childhood by writing about it. Their reports have focused public attention on the victimization of the child and its consequences in adult life, and above all, on the danger of having to keep silent about this situation. They have revealed an ominous cancer in our society, the existence of which has scarcely been suspected by the general public until now. At the same time, by their candor they have been of help to many others. It has been a great relief for countless women readers to be able to speak out about their own experiences, no longer to feel condemned to silence, to know they are not alone with their fate and are not themselves to blame for what happened. "The best kept secret," whose history in our culture is traced by Florence Rush in her moving book of that title, is a secret no longer. Women have revealed it, and they are offering support to other victims in their lonely struggle to overcome their bewilderment and to keep their experiences from being distorted by uncomprehending psychiatrists. (There are also a few American men who are taking an interest in this long-hushed-up subject because they too see that the problem can be solved only by exposure and not by secrecy.) These women explain in their books what happened to them, telling about their fears and their attempts—when they were little girls, often long before puberty—to escape being sexually abused on a more or less regular basis by their fathers, grandfathers, uncles, or others. Most of the women in question lived under the constant threat of being killed or sent to jail if they ever told anyone about it. Their relationship with their mothers was generally a bad one, and even teachers and psychiatrists regularly took the guilty parent's side if anything ever did come out. As a result, the child or adolescent had no choice but to remain silent until the symptoms she later developed as an adult provided her with a substitute language in which she was able—and compelled—to tell the truth.

Charlotte Vale Allen describes her own distress in her book *Daddy's Girl*. She says that it was writing this autobiography that finally released her from the terrible burden of her past. From the time she was six, every Tuesday and Thursday evening when her mother went out to play cards, Charlotte was at her father's disposal for his sexual games. She writes: "Once it was over, I'd rush to the bathroom to scrub myself raw, trying to scrape away the bad feelings; I'd look down at my formless body wanting to kill it. I wanted to murder my body so that I might, somehow, be able to continue on in the world with only a brain. It was my body's fault that this was happening to me. Without it, Daddy wouldn't be able to touch me."* Suicidal thoughts, frequent accidents, hearing voices, and physical illness were the outward signs of her growing despair and self-loathing. She was filled with bewilderment combined with the fear of giving herself away or of being found out and then put to death. She describes what went through her mind when a friendly teacher asked her how she was getting along. What she really wanted to answer was: "I'd like to be dead, Miss Redfield. Or taken away somewhere. I want someone to save me. Will you? Will you risk your probably quiet and peaceful life by coming to where I live and presenting yourself, properly infuriated on my behalf, to my mother? My mother wouldn't believe a word you had to say and might even get mad and start shouting words you'd probably never say in your entire life. Would you do that for me, Miss Redfield? Would you go to the authorities and defend me, stay with me and then take me to live with you, make me your child and keep me safely away from Daddy so I don't have to do any of those things anymore and I can stop hating myself so hard?"†

Charlotte imagines what would happen if she were to say these words out loud: her horrified teacher might tell the principal; he would tell others, who would go to her parents, and they would shake their heads incredulously. Her father would put on an act and calmly tell his lies. Charlotte would be taken out of school and sent

---

* Charlotte Vale Allen, *Daddy's Girl* (Berkley, 1982), p. 120.
† Ibid., p. 113.

to prison. Thus, the child has no choice but to answer her teacher's question with a polite "I'm fine, thank you."

The extent to which Charlotte's fears were justified can be seen in an example taken from Florence Rush's book. A young woman tells this story:

> Jill, my sister's daughter, is fourteen. Her stepfather has been feeling her up and going into her bedroom at night for the past six months. I know she's telling the truth because he did the same to me when I lived with them. Jill couldn't stand it and finally told her teacher. The teacher told the school psychologist, who said that either the child was lying and very sick or the family was in great trouble. The father could go to jail.
>
> When confronted, the stepfather said Jill lied. Jill's mother believed her husband. Wringing her hands, she pleaded with her daughter to "confess." Otherwise who would support them and her younger brothers? Jill tried to stick to her story, but with persistent pressure and increased guilt at depriving the family of support, she finally "confessed" that she lied.*

Jill was denied her request to live with her aunt and was placed under psychiatric care. That could mean the beginning of lifelong psychiatric treatment.

It would be much easier to break free from the tormenting burden of the dark secret and not become ill if the abusive adult were not one's own father and often an object of sympathy. The child has scarcely any recourse but to hope that her emotionally ill father, who is causing her anguish, will someday, because of the daughter's docility, become the father she so desperately needs: someone she can trust, who will be affectionate toward her but not exploit her. And so the child continues to do what is expected of her and to keep the secret. She tries to appear "normal" and composed and to forgive everything, although her true self and the whole range of her feelings (which include rage, indignation, disgust, shame, and a desire for revenge) remain stifled. Since soul murder cannot be totally successful, her split-off feelings remain unconscious and are not activated until the child grows into an adult and meets a partner with whom she feels free to express them. If this should prove to be unfeasible because the partner responds in kind to these outbursts

---

* Florence Rush, *The Best Kept Secret* (Prentice Hall, 1981), pp. 3–4.

of feeling, in any case she will have no difficulty "expressing herself" later on when she has a child of her own. The child in his or her helplessness will be sure to accept the mother's outbursts and mistreatment and forgive everything. It is this tragic tolerance on the part of children that is responsible for their inability to defend themselves, to denounce the person who abuses them, and often even to recognize the abuse as such.

There was a brief period in the history of psychiatry when one young man came to these same conclusions as a result of his initial encounters with the unconscious of his patients. His name was Sigmund Freud, and he published his discoveries in 1896 in his *Studies on Hysteria*. But only a few years later he had already come to believe that the sexual abuse in childhood reported by one female patient after another had never really taken place. In other words, Freud shrank from the reality that was being revealed to him, instead of allying himself from that time on with the patriarchal society of which he was a member (especially once he was over forty and, as a family man, had become a respected authority figure). He founded the psychoanalytic school, which likes to think of itself as revolutionary but in fact remains committed to the old ideas of casting blame on the helpless child and defending the powerful parents. When a patient who has been sexually abused as a child enters analysis, she will be told that it is her fantasies and desires that she is relating, because in reality she dreamed as a child of seducing her own father. Thus, with the aid of the invention of the concept of "infantile sexuality," which was a figment of Freud's imagination, the absurd childhood situation is repeated: the patient is dissuaded from recognizing the truth the same way the child was once dissuaded from recognizing her perceptions. The onus of what was inflicted on her is laid at her own doorstep.

Women seeking psychiatric help today are now beginning to see through this deception, which is sanctioned by society and comes packaged in complicated theories. Some women have been able to recognize that their struggle to deny their knowledge of the degrading things that happened to them in childhood is the cause of their often severe symptoms. They have given up this struggle and have started talking and writing about their experiences, have overcome their depressions, and have gained strength, self-respect, and courage. This may sound too good to be true, but not if we take into account that they were absolutely forbidden to speak to anyone about the major part of their childhood traumas, and particularly about that part which led to their symptoms. It is easy to imagine how damaging such a prohibition dating back to childhood can be to a person's psyche.

Once this prohibition has been removed, however, the power of those who are supposedly on the patient's side—those who tried to talk her out of what she knew to be true—disappears along with it. The mistreated child imprisoned in her ailing psyche is finally allowed to speak, and now people listen. Women who hear about these things and take them seriously, who read books such as Louise Armstrong's *Kiss Daddy Good Night*, will be able to resist new manipulation, whether in pedagogic or therapeutic guise. They will find the strength they need to ally themselves with the child they once were and to give that child credence.

Not all writers who deal with the sexual abuse of children are speaking from personal experience. Sandra Butler, for example, in *Conspiracy of Silence: The Trauma of Incest*, initially intended to investigate the question of why so many adolescents leave home and then fall into a life of crime, drug addiction, and destitution. She won the confidence of the many adolescents she talked to within the street subculture in San Francisco and discovered to her growing amazement that in most cases these young people, both male and female, had been abused by their fathers over the years. When they could no longer bear the degradation and were old enough to leave home, they tried to improve their situation by getting a new start somewhere else, but they usually ended up as prostitutes. When they were apprehended by the police, they told the truth about their background, hoping that the defenders of law and order would protect them, but they were only accused of making up stories and were sent back to their parents.

It was through these interviews that Butler became aware of the problem of sexual abuse of children, which she then made the center of her study. She also spoke with fathers who were serving prison sentences for abuse and learned that they had been victims of similar treatment as children. She spoke with the victims' mothers, who had gone through the same thing in *their* childhood and then turned a blind eye to their children's victimization, just as society had to theirs. When one mother tried to tell her church group what her husband had done to their little girl, everyone left the room without saying a word, and the next day she was asked not to come back.

According to the statistics published by Florence Rush, 70 percent of all prostitutes and 80 percent of female drug addicts have had a history of severe sexual abuse as children, and 85 percent of the crimes committed against children are of a sexual nature. We shall learn nothing from these figures as long as we adhere to the commandment "Thou shalt not be aware" and feel compelled to remain silent. But once the silence has been broken, daughters will not have to fear their mothers but will turn to them for protection. They will be able to speak freely and openly if something has been done to them that—should it be continued in secret—could ruin their whole life. Ruining the child's life will only cover up the parent's illness, not cure it. However many sexually abusive fathers there may actually be, their number will probably decline once the dire consequences of their actions become widely known.

Bibliography*

Allen, Charlotte Vale. *Daddy's Girl*. New York, 1980.

Ariès, Philippe. *Centuries of Childhood: A Social History of Family Life*. Translated by Robert Baldick. New York, 1962.

Baudelaire, Charles. *Flowers of Evil*. Translated by Florence Louie Friedman. Introduction by Richard Church. Philadelphia, 1966.

———. *The Letters of Baudelaire*. Translated by Arthur Symons. New York, 1927.

Beckett, Samuel. "Assumption," *transition* 16–17 (June 1919), 268–71.

Bell, Quentin. *Virginia Woolf: A Biography*. New York, 1972.

Bible, The New English. With the Apocrypha. Oxford and Cambridge, 1970.

Birkenhauer, Klaus. *Samuel Beckett*. Rowohlt Monograph 176. Reinbek, 1971.

Bourdier, Pierre. "L'hypermaturation des enfants de parents malades mentaux," *Revue française psychoanalyse 36* (January 1), 19–41.

Brigitte. Als Kind missbraucht: Frauen brechen das Schweigen [Abused as Children: Women Are Breaking Their Silence]. Munich, 1983.

Brod, Max. *Franz Kafka: A Biography*. Second, enlarged edition. Translated by G. Humphreys Roberts and Richard Winston. New York, 1960.

Cardinal, Marie. *The Words to Say It: A Personal Account*. Translated by Pat Goodheart. Newton, Massachusetts, 1983.

---

* This bibliography does not include those American writers whose works I read after the original German edition of this book appeared (cf. footnote on page 309 and Appendix page 319).

Ciompi, Luc. "Ansatz einer psychoanalytischen Systemtheorie" [Toward a Psychoanalytic System Theory], *Psyche* 35 (1981), 68–86.

Drigalski, Dörte von. *Blumen auf Granit: Eine Irr- und Lehrfahrt durch die deutsche Psychoanalyse* [Flowers on Granite: Negative and Positive Experiences with Psychoanalysis]. Frankfurt, 1980.

Flaubert, Gustave. *Oeuvres de jeunesse inédites: I 183?–1838: Oeuvres diverses—Mémoires d'un fou.* Paris, 1910.

———. *Sentimental Education.* Translated, with introduction and notes, by Anthony Goldsmith. Everyman's Library. Edited by Ernest Rhys. London and New York, 1942.

Fleischmann, Lea. *Das ist nicht mein Land* [This Is Not My Country]. Hamburg, 1980.

Freud, Anna. *The Ego and the Mechanisms of Defense.* Translated from the German by Cecil Baines. New York, 1958.

Freud, Ernst; Freud, Lucie; Grubrich-Simitis, Ilse, eds. *Sigmund Freud: His Life in Pictures and Words.* With a biographical sketch by K. R. Eissler. Translation by Christine Trollope. Design by Willy Fleckhaus. New York and London, 1978.

Freud, Sigmund. *The Origins of Psycho-analysis: Letters to Wilhelm Fliess: Drafts and Notes 1887–1902.* Edited by Marie Bonaparte, Anna Freud, Ernst Kris. Authorized translation by Eric Mosbacher and James Strachey. Introduction by Ernst Kris. New York, 1954.

———. *The Standard Edition of the Complete Psychological Works.* Translated from the German under the general editorship of James Strachey. In collaboration with Anna Freud. Assisted by Alix Strachey and Alan Tyson. Volume III (1893–99) *Early Psycho-Analytic Publications.* London, 1961. Volume XVII (1917–19) *An Infantile Neurosis and Other Works.* London, 1955.

Gardiner, Muriel, ed. *The Wolf-Man by the Wolf-Man.* With the Case of the Wolf-Man by Sigmund Freud and a Supplement by Ruth Mack Brunswick. Foreword by Anna Freud. Edited, with notes, an introduction, and chapters by Muriel Gardiner. New York, 1971.

Grimms' *German Folk Tales.* Translated by Francis P. Magoun, Jr., and Alexander H. Krappe. Carbondale and Edwardsville, London and Amsterdam, 1960.

Grubrich-Simitis, Ilse. "Extremtraumatisierung als kumulatives Trauma" [Extreme Traumatization as Cumulative Trauma], *Psyche* 32 (1979), 991–1023.

Haley, Jay. *Uncommon Therapy: The Psychiatric Techniques of Milton H. Erickson, M.D.* New York and London, 1973.

Helfer, Ray E., and Kempe, C. Henry. *The Battered Child.* 3rd ed. Chicago, 1980.

Herman, Judith Lewis. *Father-Daughter Incest.* Cambridge, Mass., 1982.

―――. *The Feeling Child.* New York, 1973.

Janov, Arthur. *The Primal Revolution.* New York, 1972.

―――. *The Primal Scream.* New York, 1971.

Jones, Ernest, M.D. *The Life and Work of Sigmund Freud, I: The Formative Years and the Great Discoveries 1856–1900.* New York, 1953.

Jung, Carl Gustav. *The Collected Works of C. G. Jung, X: Civilization in Transition.* Translated by R. F. C. Hull. Bollingen Series XX. New York, 1964.

Kafka, Franz. *Amerika.* Translated by Willa and Edwin Muir. Preface by Klaus Mann. Afterword by Max Brod. Illustrations by Emlen Etting. New York, 1946.

―――. *Briefe 1902–1924* [Letters]. Fischer Taschenbuch 1575. Frankfurt, 1975.

―――. *Briefe an Ottla und die Familie.* Frankfurt, 1974.

―――. *The Castle.* Translated by Willa Muir et al. Definitive edition. New York, 1976.

―――. *The Complete Stories.* Edited by Nahum N. Glatzer. New York, 1972.

―――. *Letter to His Father/Brief an den Vater.* Translated by Ernst Kaiser and Eithne Wilkins. New York, 1966.

―――. *Letters to Felice.* Edited by Erich Heller and Jürgen Born. Translated by James Stern and Elisabeth Duckworth. New York, 1973.

―――. *Letters to Milena.* Edited by Willi Haas. Translated by Tania and James Stern. London, 1953.

Kentler, Helmut. *Sexualerziehung* [Sex Education]. Rowohlt Monograph 8034. Reinbek, 1970.

Kierkegaard, Sören. *Diary of a Seducer.* Translated by Gerd Gillhoff. New York, 1966.

Kohut, Heinz. *The Restoration of the Self.* New York, 1977.

Korczak, Janusz. *Das Recht des Kindes auf Achtung* [The Child's Right to Be Respected]. Göttingen, 1970.

―――. *Verteidigt die Kinder* [Defend the Children]. Gütersloh, 1981.

Krüll, Marianne. *Freud und sein Vater* [Freud and His Father]. Munich, 1979.

Langegger, Florian. *Mozart—Vater und Sohn* [Mozart—Father and Son].
Zurich, 1978.

Leboyer, Frédéric. *Birth Without Violence.* New York, 1975.

Liedloff, Jean. The Continuum Concept. Revised edition. New York,
1977.

Mause, Lloyd de, ed. *The History of Childhood.* New York, 1974.

Mecke, Gunter. "Franz Kafkas Geheimnis" [Franz Kafka's Secret],
Psyche 35, 1981, 209–36.

Mehr, Mariella. *Steinzeit* [Stone Age]. Bern, 1981.

Miller, Alice. *For Your Own Good: Hidden Cruelty in Child-Rearing and
the Roots of Violence.* Translated by Hildegarde and Hunter
Hannum. New York, 1983.

———. *Prisoners of Childhood.* Translated by Ruth Ward. New York,
1981. (Published in paperback [1983] as *The Drama of the Gifted
Child.*)

———. Review of Florian Langegger's *Mozart—Vater und Sohn, Psyche*
35 (1981), 587–88.

———. "Die einsame Not der kleinen Mädchen" [The Lonely Anguish
of Little Girls], *Brigitte* (September 7, 1982).

———. "Die Töchter schweigen nicht mehr" [Daughters Are Breaking
Their Silence], *Brigitte,* Special Issue (October 1982).

———. "Zur Behandlungstechnik bei sogenannten narzißtischen Neuro-
sen" [Methods of Treatment of So-called Narcissistic Neuroses],
Psyche 25, 641–68.

Montagu, Ashley. *Touching: The Human Significance of the Skin.* New
York, 1971.

Moser, Tilmann. *Lehrjahre auf der Couch* [Apprenticeship on the Couch].
Frankfurt, 1974.

Niederland, William G. "The Ego and the Recovery of Early Memories,"
Psychoanalytic Quarterly, 34:4 (October 1965), 564–71.

Obholzer, Karin. *Gespräche mit dem Wolfsmann* [Conversations with the
Wolf-Man]. Reinbek, 1980.

Pernhaupt, Günter, and Čzermak, Hans. *Die gesunde Ohrfeige macht
krank: Über die alltägliche Gewalt im Umgang mit Kindern* [A
Healthy Box on the Ears Causes Illness: Everyday Violence Applied to Children]. Vienna, 1980.

Petri, Horst, and Lauterbach, Matthias. *Gewalt in der Erziehung:
Plädoyer zur Abschaffung der Prügelstrafe* [Violence in Child-
Rearing: A Plea for the Abolition of Corporal Punishment].
Fischer-Athenäum Taschenbuch 4060. Frankfurt, 1975.

Pizzey, Erin. *Scream Quietly or the Neighbors Will Hear.* Hillside, N.J.,
1977.

Richter, Horst Eberhard. *All Mighty.* Translated by Jan Van Heurck. Claremont, Calif., 1983.

————. *Eltern, Kind, Neurose* [Parents, Child, Neurosis]. Stuttgart, 1963.

Sanford, Linda Tschirhart. *The Silent Children.* New York, 1980.

Sartre, Jean-Paul. *The Family Idiot: Gustave Flaubert: 1821–1857,* Volume I. Translated by Carol Cosman. Chicago, 1981.

Schatzman, Morton. *Soul Murder: Persecution in the Family.* New York, 1973.

Schreber, D. G. M. *Das Buch der Erziehung an Leib und Seele* [Educating Body and Soul]. Leipzig, 1865.

Schreber, D. P. *Denkwürdigkeiten eines Nervenkranken* [Memoirs of a Neuropath]. Leipzig, 1903; Frankfurt, 1973.

Schwab, Gustav. *Gods and Heroes: Myths and Epics of Ancient Greece.* Translated by Olga Marx and Ernst Morwitz. New York, 1946.

Sebbar, Leila. *Gewalt an kleinen Mädchen* [Violence against Little Girls]. Naumburg-Elbenberg, 1980.

Segal, Hanna. *Introduction to the Work of Melanie Klein.* New, enlarged edition. New York, 1973.

Stierlin, Helm. *Separating Parents and Adolescents: Individuation in the Family.* New York and London, 1981.

Thomas, Klaus. *Selbstanalyse* [Self-analysis]. Stuttgart, 1972.

Tuschy, Gerhard. "Zum Problem von Individuum und Gesellschaft aus der Sicht der Tiefenpsychologie" [The Problem of Individual and Society Seen from the Perspective of Depth Psychology]. A Lecture Delivered at a Conference Held at the Gustav Stresemann Institute in Lenbach (Cologne), April 1979.

Vegh, Claudine. *Ich habe ihnen nicht auf Wiedersehen gesagt: Gespräche mit Kindern von Deportierten* [I Didn't Say Goodbye: Conversations with Children of Deportees]. Cologne, 1981.

Vinke, Hermann. *Das kurze Leben der Sophie Scholl* [The Short Life of Sophie Scholl]. Ravensburg, 1980.

Wagenbach, Klaus. *Franz Kafka.* Rowohlt Monograph 091. Reinbek, 1976.

Winnicott, Donald W. "Hate in the Counter-Transference" in *Collected Papers: Through Pediatrics to Psycho-Analysis.* New York, 1949.

————. *Piggle.* New York, 1977.

Zenz, Gisela. *Kindesmisshandlung und Kindesrechte* [Mistreatment of Children and Children's Rights]. Frankfurt, 1979.

Printed in the USA
CPSIA information can be obtained
at www.ICGtesting.com
LVHW091129150724
785511LV00001B/47